WITHDRAWN

The Teacher As Writer: Paul T. Nolan, Example

Edited by

James M. Salem

The Scarecrow Press, Inc.
Metuchen, N.J.   1970

For Provincia

Contents

Introduction

Introduction

In an essay concerning the writing activities of a classroom teacher--Dr. Paul T. Nolan of the University of Southwestern Louisiana--Professor Katherine P. Finley, Dean of Instruction at Artesia College, New Mexico comments that her interest in Nolan's work is limited to its value as "an example" of the kind of writing that may be expected from the professional teacher. Professor Finley makes no distinction, although she implies one, between the teacher who writes and the writer who teaches, but this distinction needs to be made here.

Higher education has long served the useful function of providing a steady (if modest) income for the writer-in-residence, both for the scholar and the creative writer; and in return, the writer-in-residence has given the sponsoring institution a first-hand association with the active writer. It is a fair exchange, and nothing in this book is meant to suggest that such relationships should be discouraged or limited. In fact, it is hoped that more writers will use academia as a some-time address and that more academic institutions will provide the money for in-residence sponsorship. The University of Virginia and William Faulkner, Yale University and Marc Connelly, Lionel Trilling and Columbia University all profited from their relationships.

The value of educational-literary relationships is so obvious, in fact, that both colleges and teachers have come to accept the theory that the writer is a more useful teacher than the non-writer, a theory that has led to the sometimes unfair and illogical dogma of "publish or perish."

In her study of Dr. Nolan's writing, Mrs. Finley makes a case for the educational use of publishing from the teacher's point of view. Since this collection begins with her essay, I do not intend to anticipate her argument, but it should be noted here that I am in agreement with the general assumption that a teacher who also writes is able to perform educational services which in both style and scope are superior to the services that the same teacher would make without writing. It is, of course, assumed that a teacher who writes must give his first attention to his teaching, not merely because of his professional obligations to his students, but also because his teaching is the main source for his writing.

The teacher who writes, unlike the writer who teaches, cannot really survive as a writer if he ceases to be a teacher. As long as he is a teacher who writes, he is writing from a teaching point of view. There is, thus, not only no conflict between his teaching and writing activities, but there is a necessary harmony and a mutual dependence.

Mrs. Finley demonstrates her argument by a selective bibliography of Nolan's published work. She wishes to show that the teacher has a variety of audiences outside the classroom willing "to be taught" by the teacher in print. I wish to show in this anthology that what a teacher does in print is not unlike what he does in the classroom, and thus, for my purposes, the complete text is necessary.

In an early plan I made for this collection, a variety of teacher-writers were selected. This plan was discarded, not without some regrets, because while it demonstrated that many teachers also write and that one subject matter has various applications, it failed to suggest the variety of ways in which a single teacher may write about his subject.

In the years between Professor Finley's essay and the composition of this introduction, some of Nolan's separate works have received some praise for their own merits. His Chaucer for Children has become a minor classic in children's theater with productions from Bombay, India, to Mansfield, Ohio. Another of his children's plays, "The Double Nine of Chih Yuan," was taken from his original Round-the-World Plays for Young People and anthologized cheek-to-jowl with Shakespeare and Elizabeth Barrett Browning in the Ginn reader, This Is Our Heritage. Editors of magazines about the American West, such as Real West, now suggest topics to him, not because he is a teacher, but because he writes a "good yarn." For the purposes of this study, however, the question of the literary merit or want of it is beside the point. For the purposes of demonstrating what the teacher-as-writer is--a teacher-- the quality of the writing, like the quality of the teaching, is of interest only in showing how good he is.

This collection, in fact, is not based on literary merit except that on occasions when two or more works would serve the same purpose as an "example," I took the one I liked the best. In the plays, for example, I had a choice in community-theatre plays between "There's Death for the Lonely," a play that won the Players Workshop Award in 1964, and "Last Week I Was Ninety-Five." I took the latter, without the award, because I liked it better. At the same time, however, I neglected to take any one of Nolan's recent one-act plays being published in <u>Plays: The Drama Magazine for Young People</u>. Plays like "An Anton Chekhov Sort of Evening," "The In-Group," and "Hi, Down There" are, in Nolan's opinion at least, among the best work that he has done in the short drama. But such works did not illustrate the relationship between his teaching and his writing as closely as did other selections, perhaps of less literary value.

The works in this collection were selected to show the natural ways in which the ideas and factual content of the teacher's in-class work can be used in writing. The collection is less an anthology of Nolan's writing than it is a how-to-do-it book for teachers seeking to find the proper relationship between teaching in the classroom and teaching in print. Any reader may, and should, know hundreds of other teachers who would serve equally as well as an "example" of the teacher who writes. Nolan's work is just one example, and the intention is to call attention to the methods, not the man.

In preparing this work, I received considerable aid from various people. I am responsible for the application I have made of Professor Finley's original essay, of course; but her essay was the "germ" from which this collection grew. I am under obligation to Professor Nolan both for permission to reprint the various works in this collection and for the information he so freely gave me concerning his work. Finally, I am grateful to the various journals and publishing companies for permission to reprint works first published by them. The specific journals and publishers are noted in the context of the book.

I

The Example:
Professor Paul T. Nolan

This introductory essay by Professor Katherine P. Finley was first published in The Serif: Kent State University Library Quarterly, III (March 1966), 9-16. Although the bibliography is now some several years out of date, it is still fairly representative of Nolan's work. One recent publication, Provincial Drama in America (Scarecrow Press, 1967), should probably be mentioned, however. The book contains a variety of literary forms (play editions, critical and historical essays, popular features, and bibliographies) that Professor Nolan used in his "teaching-in-print" of one subject from his classroom experience.

Paul T. Nolan, An Example:
The Teacher in Print: A Check List

During the past ten years, Dr. Paul T. Nolan, a professor of English at the University of Southwestern Louisiana, has published over one hundred and fifty books, articles, editions, and plays. He is listed in a dozen of the standard reference works of writers and teachers: Contemporary Authors, Who's Who in American Education, and The Directory of American Scholars. His works are annually reviewed, footnoted, listed, or mentioned in a variety of journals: Dramatics, Southern Speech Journal, Players Magazine, Library Journal, PMLA, American Literature, American Quarterly, Louisiana Schools, Educational Theatre Journal, and Abstracts of English Studies. By a conservative estimate, probably five million people have, at one fleeting moment or another, read his works or heard them from a stage. Probably another five million have read about his writing or seen some of it listed.

Yet, if all these people were polled, probably not
five thousand could identify him or even recall ever having
seen his name in print. Judging from his present works
(and he was forty-six last spring), he seems never to be
intended for a Pulitzer Prize or a place on any "Best
Sellers" list. He is, however, an example--perhaps a successful example--of the "teacher in print"; and his career
should be of some value in the current argument about the
role of "the publishing teacher" in American education today.

Dr. Nolan is a teacher. It is not only his principal
occupation; it is his only occupation. During the past ten
years, while averaging about twenty publications a year,
he has taught every semester (summers included) in the
USL English department. His teaching assignment has
always been a full load, normally fifteen classroom hours;
and they have included not only courses in his specialty--
dramatic literature, but also the "stock courses" in the
department, freshman composition, introduction to literature, and surveys of English literature. Most of his
students are not English majors, and he receives no
"special considerations" on the sizes of his classes, no
graders, no student assistants to take care of "the routine
work. " This is not the teaching schedule of a research
scholar who is, to echo the complaints in the popular journals, "encouraged to neglect his teaching duties for research. "

Nor are his duties limited to the classroom. He
serves on a variety of committees, directs theses, is active
in a number of professional organizations: American Studies
Association, American National Theatre Academy, South-
Central Modern Language Association, Deep South Writers
Conference, College Writers' Society of Louisiana, Louisiana
Historical Association, English Section of the Louisiana
College Conference, the Louisiana Folklore Society, and
the Educational Theatre Association.

And he has been active in these organizations. He
is one of the founders of both the College Writers' Society
and the Deep South Writers Conference and established a
chapter of the English fraternity, Sigma Tau Delta, on the
USL campus. He serves annually as a judge for such
national writing contests as those sponsored by the Pioneer
Drama Service and the Student Writer. He is a reader for
American Quarterly, and a reviewer for the Educational

Theatre Journal, the Southern Speech Journal, and the
Journal of the Illinois Historical Society.   For eight years
he was one of the bibliographers for the Educational Theatre
Association.   He has been a program chairman at one time
or another for most of the groups--the S-C Modern Language
Association, the Louisiana Folklore Society, the College
Wrtiers' Society, the English section of the state College
Conference.   He is a campus representative for the Woodrow
Wilson Foundation; and he, finally, serves on several on-
campus faculty committees.

Such a listing is not, of course, intended to impress
anyone that here is a teacher of special merit.   It is merely
to demonstrate that here is a teacher who is not neglecting
his teaching duties.   Obviously, his record both as a teacher
in the classroom and in print can be matched by teachers in
almost every college and university in the United States.
And this activity--and his publishing activity--is, according
to Dr. Nolan, the normal schedule of the American college
teacher.

Too many critics of education--inside and outside the
profession--have jumped to the defense of those teachers
"burning in the hell's fire of a publish-or-perish inferno."
It is time, the argument goes, that the natural relationship
between teaching-in-the-classroom and teaching-in-print be
exhibited.   If we are to stop waving the "publish or perish"
banner, it is at least equally dangerous to wave the "publish
at your own risk" flag in its place.

"No one," Dr. Nolan comments, "points out that the
academic community punishes as well as rewards its publishing professors.   Every issue of AAUP Bulletin carries
advertisements for 'teaching teachers' with the blunt im-
plication that one who teaches in print cannot possibly teach
in a classroom.   Some schools favor their nonpublishing
faculty members, especially those still working on terminal
degrees, when it comes to the granting of leaves.   There
is even a mild suspicion that the publishing professor is
leading a riotous life on the royalties from his articles in
PMLA, Notes and Queries, and the Book Lovers' Review."

According to Nolan, the whole objection to the publication activity of college teachers arises from some serious doubts as to its worth and to its need.   "If the college
teacher would admit that the average college student is at
least as intelligent as the average reader and that the aver-

age reader is at least as interested in learning as the
average college student, he would start with a more realistic view of what his job is and what his opportunities
are. "

(Nolan's basic argument is that what is taught in the
classroom should be of enough interest to satisfy the reader
as well as the student.) "If not, it's probably not good
enough to be said.   Teachers often argue against writing
on the basis that they have nothing to say, and if they are
telling the truth, we should expect more--not fewer--riots
on the campus. "

Secondly, he argues that in spite of Shaw's quip
about teachers being people who cannot do, teachers should
at least be able to do what they expect of their students.
Speech teachers should speak; English teachers should write;
philosophy teachers should philosophize.

And, finally, he argues, it is not the teacher's job
to take upon himself the responsibility of judging the whole
world.   "Any teacher who finds it necessary to defend his
subject against the world will be too busy defending to have
any time left for teaching.   His responsibility is to his subject matter, to tell what he knows in the best possible manner.   If he does, he has kept the faith with his profession. "

"Few teachers," he argues, "would object to this
theory in the classroom.   In fact, no question so irritates
the teacher as the one asking, 'Why do I have to take this
course?'; yet many object to following it when teaching in
print. "

The teacher-in-print, according to Nolan, should
write the best he can and then submit what he has written.
It is the editor's responsibility to accept it or reject it.
"This is always the teacher's argument about his in-class
teaching; and it is more true of his in-print teaching.   After
all, the teacher-writer cannot flunk the editor for failing to
see the worth of his teaching. " Nolan says that many teachers worry themselves to death about the worth of their
writing without any concern for the obvious fact that the
editor--not the writer--is responsible for it being in print.

Following his own credo, Nolan writes about what he
teaches, following the rules that he preaches, and he publishes with those editors who will accept his material--

"those students who sign up for the course."

"The best part of teaching," he says, "in the classroom or in print is the action--the speaking or writing itself. It is the only part over which the teacher has control.
The uses made of the teaching, the abuse of it, the worth
of it, all these are matters beyond the teacher's real control. Few teachers worry much about this in their classroom practice, but many are paralyzed by such considerations when it comes to teaching in print."

Nolan teaches classes in literature, especially dramatic literature--from the Greeks to Albee. Largely, his
"teaching in print" is in the same field--drama. "It is
not merely," he says, "that one teaching in print should
teach what he knows best; it is, also, that one teaching in
the classroom should be willing to test his materials and
his approach on a wider and freer audience."

The teacher-in-print is not a professional writer.
He is a man who is using the printed word, rather than the
spoken one, to tell things he knows to those who want to
consider them. Unlike the professional writer, he does not
look for subjects to interest his readers; rather he makes
himself available for readers looking for information about
his subject.

The check list that follows (a rather large sampling
of Nolan's publications in the past ten years) is a demonstration that a wide variety of readers are interested in
what the teacher has to say in print; and it has been loosely
arranged to suggest the various audiences available.

1. For the Literary Critic

"Classical Tragedy in the Province Theater," American Quart-
    erly, XIII (Fall, 1961), 410-13.
"Comic Style of Beaumarchais: Books in Review," Education-
    al Theatre Journal, XIV (March, 1962), 76-77.
"Congreve's Last Works: The Artist in Escape," Southwestern
    Louisiana Journal, I (October, 1957), 245-69.
"Congreve's Lovers: Art and the Critic," Drama Survey, I
    (February, 1962), 330-39.
"John Dryden's 'All for Love, Barron Edition: A Review,"
    Southern Speech Journal, XXVIII (Fall 1962), 76-77.
"Journal of a Young Southern Playwright," Louisiana Studies

[Two parts.], I (Fall and Winter, 1962), 30-50 and 33-54.
"J. W. Crawford's 'The Dregs': A New Mexico Pioneer in
the Short Drama," New Mexico Quarterly, XXXIII (Winter,
1963-64), 388-403.
"J. W. Crawford: Poet-Scout of the Black Hills," South
Dakota Review, II (Spring, 1965), 40-47.
"Life and Death of a Southern Play: Williams' 'Unorna',"
Louisiana History, V (Spring, 1964), 143-59.
"Shakespeare Idol in America," Mississippi Quarterly, XII
(Spring, 1959), 67-74.
"Southern Playwright: Arthur Lee Kahn," Southern Speech
Journal, XXVIII (Spring, 1962), 202-12.
Three Plays by J. W. (Capt. Jack) Crawford: An Experiment
in Myth-Making. The Hague, The Netherlands: Mouton
Publishing Company, 1965.
"Tolstoy's 'Power of Darkness': Genre as Meaning," Educa-
tional Theatre Journal, XVII, (March, 1965), 1-9.
" 'Way of the World': Congreve's 'Moment of Truth'," South-
ern Speech Journal, XXV (Winter, 1959), 79-95.
"Williams' 'Dante': The Death of Ninteenth-Century Heroic
Drama," Southern Speech Journal, XXV (Summer, 1960),
225-63.

II. For the Regional Historians

"Alabama Drama, 1870-1916," Alabama Review, XXIV (Jan-
uary, 1965), 65-72.
"Arkansas Drama Before World War I: An Unexplored
Country," (with Amos E. Simpson), Arkansas Historical
Quarterly, XXII (Spring, 1963), 61-75.
"Arthur Lee Kahn: The Sardou of Shreveport," Bulletin of
the Louisiana Library Association," XXIV (Summer, 1961),
55-58, 83.
"Boomers: Oklahoma Playwrights Opened the Territory,"
Chronicles of Oklahoma, XLI (Autumn, 1963), 248-52.
"Captain Jack Crawford: Gold Searcher Turned Playwright,"
Alaska Review, I (Spring, 1964), 41-47.
"Captain Jack Rides Again," New Mexico Magazine, XLIII
(January, 1965), 3-5.
"Case for Louisiana Drama," Southwestern Louisiana Journal,
IV (January, 1960), 35-43.
"Ernest J. Whisler: Arizona's 'Lost Playwright'," Arizona
Teacher, LII (May, 1964), 19-20.
"Espy Williams: New Orleans Playwright," Bulletin of the
Louisiana Library Association, XXI (Winter, 1958), 137-
39.
"Forgotten Playwrights," New Mexico Magazine, XXXX

(September, 1962), 37, 39-40.

"From Shakespeare to Nagel," New Mexico School Review, XXXXII (March, 1963), 14-15.

"Mississippi Drama Between Wars, 1870-1916," (with Katherine P. Finley) [Two parts], Journal of Mississippi History, XXVI (August, 1964), 219-28 and (November, 1964), 299-306.

"S. C. Drama: The Lost Years Between the Wars," South Carolina Magazine, XXVI (Spring, 1962), 20-29.

"Southerner's Tribute to Illinois' 'Pagan Prophet'," Journal of the Illinois Historical Society, LI (Autumn, 1958), 268-83.

"Terrill's Purgatory: First Play Printed in Oklahoma," Chronicles of Oklahoma, XLII (Autumn, 1964), 246-52.

"When Curtains Rise, Scouts Fall Out," Southern Speech Journal, XXIX (Spring, 1964), 175-86.

III. For the Teacher of Literature

"Children Can Read Plays, Too," Elementary English, XXXIX (November, 1962), 699-701.

"Crashaw's 'To Lesbia,'" Roundtable, I (April, 1960), 2.

"In Search of the Solitary Figure," Phi Kappa Phi Journal, XLIV (Fall, 1964), 30-36.

"Marc Connelly's 'The Green Pastures' as an Introduction to Folk Drama," Exercise Exchange, XII (November, 1964), 8-10.

"So Long in Silence: The Voice of J. D. Salinger," Student Writer, III (February, 1964), 20-23, 40-41.

"Shakespeare's 'Romeo and Juliet' as an Introduction to Lyric Drama," Exercise Exchange, X (March 1963), 26-28.

IV. For the Creative Writing Teacher

"Freshman Research and Native Materials," English Record, XIII (April, 1963), 9-12.

"Kodak-Kiver: The School of George Eastman," Word Study, XXXVI (February, 1961), 6-7.

"Louisiana Drama and a Study Program," Louisiana Schools, XXIV (May, 1957), 43-44.

"'New' Old Fashioned Melodrama," Players Magazine, XXXVIII (November, 1961), 53-55.

"Research Projects Waiting: The Forgotten Drama of Provincial America," Western Speech, (Summer, 1963), 142-50.

"Some Reconsiderations on Playwriting," Dramatics, XXXIV (November, 1962), 11, 25-26.

"Sources for Articles: Your Specialty," <u>Louisiana Schools</u>,
   XXXVIII (February, 1961), 8-9, 31.
"State Educational Journals," <u>Louisiana Schools</u>, XLI (October,
   1963), 16-18.
"Teaching and Research in the Feature Article," <u>Louisiana
   Schools</u>, XXIV (May, 1957), 42-44.
"Turning Fiction into Drama," <u>Student Writer</u>, III (January,
   1964), 15-16, 25.
"What the Editors Want," <u>Author & Journalist</u>, XLIX
   (February, 1964), 15.
"What to Do with the Finished Product: Markets for the
   One-Act Play," <u>Student Writer</u>, IV (February, 1965),
   17-19.
"What's Good for the Editors," <u>English Record</u>, V (December,
   1963), 23-27.
"Writing a Drama of the Absurd," <u>Dramatics</u>, XXCI (Jan-
   uary, 1965), 15, 31.
"Writing Plays for Children," <u>Southern Speech Journal</u>, XXVI
   (Spring, 1961), 224-34.
<u>Writing the One-Act Play for the Amateur Stage</u>. Cody,
   Wyoming: Pioneer Drama Service, 1964.

V. <u>Plays for the Schools</u>

"After the Last Class," <u>Louisiana Schools</u>, XXVI (May, 1959),
   8-11.
"Birthday of the Infanta," <u>Plays</u>, XXIV (April, 1965), 85-95.
"Blades of Grass," <u>Little Red Schoolhouse Bulletin</u>, II
   (Spring, 1963), 24-25.
<u>Children's Chaucer: An Evening's Entertainment from The
   Canterbury Tales</u>. La Farge, Wisconsin: Little Red
   Schoolhouse Press, 1964.
"Cocks Should Crow," <u>Instructor</u>, LXXV (May, 1958), 24-
   25.
"Goannas," <u>Grade Teacher</u>, LXXVIII (October, 1960), 87-96.
"Moon's Up There," <u>Plays</u>, XXII (April, 1963), 1-10.
"Still Another Play: 'Two Irish Orphans,'" <u>Louisiana Schools</u>,
   XL (March, 1963), 6-10.
<u>Round-the-World Plays for Young People</u>. Boston: Plays,
   Inc., 1961.
"Three Sundays in a Week," <u>Plays</u>, XXII (November, 1962),
   54-60.
"Tony Kytes: The Arch Deceiver," <u>Plays</u>, XXII (February,
   1963), 87-94.
"Value Room: A Two-Act Play," <u>Grade Teacher</u>, LXXIX
   (May, 1962), 38, 102-03.
"View of the Sea," <u>Plays</u>, XXIV (March, 1965), 11-24.

VI. Plays for the Community Theatre

"Bride Comes to Yellow Sky. " Cody, Wyoming: Pioneer Drama
   Service, 1963.
"Christmas Dress. " Cody, Wyoming: Pioneer Drama Service,
   1963.
"Herman M. Bien: The Feast of Lights or Chanukoh" (edited).
   Lexington: University of Kentucky Press, 1963, K. Micro-
   cards, Series A, no. 145.
"Life on the Border: Written Especially for William F. (Buf-
   falo Bill) Cody. " (edited) Cody, Wyoming: Pioneer Drama
   Service, 1965. (A production of this play opened the 75th
   anniversary of statehood in Cody, Wyoming, May 7, 1965.
   Nolan found the ms. and edited it. It is the only extant
   copy of an original Buffalo Bill play.)
"There's Death for the Lonely. " Burlington, Iowa: Players
   Workshop, 1964. (This three-act play won the 1964 Players Workshop award and was printed by the Workshop for
   its December, 1964, production. It has not been published.)

VII. For the Sunday Reader

"Arkansas Was Once a Theatrical Center, " Arkansas Gazette
   Magazine, Sept. 16, 1962, 4E. (with Amos E. Simpson)
"Arthur Lee Kahn of Louisiana, " Southern Israelite, XXXVJ
   (September, 1961), 27-31.
"Buffalo Bill's Life on the Border, " Dime Novel Round-Up,
   XXX (August 15, 1964), 68-69.
"Captain Jack, The Poet Scout, " Real West, VIII (January,
   1965), 22-25, 44-45.
"Changing Face of a Legend: Harriet Beecher Stowe . . . , "
   Ark-La-Tex Magazine, September 13, 1959, 4G.
"In Mississippi: These Playwrights Started a Renaissance, "
   Advocate Sunday Magazine (Baton Rouge, La.), Jan. 13,
   1963, 1-E.
"In the Last, Hot Summer: Louisiana Playwright Struggled with
   Shakespeare, Marlowe, and Fame, " Advocate. Sunday
   Magazine, July 29, 1962, 1-E.
"Lost: One Playwright, " Dixie Roto Magazine, Dec. 23, 1956, 9.
"Playwright Judge Howe Pokes Fun at Antebellum Eden, "
   Advocate Sunday Magazine, March 13, 1961, 3E.
"Victor H. Smalley: Louisiana Playwright, 1880-1910, " South-
   west Magazine, II (June-July, 1960), 12.
"Whiff of Greasepaint, " Dixie Roto Magazine, Dec. 23, 1956, 9.
"Witch that Toured the South, " Advocate Sunday Magazine,
   Jan. 13, 1963, 1-E.

This check list, representative and incomplete, pretty
much speaks for itself, and it shows clearly the relationship
between the in-class and in-print activities of the teacher.
As the teacher recognizes the need of the same material
for different classes, so is it obvious that Nolan draws
from the same material for different readers.   His edition
of Crawford's plays, An Experiment in Myth-Making, is
his most complete statement on the part of the "Western
hero" in American drama, but he earlier published shorter
studies on the same subject in a variety of journals for a
variety of readers--literally from Alaska to the Gulf of
Mexico and for the professional theatre critics of Southern
Speech, the dime-novel collectors of the Round-Up, the
state historian of New Mexico Magazine, the drama critic
of the New Mexico Quarterly, and the Sunday readers of the
Advocate.

Some of his in-print teaching is, of course, merely
a more detailed presentation of classroom materials, his
article on Tolstoy's "Power of Darkness" for example.   But
in his plays for the schools--his adaptations of Chaucer,
Poe, Hawthorne, Greek drama, the Japanese Noh play--he
is presenting materials for students in ways not easily
handled in the normal classroom.

The selections for this check list were made, in part,
to show the variety of audiences willing to be taught by the
teacher-in-print.   But these readers are also capable of
teaching the writer, and they do so.   Nolan's little article,
"Lost, One Playwright, " for example, got a response from
the daughter of the "lost playwright, " who finally turned
over to the USL Library the complete collection of her
father's published and unpublished plays, many of them the
"only extant" copies. Nolan's discovery of the only known
copy of a Buffalo Bill play came through one of his readers,
Mrs. Buford Richardson, who found the copy in her attic
and thought he might be interested.   These manuscripts
would eventually have been permanently lost if Nolan had
not been teaching in print.

Some would argue that Nolan's field, drama, lends
itself more easily to teaching-in-print than do other fields.
He agrees that this argument is valid.   But it is difficult
to think of a single field of academic study--religion, economics, home economics, physical education or philosophy--
in which there is not a large number of readers, for which
there is not a number of markets.

According to Nolan, ("The teacher who wishes to teach in print as well as in the classroom needs merely to ask himself <u>who</u> is interested in what he knows and <u>what</u> publications <u>does</u> he read.) The answers to these two questions give him his markets, and the markets themselves suggest the teaching-writing methods to be employed. "

"It is, " he says, "not a question of writing <u>up</u> or writing <u>down</u>, but rather writing <u>to</u>. "

II

The Lecture in Print

Few teachers think of the classroom lecture as
publishable material. In fact, in the normal give and take
of the classroom the formal lecture has just about disappeared, being replaced by explication of the text, discussion,
and evaluations or comments on the existing critical studies
in print. Classroom lectures are, moreover, things of
"rags and patches"--chunks of scholarship done by others,
statements made to suit the particular needs of particular
classes, and statements of ideas offered as starting points
for discussion.

There are, however, parts of classroom lectures
worth repeating, comments worth more formal development;
and the teacher who thinks of writing as an extension of his
classroom teaching gets in the habit of listening to himself
with some degree of objectivity--listening for the spoken
words that might be of use in print.

It is common to think of the scholarly journals
as the only outlet for serious teachers, and it is generally
assumed that scholarly journals are intended "for members
only." Privately, teachers may agree that the chief readers
of such journals are probably graduate students, but it is
all but ignored that undergraduate students, too, go to the
scholarly journals for some light on a subject which the
classroom lecture left in the shadows. In the field of English
teaching alone there are scores of journals read by undergraduate students looking for help: a review, a precise
explanation, a new approach to the subject matter of a
standard course. One who writes for the "scholarly" and
subject-related journals is not necessarily reporting to other
scholars on "new contributions to knowledge."

The three selections in this chapter illustrate the
various kinds of classroom material that have some use in
print: a formal lecture, an outlined study guide, and a
mechanical how-to-do-it report. The works appeared in

three different kinds of journals interested in the work of
the teacher as writer.

The first, a study of Marc Connelly's "The Green
Pastures, " was published on pages 216-224 of Western
Speech, XXX (Fall 1966), a professional journal for
speech teachers.   Although Nolan has written elsewhere
of the works of Marc Connelly, including a biography that
called for major research effort, this essay is essentially
an introductory lecture about a single play, exactly the
kind of lecture he gives in a survey course in modern drama.
The second, an exercise concerning Eugene Ionesco's
"The Chairs, " appeared first in pages 9-10 of Exercise
Exchange, XIV (April, 1967), a study guide publication
for teachers, supported by Holt, Rinehart, and Winston
Company.   This work is little more than an outline by
which a single play is taught.   The third example, a discussion of marketing one-act plays, was, in fact, first
prepared for an undergraduate class writing one-act plays.
It was first published on pages 17-19 of The Student Writer,
IV (February, 1965), a writers' guide book for high school
and college would-be-writers.   This article is, Dr. Nolan
says, little changed from the form used in the classroom.

1. The Formal Lecture

Marc Connelly's Divine Comedy:
Green Pastures Revisited

I

Some plays are forever surprising their audiences
into re-evaluations. They come announced as one thing;
and when they are revealed as something else, they delight
and frustrate their critics from the first to the last. Such
plays as Euripides Medea, Shakespeare's Romeo and Juliet,
and Congreve's The Way of the World seem to possess the
quality of making critics uncomfortable with both their past
praise and censure. This constant re-appraisal seems
especially needed in modern dramas with some religious
intents or associations. Tolstoy's Power of Darkness,
for example, has demonstrated its power to move the
critic in performance and later to leave him uncomfortable
about the feeling. [1] Perhaps no other play in American
drama has made its critics give as many second thoughts
to their last responses as Marc Connelly's Green Pastures,
and the problem, I think, lies in Connelly's use of two
elements--folk literature and religion--to achieve a purpose
consistent with both, but different from either.

Thirty-five years ago, in 1930, when Connelly's
Green Pastures[2] first appeared on the American stage,
the United States was, as Tennessee Williams was later to
phrase it, "matriculating in the school for the blind."[3]
The Crash of '29 was still echoing, and the Depression had
become "the American Way of Life." Theatre-going Americans, if we may judge from the plays of the 1930's, were
involved in soul searching, in testing their dreams, their
illusions, their biases against the hard realities of the new
world.

For those who know Connelly as a collaborator with
George S. Kaufman on such plays as Dulcy (1921), Merton
of the Movies (1922), and Beggar on Horseback (1924), and
for his own The Wisdom Tooth (1926), Green Pastures must
have come as something of a surprise. Connelly, like
Philip Barry, was a "bright young man of comedy"; and as
Professor Joseph P. Roppolo has pointed out so ably, when
such a playwright turns to drama with religious intent,

there is a general uncomfortable feeling that he is "simply
being perverse ... courting disaster by deserting his 'true
forte' ...."[4] If Barry's John, which was at least conventional
in both its use of Shakespearean form and Biblical content,
left its audiences uncomfortable, what could Connelly have
expected from Green Pastures?

Connelly, in fact, knew that when he took Roark
Bradford's collection of Negro dialect stories of the Old
Testament, Ol' Man Adam an' His Chillun, as the basis for
his drama, he was in danger of offending many of the New
York theatre-goers. To be sure, metropolitan theatre-goers
are perhaps more sophisticated about racial and religious
matters than the average American, but Green Pastures
contained materials that, fifty years earlier, might have
caused riots--a Negro God the Father, Biblical language
in Negro dialect, a comic treatment of the Judaeo-Christian
story.

In an Author's Note to the play,[5] Connelly argued
for indulgence from white educated Christians for this treatment. "The Green Pastures," he wrote, "is an attempt
to present certain aspects of a living religion in terms of
its believers. The religion is that of thousands of Negroes
in the deep South. With terrific spiritual hunger and the
greatest humility, these untutored black Christians--many
of whom cannot even read the book which is the treasure
house of their faith--have adapted the contents of the Bible
to the consistencies of their everyday lives." Connelly
strengthens the suggestion that this is a play about "their
religion, not our religion" by commenting that Green Pastures
is not intended to be Biblically sound. It merely attempts
"to translate" the beliefs, "the meditations of some of the
old Negro preachers ..." into drama.

The tone of the play and of Connelly's private approach to his audience was successful in avoiding a disturbance. Green Pastures was not popular in the South
(I know of no production in Louisiana, for example), but
neither did it cause any cries of outrage. A few critics,
like Richard Dana Skinner,[6] to be sure, did complain about
the theology of the play, but even Skinner was more offended
by the "intrusion of cuteness"--the heavenly fish fry, for
example--than by any lack of Christian orthodoxy. Connelly
had sinned "against real simplicity," he concluded. Most
of the critics, like John Mason Brown, approved of the play
as good entertaining theatre; but, at the time of its initial
production, they had reservations about the play as genuine

folk or religious drama.

In part, the critics felt a need to hold their tongues. They knew the history of objections to dramatizations of God on stage; they knew the average New York audience did not take kindly to religious plays of any sort; and they knew, too, that a play with an all-Negro cast might run into racial biases. Mr. Brown, for example, although he concluded that the play "somehow fell short of its ultimate goal, " saluted Green Pastures as being "brave and meritorious. "[7] Some critics were prepared to defend the play to the death; Brooks Atkinson, for example, called Green Pastures the "divine comedy of the modern theatre. [8]

Audiences, in the main, approved of the play. The role of the Lawd established Richard B. Harrison as a permanent fixture on the professional stage; and since his death, the part has done the same for his successor, William Marshall. As a filmed drama, Green Pastures was successful in both the United States and Europe, even in England where a law exists forbidding the dramatization of God on stage. [9]

Green Pastures has never become one of the favorite plays of academic critics as O'Neill's or Miller's or Williams' plays have been. It has never been argued that it is a matter of taste and an evidence of critical maturity to approve the play. It has, however, without the professional support of the academic critic, quietly established itself as one of the "great plays" in American theatre history. Just two years ago, in 1963, for example, Mr. Brown re-examined the play in the light of his earlier qualifications and concluded, "Let's face it with proper gratitude. The Green Pastures is a masterpiece. "[10]

The original danger of protest concerning the tone and subject matter--merely hinted at in such comments as Skinner's complaints--has in the past dozen years come, not from the racists, but from the occasional Negro leader. The Bishop of the African Methodist Episcopal Church, for example, a few years ago charged that the play was "irreligious" and that it "perpetuated out-moded stereotypes" of Negroes. [11] Mr. Brown has little sympathy now, at least as of 1962, with the objection; but in truth his own earlier qualifications had been based on a feeling that Green Pastures was guilty of some offense of that nature.

Seemingly, he had then decided that the general intent of
the whole play was of sufficient merit for him to overlook
its weaknesses. He may well have reassumed that folk
plays, religious dramas, and social protest plays were
not successful enough in 1930 to risk success for this one
at that time by complaints.

Folk dramas, religious plays, plays about Negroes
were, of course, not completely new to the American stage
of 1930. Perhaps no other folk play, however, not even
Porgy; no other play about the "problem of the Negro,"
not even O'Neill's All God's Chillun; and no other religious
play, certainly not Barry's John, had quite so favorable
an initial reception and none has had the holding power of
Green Pastures. The secret of this power, it seems to me,
lies in its odd mixture of folk materials, religious matter,
and, finally, in its obvious social-moral theme. Green
Pastures, strangely enough, caters to everyone's biases
about race, about religion, about sentimentality; but finally
it rises above all questions of theatrical and social forms
and biases to make an obvious--a tragically obvious--com-
ment about the nature of man and the world in which he
lives.

Stated simply, the theme of Green Pastures is "No
one (including God) can judge mankind from the outside, and
the only way to join the human race is to share in its
suffering." Such a statement is, of course, fundamental
to most tragedy of the western tradition--from Oedipus
to Death of a Salesman--and to most humanistic philosophy.
Connelly did not invent the statement, but he did give it a
fresh interpretation in 1930 by a skillful manipulation of
familiar materials; moreover, it is in the manipulation--not
in the materials themselves--that Green Pastures achieved
the success denied to Barry's John.

II

Green Pastures is made up of two parts, the first
in ten scenes and the second in eight. Obviously, such a
play with its rapidly changing scenes, its multiplicity of
actions, and its actor-filled stage must depend upon the
"memory" of the audience to give it a continuity. Indeed,
the play is cast, like Williams' Glass Menagerie, in the
design of a "memory play," or to use Connelly's term, a
"meditation" play. Green Pastures, however, is not Mr.
Deshee's "private memory." Rather, Connelly first gives

its subject--the history of man (not a man) from the creation to the death of Christ--a private coloring, Mr. Deshee's,
merely as a preparation. The play, finally, is the race
memory of all men. It is intentional that, unlike the narrator in The Glass Menagerie, Mr. Deshee departs from
the play long before the final curtain.

Modern Negroes, weary of the "Uncle Tom" pose of
the "Good Ol' Darky, " may well be offended at the opening
scenes of Green Pastures. While it is true that Mr. Deshee
is shown as a "good man, " he seems so simple that his
goodness seems to be the result of ignorance rather than
virtue. In the first scene in the Louisiana Sunday School,
for example, he is teaching a class of small Negroes. In
his opening speech, he summarizes for his young charges
the first five chapters of Genesis, and this summary is
little more than a list of begats and deaths. His main concern is with age: "Adam lived a hundred and thirty years
an' begat a son in his own likeness ... Seth. An de' days
of Adam after he had begotten Seth were eight hundred years!"
The only reference he makes to contemporary life is that
"ol' Mrs. Gurney's mammy" is called "ol' Mrs. Methusaleh
caize she's so ol'. " This summary of ages, Mr. Deshee
calls, "de meat and substance" of the first five books, and
he concludes with the question, "Now, how you think you
gonter like de Bible?"

All queries from the children are answered by Mr.
Deshee with a proper respect for conventional morality and
a complete dependence upon the literal truth of the Bible as
he understands it. In scene iii, for example, which is also
set in the Sunday School class, one boy wants to be sure
that Adam and Eve were married the proper length of time
before the birth of Cain. "My mammy say it was a hund'ed
years, " the Boy says. Mr. Deshee admits that is now
difficult to give an answer in the exact number of years,
but his answer assures the Boy that at least the proper number of months passed.

This concern with age and with proper behavior seems
to suggest a lack of understanding of the "central truths" of
the religious story; at least, modern, metropolitan, educated
Americans would probably think so, and 1930 theatre critics
and 1965 Negro leaders have been made uncomfortable by
the suggestion. But for the leader (Mr. Deshee) of a people
who live hungry, die young, and face day-after-day indict-
ments that they are "by nature" immoral because of their
transgressions against the conventional code, such a concern

is no more than an attempt to make an abstract religion a
practical guide, and, a people who die young must be im-
pressed by age.

Connelly avoids making obvious social-protest associations. Mr. Deshee's life among the poor, the hungry,
and the shamed--the Negro scene--is never mentioned.
Rather, a kindly, old preacher and a chorus of innocent
children set the stage. No one, in or out of the Ku Klux
Klan, would deny the basic goodness of such a group; but
the audience's sympathy for this group must also be mixed
with some mild sophisticated contempt. Undoubtedly in
such a state, the folks are good; but the suggestion must
be there that "such a state" is, therefore, necessary for
them. The first scene in Heaven, scene ii, develops the
same concept of the good, simple "Darky." The Heavenly
scene does show "adults"--Angels, God, Gabriel; but, in
addition to being child-like, they are in terms of the religious story being used, naturally good beings. Connelly
has, moreover, surrounded them with children, Cherubs.
The use of characters who are given all the qualities of the
stereotype of the "good Darky," and who are yet loosely
drawn from the Biblical story, makes a sentimental appeal
to the audience. It shows the "naturally" simple Negro in
his pursuit of "naturally simple" goals, and it reinforces
this sentimental view with a simple religious view. The
Angels, even white, Anglo-Saxon ones, may be simpler
than man by the popular sentimental view, but they do
possess superior advantages; and it is well, even in one's
thoughts, not to offend them. The total view of the first
three scenes is one of the Negro as simple and good--the
Uncle Tom figure.

III

In the following scenes--with Cain, with the blues-
singing Zeba, with the Children of Noah, and with the Children of Israel--the Lawd and the audience get another view
of man, the Negro. Here is the "depraved being" who--for
the sake of our wives and daughters--must be kept in
isolation. The evidence is overwhelming--he kills his brother, he steals, he lies, he betrays. He does, in fact,
everything that all the imperfect heroes and villains of the
Old Testament did; and he does it all in a fashion that will
allow those who view the Negro actors in the play to conclude, "That's the Negro in society. That's how he behaves."

Anyone who has ever worked with "the folk" in any
position of law enforcement or guidance--as policeman,
teacher, social worker, parole officer, or simply as one
whose sympathy has led him to join a movement for the
"oppressed" group--is ready to join in the weariness of the
Lawd after so much sin. "Dat's about enough," God concludes. "I'se stood all I kin from you. I tried to make
dis a good earth. I helped Adam, I helped Moses, an' I
helped David. What's de grain dat grew out of de seed?
Sin! Nothing but sin throughout de whole world. I've given
you ev'y chance. I sent you warriors and prophets. I've
given you laws and commandments, an' you betrayed my
trust. ... So, I renounce you. Listen to the words of yo'
Lawd God Jehovah, for dey is de last words yo' ever hear
from me. I repent of dese people dat I have made and I will
deliver dem no more."

Connelly's insight into the nature of the "Good Outsider," weary with the "transgressions of the folk," seems
so fresh that his characterization might have been created
in 1965 rather than in 1930, as this insight relates to the
currect race problem. In 1965, for example, more than
sixty percent of white America has complained that the Negro
drive for "equal rights" is moving too fast, obviously suggesting a repentance of past "deliverances."

The accumulative view of these central scenes of
the play stands in contrast to the first three scenes and
shows the Negro as violent and depraved--the Ku Klux Klan
image. One accepting both views might reasonably argue
that the solution of the race problem lies in moving the
Negro from the world of Cain and David back to the Sunday
School of Mr. Deshee.

IV

With the Lawd's renunciation scene, however, a
pronounced change takes place in the tone of the play and,
I would think, in the response of the audience. Until the
last few scenes, the white sophisticated audience has been
watching--with some amusement, some sympathy, and probably some impatience--the history of "the folk" from the
point of view of the Lawd. In another place, [12] I have argued
that the character of the Lawd is based on a stereotype of
the "Good White Man," as he sees himself in relationship
to the folk. There may be some question of the validity
of that argument; but there is none, I think, of the assump-

tion that the Lawd through his renunciation speech reflects
the varied attitudes of the well-meaning, sympathetic outsider to the problems and errors of the folk.

From the moment of his renunciation, however, the
Lawd, in dramatic terms, loses his superiority. In scene
vi, Part II, the Lawd recognizes the righteousness of Hosea,
now a resident of Heaven, who, unlike the Lawd, is not
willing to renounce mankind. He is, in terms of dramatic
conflict, the Lawd's superior; and in their conflict--their
unspoken agon--he overwhelms the Lawd. The Lawd's
final speech in this scene shows his capitulation to the
superior force. "You know I said I wouldn't come down, "
the Lawd shouts down to the voice of goodness on earth
after Hosea's silence has weakened his resolve. "Why
don't he answer me a little? Listen, I'll tell you what I'll
do. I ain't goin' to promise you anythin', an' I ain't goin'
to do nothin' to help you. I'm just feelin' a little low, an'
I'm only comin' down to make myself feel a little better,
dat's all. "

In the last long scene of the play, scene vii, the
Lawd comes into conflict with Hezdrel, one of the characters
Connelly created without Biblical authority. If the characters
to this point could be divided into "good simple" and "bad
smart alecky" Negroes, Hezdrel is a new kind of being.
He is good, courageous, faithful. Unlike those who have
gone before him, he is a complicated human being, wiser
in the matters of man than the Lawd himself. God, in fact,
finally has to ask Hezdrel for the secret of his knowledge--
how does one (even God) discover mercy?

Hezdrel answers him, "De only way he could find it.
De only way I found it. ... Through suffering. " God leaves
the scene, puzzled and full of admiration, the "inferior being"
who must be removed for his own safety; and the curtain
falls on the heroic Hezdrel as he gives the battle cry of man,
"Give 'em eve'ything, Boys. "

In these two scenes, the audience's sympathy must
shift from the Lawd to Hosea and Hezdrel. They are, in
the terms of Green Pastures, the more knowledgeable, the
morally superior. They are in terms of their agons with
the Lawd in the same position Tiresias holds with Oedipus,
Antigone with Creon. At about this point in the drama, the
audience must become sharply aware that although the actors
are Negroes, the subject is man; and God's repentance of

"dese people" includes not merely the <u>folk</u> in the play, but the <u>folk</u> in the audience.

The audience's identification with the Lawd has now stopped. The basic history of man in this play--in spite of the actors and the dialect--is not the story of the Negro race, but the story of Christian man. If the white outsider in the audience is going to sympathize with the Lawd's decision to withdraw from the Negro world, he must--in the next step--put himself in a world from which God has withdrawn and he must approve of that withdrawal. The white audience has convicted itself by its own biases to a God-forsaken world.

The Lawd's argument for his withdrawal from man, in terms of the current race problem, pretty much represents the doctrine of "separate but equal" treatment of the folk. The Lawd of <u>Green Pastures</u> finally concludes that he cannot judge men fairly from without, and the play ends with the sacrifice of Jesus on the cross. Whether <u>Green Pastures</u> is orthodox Christian doctrine is a matter for the theologians.

From a dramatic point of view, however, Connelly's <u>Green Pastures</u> offers a successful pattern for the writer of folk drama. All folk drama must assume that there are apparent differences between the audience and the folk; it must further assume that the audience considers itself superior (in some form) to the folk. The playwright must then find some way to cause this audience to sympathize-- and to identify--with the folk characters. Connelly with his characterization and language shows the "typical behavior" of the Negro as this behavior is understood and observed by the outsider audience. Critics who have complained that his characterizations are stereotypes have some reason for their complaints. But Connelly is not concerned merely with the characters. He also has an action, a story; and the basis of this story is taken from the religious history of the outsider group. It is a history, however, that fits both the folk and the audience; and because folk and audience are welded together, it becomes clear that is the race of man, not the Negro race, that needs apology and mercy.

Joseph Conrad in his <u>Heart of Darkness</u> uses the same technique when he has his narrator, Marlow, interrupt a panegyric about British colonialism with a reminder that

London itself was once a colony, one of the dark places of
the earth.   But no other playwright and no other play, to
my knowledge, so carefully caters to the variety of biases
of its audience and then so artfully places the audience in
a position in which it must either surrender these biases
or prove victim to them.   Oedipus, to be sure, thinking
he is an "outside observer, " makes objective judgments
that ironically destroy him, but in Green Pastures the audience is given the Oedipus role.

It is the magic of Green Pastures, I think, that it
has from its beginning seemed exactly the right comment
for the times.   In the 1930's, with that wise, old actor,
Richard B. Harrison in the role of the Lawd, Green Pastures
was a play about mercy that almost grows out of sentimentality.   In the 1960's, when kindness is not enough,
the role of the Lawd played by the younger, the physically
larger William Marshall, has become a play about courage
and suffering--the suffering that comes when the "outsider"
acknowledges that he is a member of the human race, all
of it; and that he can do no less than his God did--suffer
with it.

Notes.

1.   See Paul T. Nolan, "Tolstoy's 'Power of Darkness':
Genre as Meaning, " Educational Theatre Journal, XVII
(March, 1965), p. 1-9, for a more complete argument.

2.   All citations from the play are from the edition
in John Gassner, A Treasury of the Theatre (New York,
1960), p. 897-927.

3.   The Glass Menagerie, scene i.

4.   Philip Barry (New York, 1965), p. 56.

5.   Gassner, Treasury of the Theatre, p. 897.

6.   Ibid., p. 896.

7.   Dramatis Personae (New York, 1963), p. 88.

8.   Cited in ibid., p. 15.

9.   It was, however, forbidden stage production.
See E. Bradlee Watson and Benefield Pressley's introduction

to Green Pastures in Contemporary Drama: Eleven Plays (New York, 1956), p. 45-56.

    10.   Brown, Dramatis Personae, p. 88.

    11.   Cited in ibid., p. 88-89.

    12.   "God on Stage: A Problem in Characterization," Xavier University Studies, IV (May, 1965), p. 75-84.

2. The Lecture Outline

Eugene Ionesco's The Chairs as an
Introduction to the Drama of the Absurd

Author's Comment: Although the "drama of the absurd"
probably contains a good deal of nonsense and trickery,
there can be little doubt about its influence in the modern
theater of the past twenty years.   On the kitsch level, the
assumptions of absurdist drama have gained widespread
popularity in such TV fare as "Batman."   In the legitimate
theater, the absurd movement as reflected in the varied
works of such men as Jean Genet, Edward Albee, Samuel
Beckett, Arthur Kopit, Jack Gelber, and Leroi Jones has
assumed major importance with serious critics.   Both senior
high school and college students have found it easy to identify
with the absurd movement, but they often assume that the
drama of the absurd merely reflects an attitude--wild. ir-
responsible, fun-and-gamish, perverse--that requires no
more understanding of drama than the humdrum of the
Beatles requires an understanding of music.

The problem for the teacher dealing with dramas of
the absurd is to help the student develop some sort of poetics by which he can approach the drama as a conscious
work of art, not merely as a protest against everything.
Oddly enough, the dramas of the absurd--since they are
protests not merely against social forms and social mores,
but also against theatrical forms--require a greater famili-
arity with conventional drama than do conventional plays
themselves.   To some degree, every absurdist playwright
consciously violates established dramatic principles as a
means of "shocking his audience into a new awareness."
Obviously, an audience must know the established principles
to be shocked by the violation.

Conventional drama--from Oedipus to Death of a
Salesman--assumes that something happens, an action, that
has meaning.   The drama of the absurd--in such plays as
Endgame and Waiting for Godot for obvious examples--de-
pends upon the audience's expectation of a meaningful action.
Without the anticipation, the lack of an action would mean
nothing.   Conventional drama uses characters whose natures
are suggested by their choices; the drama of the absurd uses
characters--who sound like the characters of the conventional

drama--but either they make no choices at all, or their choices are meaningless in terms of the result of an action. Conventional drama uses dialogue to indicate the action, the choices, and the natures of the characters; the drama of the absurd uses language that stands in opposition to the characters and events. In The Bald Soprano, for example, Ionesco has no bald soprano, hence by the logic of the absurd, the title.

Ionesco's The Chairs is a particularly good play to use as an introduction to the drama of the absurd, both because it is a relatively simple play and because the absurdist techniques are used in such a way that the student may observe them as easily as he can identify blank verse, tragic flaw, or climax in conventional drama.

Each of the following assignments starts as a conventional analysis of the standard "parts"--action, character, and dialogue--of all drama; but after the student has made his conventional analysis, he should comment on what is being said about the "part" itself through the absurdist methods.

1. Action: The student should write (or discuss) the central action of the play. An old man prepares a paper that is the sum total of his experience. He then hires an orator to read the paper to a distinguished audience, but the orator proves to be a mute. The student will recognize immediately that this action is absurd, a kind of "sick" joke; but he should, also, be concerned with whether there is any truth in this action. Is it representative? Do people, as the student observes them, give the "philosophy of life" to a mute orator?

2. Characters: The Chairs has only three characters represented by actors--the Old Man, the Old Woman, and the Mute Orator; but, as the list of dramatis personae shows, there are "many other characters," the invisible, perhaps nonexistent, members of the audience that the Old Man has invited for his speech. The student should first assume that all the characters are real. (The stage directions at the end of the play insists they are: "We hear for the first time the human noises of the invisible crowd.") The student should evaluate all the characters, as we would make a character analysis for any play. Throughout the play, however, there is every reason to assume that the "many other characters" are mere figments of the old people's

minds; so the student should also evaluate these characters
as symbols of the values of the visible characters.

3. <u>The Tragic Protagonist</u>: The Old Man, aged 95,
may be readily seen to be a caricature of the tragic hero.
In terms of conventional tragedy, his "heroic achievements"
are obviously absurd. He is a general, but a general
<u>factotum</u> (a janitor); and the "209" he killed in battle were
"flies." It should also be observed, however, that all
"heroic achievements" are absurd in this play. The Colonel,
who is a genuine military hero, must be told to behave himself and not to throw cigarette butts on the floor; and he is
asked of his military victories, "... Colonel, it's slipped
my mind--in the last war did you win or lose?" If, on the
one hand, all heroic protagonists are absurd, then, on the
other hand, are even the absurd "heroic"? Is the protagonist a genuine tragic hero?

4. <u>Language</u>: It is in the dialogue of the theater
of the absurd that the student will have the most trouble
and the critic has shown the most interest. <u>The Chairs</u>
is, in part, a broad burlesque of speech forms. The student
should be prepared to point out the clichés, but he should
also note that it is not merely the trite expression, but the
trite form as well, that is being burlesqued. When he is
aware that <u>The Chairs</u> makes fun of formal speeches, of
dedications, of polite conversation, the student will conclude
that not merely speech but all social form is being burlesqued.

<u>Written Assignment</u>: Putting together his observations of
the separate parts of the play, the student should first draw
a conventional thesis in terms of these parts, defending this
thesis with his matter-of-fact analysis of action, character,
and language. Then he should indicate what attitude the
audience is expected to take toward this thesis by a consideration of the jokes, the ironic tone, and the burlesque. The
conventional analysis will tell him what <u>The Chairs</u> would
mean if it were conventional drama; the "absurdist elements"
tell him what attitude he should have toward the conventional
thesis.

3. <u>How-to-do-it-Details</u>

Markets for The One-Act Play

Although most fiction writers hope that their works
will be dramatized--for screen, stage, and/or TV, most
young writers seldom think of drama as a direct field in
which to work. It is, of course, true that Hollywood,
Broadway, and the national TV networks are about the most
difficult markets in the world for the beginning writer, but
the market for plays written for the amateur theater is
about as free as--and much more rewarding than--the market
for any other field of writing.

The fledgling playwright, it seems, would do well
to work in the one-act play. It is not that it is any easier
to write a brilliant one-act play than a brilliant full-length
drama; it is rather that it is certainly easier to write a
competent one-acter than it is a competent full-length drama;
and the amateur theater, while it hopes for occasional flashes
of brilliance, demands only competence.

There already exists a vast number of "how to write"
books on the drama. No would-be playwright need expect
much help with basic dramatic "rules" in an article the
scope of this. He does need some help in the work that
follows the composition of the play. It goes without saying,
of course, that the script of a play is merely the <u>score</u>
for a drama. A playwright should no more send <u>his play</u>
off for consideration before testing it than a musical com-
poser would send off a composition before playing it. The
means available to the beginning playwright are many:
school and community public performances, private performances, private performances with friends, and readings. It
is, therefore, assumed that the young playwright has written
a one-acter, tried it out with a group of actors or readers,
straightened out the "kinks," rewritten it, and is now ready
"to be discovered."

There are a great many academic and civic contests
for drama--the University of Arkansas Collegiate Contest,
and the Abilene, Texas, Children's Drama Contest, for examples. These contests are intended to serve largely as
scouts for the professional theater. If the playwright is
convinced that what he has written belongs on the national

stage, he should by all means use such contests as a means
to reach Broadway or Hollywood. Such contests are, however, a waste of time for the playwright who is merely
convinced that he has written a "competent play" which will
give pleasure if done by some amateur group. These contests usually draw from a hundred to several hundred entries,
and even the most generous of them limit their selections
to two or three "winners." They are intended to tell the
playwright how his work compares with that of other aspiring
playwrights; they are not intended to tell him whether his
work is adequate for the stage. These contests, moreover,
take a great deal of time. Usually, the playwright submitting a dramatic composition for consideration should
allow a year between the time of submission and the announcement of a decision.

Another market exists for plays--the publishers of
Broadway successes. Most of the publishing done by Samuel
French, Inc., for example, is of plays that have proved
their popularity with long commercial runs. To send a play
to such a market is to apply for admission to Who's Who.
When the play is ready for this market, the editors will
seek it out.

The market for plays--new plays, untried plays, plays
with nothing but a local production--is of two types; the
commercial publishers like Walter H. Baker Company who
supply the amateur theater with stage vehicles for a modest
royalty; and the magazines like Plays: The Drama Magazine
for Young People who supply their readers with plays that
may be read and produced without royalty. This market is
the reason for this article.

When one compares this list to any "possible list"
for poems or short stories, it may seem to be a slight
one; but it is a "buying market." These editors need and
want one-act plays, and they encourage submissions. Some
of them--if a play shows any merit at all--will give detailed
criticism of the work, even suggesting changes that could
make the work acceptable. Some of these markets, Plays:
The Drama Magazine for Young People, buy as many as a
hundred one-act plays a year. Others, like Audience or
Fair Sex, buy only one or two. Some, again like Plays,
make an effort to see that the plays are produced on the
amateur stage; others, like Chelsa, simply make the play
available to their readers, who may, if they wish, produce
the play with no further association with the magazine or

the author.

These markets all have one thing in common: they
are all looking for good, actable one-act plays. Some, however, are interested in plays that can be acted by grade
school students; some by high school students; and some by
college and community theater actors. Some of these markets are interested in plays for all three age-level groups.

In preparing a play for submission, the playwright
should type his manuscript on white paper, double-spaced,
on one side of the page only, of course. The list of characters should come first (and there is a bias in favor of plays
with more female than male roles); and "production notes"
should come last. A cover letter is not needed, and it is
probably more of an annoyance than an aid. A title page,
however, should give this information: the market for which
the play is intended, the title of the work, and the name and
address of the playwright, thus:

> Pioneer Drama Service
> Shubert Fendrich, Editor
> Cody, Wyoming
>
> (Title)
>
> By John Doe
> 101 Main Street
> Center City, Iowa

One last word. If a play is worth sending out once,
it is worth sending out at least a dozen times. The playwright in fact, would do well to make his list of markets
for each play before his first submission. If his play is
rejected by the first market, he should change the title page
and remail it to the second market. The manuscript, of
course, should be mailed flat. If no letter is enclosed, the
manuscript of one-act play can be mailed "educational rates"
for about 10 cents going and (be sure to enclose a self-
addressed stamped, return envelope) 10 cents coming back.
For twenty cents, the playwright can set up a date with
destiny; and any playwright who is not tempted by that pros-
pect probably should be writing for tool-and-die catalogues
anyway, not the stage.

Some of the Markets

I. Plays for the Grade School Theater.
    (Mss. should run about 4 to 10 pages.)
    The Church School. 201 Eighth Avenue, South
        Nashville (3), Tenn.   Lena Mereness, ed.
        Short plays and dramatic services for Sunday
        School performances for a Methodist audience.
    Coach House Press, Inc., 43 W. Jackson Blvd.,
        Chicago 4, Ill. O. M. Forkert, pub. Publishes
        longer plays for children's theater. (Many of
        these plays are intended to be acted by adults
        before a children's audience.)
    The Grade Teacher. 23 Leroy Avenue, Darien,
        Conn. Toni Taylor, ed. Publishes about 20
        plays each year.
    The Instructor. Danville, New York. Mary E.
        Owen, ed. Publishes about 20 plays each year.
    Little Red Schoolhouse Bulletin. LaFarge, Wis.
        Mrs. Mary Bufton, ed. Publishes about 5 plays
        each year.
    Plays: The Drama Magazine for Young People.
        8 Arlington Street, Boston (16), Mass. A. S.
        Burack, ed. Publishes about 30 plays in this
        group each year.
    The Standard Publishing Company, 8100 Hamilton
        Ave., Cincinnati (31), Ohio. Ethel Uhrich, ed.
        Plays on Biblical themes for the Sunday School
        audience.

II. Plays for the High School Theater
    (Mss. should run about 11 to 20 pages.)
    Art Craft Play Company. Box 1830, Cedar Rapids,
        Iowa. Write first for free booklet, "Pointers to
        Writers of Amateur Plays."
    Walter H. Baker Company. 100 Summer St.,
        Boston 10, Mass.
    Banner Play Bureau, Inc. 619 Post St., San
        Francisco (9), Calif. Leslie H. Carter, Pres.
        "One-act Christmas comedies and mystery plays
        only."
    The Church School. (See I above) High school and
        church theater.
    Drama Guild Publishers, Tiffany Road, Norwell,
        Mass. High school and church theater.
    Drama Shop. 109 14th St., N. W. Mason City, Iowa.
        Dramatic readings and orations.

Dramatic Publishing Co., 179 North Michigan Ave., Chicago 1, Ill. Free catalogue on request.

Eldridge Publishing Company. Franklin, Ohio. Church and high school theaters.

Samuel French, Inc., 25 West 45th St., New York (36) N.Y.

Harper & Row Plays. 2500 Crawford Avenue, Evanston, Ill. V.E. Powers, ed. "... we are publishing very few scripts of any length or kind these days; and our publication plans for 1964 include only those scripts which I have previously acquired for the past two or three years."

Heuer Publishing Co. Drawer 551, Cedar Rapids, Iowa. Edward L. Heuer, ed. Write first for free copy of "Pointers to Writers of Amateur Plays."

David McKay Company, Inc. 119 West 40th Street, New York (18), N.Y. "Taboos are sex, drinking scene, and cursing."

Plays: The Drama Magazine for Young People. (See I.) Publishes about 40 plays a year in this group.

Pioneer Drama Service. Cody, Wyo. Shubert Fendrich. Plays suitable for production in high school theater, but editor has "bias" against plays that sound as though they were tailored for high school students. No taboos except "dullness."

The Standard Publishing Company. (See I.)

III. College and Community Theater. (20 to 50 pages.)
The following publishers, listed in I and II, also take plays for this market: Art Craft, Walter H. Baker, Banner Play Bureau, Drama Guild Publishers, Dramatic Publishing Co., Eldridge Publishing Co., Samuel French, Harper & Row, Heuer Publishing Co., and the Pioneer Drama Service.

Audience. 140 Mt. Auburn St., Cambridge, Mass. Firm Houghton, ed. "... short plays of highest quality."

Chelsea. P.O. Box 242, Old Chelsea Station, New York (11), N.Y.

Fair Sex. 545 Fifth Ave., New York, N.Y. Lila Rosenblum, ed. "... interested in fantasies and short plays, the kind that used to be called 'Gothic'."

First Stage. Purdue University, 324 Heavilon Hall, Lafayette, Ind. Henry F. Salerno and Harold H. Watts, editors. "Plays of outstanding quality that have not been produced professionally."

III

Shop Talk in Print

Another kind of writing that comes from the class-room lecture and from the preparation made for the class-room may be classified as "shop talk" in print. It differs from the "lecture" in print in that it is primarily directed toward other teachers--not necessarily scholars--rather than towards students. Such writing, it is true, is like the lecture-in-print in that the subject matter is the same, but the audience and the approach are different. The first article, a study of Tolstoy's "Power of Darkness," was first published in The Educational Theatre Journal, XVII (March 1965), pages 1-9. The essay has some of the general features of scholarly writing in that it is serious, exact, and offers a new view about a traditional subject. The scope of Nolan's essay, however, puts the work in the classroom rather than the scholar's study. This essay is, obviously, not the beginning of a larger study of either the problem of form in drama or of Tolstoy's entire work, but rather it is a background consideration for a single play--the subject of a classroom lecture. The second article, concerning selecting "great" plays for school pro-ductions, first appeared in Dramatics, XXXIX (October 1967), pages 21 and 32-33, a theater journal for high school play directors. This article, and the seven that followed it in the series in Dramatics, clearly grew out of the kind of shop talk that teachers engage in when faced with the practical problem of "selecting a play." The third article, a general discussion of writing plays for children, was first published in Southern Speech, XXVI (Spring 1961), pages 224-234; but Dr. Nolan commented that the essay is little more than a polished version of a dozen conversations he had had with teachers about the ways one can go about writing plays for the classroom. The fourth article, con-cerning the qualifications for graduate faculty members in new graduate schools, was first published in the Ball State University Forum, VIII (Spring 1967), pages 70-76. As did the article on writing plays for children, this article grew out of shop talk in the faculty lounge. Unlike the other,

however, this fourth articles does not represent Dr. Nolan
as speaking as a specialist to fellow teachers about his
speciality.   Rather, he is "having his say" about a subject
that is as well known by his colleagues as by himself.

1. About a Classroom Subject

Tolstoy's Power of Darkness:
Genre as Meaning

While critics, generally speaking, have treated
Tolstoy's Power of Darkness at least with faint praise, it
is almost conventional to qualify this praise with acknowl-
edgements concerning the playwrights "ignorance of the
conventional theatre" or his pre-occupation with non-
artistic matters. It is generally assumed that in spite
of the intellectual power of this play that there is something awkward, something unstageworthy, about it. John
Gassner, in his Form and Idea in Modern Theatre,[1] for example, mentions The Power of Darkness only to illustrate
his argument that the early naturalists sometimes used
inadequate theatrical devices--the soliloquy in The Power of
Darkness--because they failed to develop theatrical techniques more suitable to the new form. Janko Lavrin in
his Tolstoy: An Approach calls the play "a masterpiece"
of "peasant drama," but he speaks of the play as being a
product of that period in Tolstoy's life when "his aesthetic
and his moral sense now became definitely divorced, and
the latter won the battle."[2]

One of the problems in dealing with The Power of
Darkness comes, it seems to me, from our awareness that
with Tolstoy we are in the presence of a man of great
artistic merit in other forms, notably the novel, but of a
man who seemed to have had no affinity for the theater.
Tolstoy's own willingness to write an altenate ending for
Act IV upon being told that his original ending was "too
gruesome for the theatre"[3] is always taken as evidence of
his uncertainty as a dramatist. Then, too, Tolstoy's
criticism of Shakespeare has led many critics, including
G. Wilson Knight, to conclude that "the true Shakespeare ...
eluded Tolstoy," and to assume from this critical inability
that it is not to be expected that he could ever write great
drama. There is a "rugged beauty to Tolstoy's gospel,"
Knight concludes, "But it is not enough; not enough for a
great religious drama."[4]

A great artist is one who takes the materials available to him and shapes them to suit his personal needs.
He is one, moreover, who binds himself only to the separate

work of art and the idea contained within it.   Soliloquies
when viewed in the history of dramatic techniques may have
been labeled "old fashioned" in 1886 when Tolstoy used them
in The Power of Darkness or when Williams used them a
half century later in The Glass Menagerie, but such an
observation is entirely aside from the point.   Tolstoy's use
of a "horror scene" in Act IV may well be distasteful to the
theatergoer of the Age of Victoria, but one may wonder if
this taste should, for the artist and his critics, be the basis
of a final judgment.

What one expects from a critic facing a work of art
is that he assumes that he is to find first what it is, what
its rules are, what its harmony is.   It is not expected that
one start with a conviction as to what the work should be--a
"peasant naturalistic drama," for example--and then damn
elements in the play because they do not fit this conviction.

Tolstoy as critic set his standards for the drama:
"... the drama, to serve the importance attributed to it,
should serve the elucidation of religious consciousness . . .
art should have found, as it is now beginning to find, a new
form corresponding to the altered understanding of Chris-
tianity. "[5]

The religious truth of The Power of Darkness is
clear enough.   Evil is a force that feeds upon all it touches,
growing in strength as it corrupts all about it.   Only by
the acts of Christian compassion, confession, and surrender--
only when the protagonist is willing to take upon himself the
sins of his world--is evil destroyed and salvation possible.

Such a truth seems much closer to the aim of the
medieval morality play than to the naturalistic drama; and
yet Tolstoy used so many of the characteristics of the
naturalistic drama that no critic, to my knowledge, has ever
doubted that, in spite of some "shortcomings" in the accomplishment, the play was certainly intended for this
genre.   It is recognized, of course, that the characters in
The Power of Darkness, even the half-witted stepdaughter,
are not mere puppets in the hands of an unfriendly, or indifferent, nature; they are not mere nerves aching in an
alien body.   Man is the center of the world of Tolstoy's
drama.   He makes choices, and insofar as these choices
are good or evil, he is damned or saved.

At the same time, Tolstoy is no medievalist, and
this play--beyond the religious quality of its theme--is not
formed in the likeness of Everyman. Tolstoy, like the
naturalists, deals with the concrete manifestations of good
and evil, not with the abstract personifications.   Nikita, his
protagonist, is the separate man tempted to evil not by an
image of Lust, but rather by the highly personalized Anisya,
lured to destruction not by Satan, but by the crafty mother.
Tolstoy, moreover, sets his drama in a concrete world of
facts, and he accepts, for the purpose of the drama, that
facts may be viewed relatively.

He, in fact, shows us this world first in comic
terms, then in realistic terms, then in naturalistic terms,
then in grotesque terms, and only finally in religious terms.
Seeing good and evil in this play is not a process of reduc-
ing the temptation of the flesh to a transformation of that
temptress to a religious abstration. It is rather to recognize, on a naturalistic level, the demands of the flesh in
its own terms and then to go beyond these demands.   The
shifts in theatrical style from act to act are not a weakness
of the drama, not an evidence that Tolstoy was trying to
use a form, naturalistic drama, that did not fit his religious
temperament.   Rather they are the means by which he
demonstrates his religious, and his dramatic, truth.   The
genre employed in each act is not a device nor an evidence
of artistic confusion in this play; rather it is the meaning.

Tolstoy's "new form" is not a new theatrical con-
vention; rather it is the use of attitudes toward life, as they
are formalized in theatrical genres, to lead to an attitude
that encompasses and surpasses all others.   Tolstoy's
observation that Shakespeare "piled up in his plays all
possible events, horrors, fooleries, discussions, and effects" is damning to Shakespeare's reputation as a "dramatic
genius, " in Tolstoy's judgment, only because they are used
without conviction. "... Shakespeare, " he argued, "...
had not formed religious convictions corresponding to his
period ... had ... no convictions at all. "[6] Tolstoy's drama
is controlled by his conviction, so controlled, in fact, that
he can safely show his audience the world in views alien
to his own as a means of his conviction.

I

Act I introduces a problem in terms long familiar
to the comic theater.   Petr, a rich peasant in poor health,

and his younger wife, Anisya, differ little in this scene from
Lord and Lady Brute in Vanbrugh's The Provok'd Wife or
Pinchwife and Margery in The Country Wife. Petr, in spite
(or perhaps because) of his religious pretensions--"Of
Course! We must remember God"--is the typical cuckold.
He has taken as his second wife a woman some ten years
his junior in years and much his junior in vigor; and he
attempts to use her for his purposes. Anisya is correct
in her complaint to her husband that his plans are based on
desires for his own comfort and a disinterest in hers.

It is typical of the comedy of cuckoldry, too, that
the wife should take a younger man as her lover and that
the husband should be tricked (through his self-interest)
into keeping his wife's lover in his home. Nikita, as the
young lover, is part wit and part buffoon. In his mistreat-
ment of Marina, the girl he has "wronged," he has the kind
of logical cruelty (with less cause) that Etherege gave his
hero, Dorimant, in The Man of Mode; but there is less of
Dorimant than there is of Wycherley's Horner in Nikita.
It is true that he has seduced both the orphan girl, Marina,
and his employer's wife, Anisya; but like Horner, he op-
erates solely on the level of the flesh. He is not motivated
by his pride, as is Dorimant; his is not an assault on the
spirit. He merely wishes for the gratification of an animal
appetite. "It's all a puzzle to me," he says. "I love those
women like sugar; but if a man sins with them--there's
trouble."

The other characters, too, are presented in this
first act in comic terms. Matrena, Nikita's mother,
is the old bawd--crafty, vulgar, hypocritical. She takes a
special pleasure, for example, in bringing her husband to
the man her son has cuckolded so that the cuckold himself
can advise the father to leave the boy alone. Horner in
The Country Wife, for example, takes special pleasure in
using Pinchwife as the means of reaching his wife, Margery.
Matrena, too, takes delight in thwarting her husband's
orders.

"Orders him?" she scoffs. "Stick his orders under
a dog's tail. I'll talk over the whole business with your old
man right away; I'll sift it so there won't be anything left
of it: my son's living in happiness [adultery] and expecting
more [wealth]--and I'm to marry him off to a vagabond girl!
Do you think I'm a fool?"

The problem for the protagonist, Nikita, in this first act is two-fold. He must free himself from his obligation to Marina, the girl he has wronged; and he must continue his position in the home of his mistress's husband. His accomplices are his mistress and his mother, both of whom are vulgar, immoral, animalistic. His chief antagonist is his father, who preaches conventional Christian morality to his son.

There is no doubt that the playwright, as a moral being, agrees with the preachments of Akim, Nikita's father, in this first act. As an artist, however, Tolstoy allows us to see Akim in comic terms. He is a religious man who makes his entrance "crossing himself before the ikon"; and all of his actions are motivated by a belief in the Christian code. The girl his son has wronged is "a decent girl" and he is sorry for her. From the mother's point of view, Marina is a "hussy, " a "streetwalker, " because she has no family and no wealth; and Akim is talking nonsense because his "sorrow on the whole world" will allow his "own folks [to] go hungry. " Akim would have his son act by God's will; Matrena would have him act by the cardinal principle of the comic world: good sense protects one's self-interest.

In the agon between Akim and Matrena, Tolstoy gives Matrena the stronger character and makes Akim something of a fool. He is, in fact, much like Foresight in Congreve's Love for Love, if we ignore the fact that Akim is preaching Christian compassion, not "Astrology, Palmistry, Physiognomy, Omens, Dreams, &c. " It is not only that his speech abounds with those mannerisms that normally identify the pompous fool in comedy--repetitions, easy irritations, cant phrases like "y'see"; it is also that he is proven to be the fool. He allows his wife, Matrena, to overcome his convictions; and then, after he has violated a fundamental moral conviction, he makes a feeble and comic attempt to save appearances by refusing to drink vodka. But he will take tea. "Tea's my sin, " he admits; and in the terms of the struggle in the way of this comic world, tea (a woman's drink) is his weakness. It is, however, not the theological sense of sin, only the social one. His confession in fact, is expressed much like those in the comedy of manners in which the fools and rogues describe social lapses with celestial language.

The dialogue throughout this first act is heavily

controlled by animalistic images.   The scene opens with
Petr calling for Nikita to control the horses.   "The horses
are loose again.   They'll kill the colt before you know it,"
Petr tells Nikita.   This seemingly naturalistic episode
serves two functions.   Most obviously in Act I it establishes
the animal world in which the first action occurs.   In this
world, Petr calls Anisya "a wet hen"; she calls him " a
mad dog."   Akulina, Petr's feeble-minded daughter, calls
Anisya a "cur."   Nikita complains that Anisya is "snorting"
and refuses to be "petted."   Anisya calls Nikita a "jackass."
Matrena defends Nikita's lovemaking with Marina by an
animal analogy: "Even calves have their fun, you know."
Petr, Matrena tells his wife, is "a scarecrow," one that
could scare away live animals.   The poison that Matrena
gives Anisya to rid herself of an old husband is "good for
cockroaches, too."

What disturbs the easy acceptances of the animal
code of the world is the multiplicity of religious utterances.
It is not only Akim who argues in terms of religious truths,
but also even Nikita and Anisya.   Anisya first refuses to
take the poison from Matrena because "I'm afraid it may be
sinful."   Petr admits, however perfunctorily, that "We must
remember God."   Nikita swears "to Christ" that nothing
has happened between him and Marina, although in his final
speech, a soliloquy, he confesses that he has "sinned" with
her.   What keeps us from viewing the expressed religious
sentiments of this play in the same light that we see Lady
Wishfort's religious pretensions in The Way of the World
is that by the use of the soliloquy Tolstoy shows that the
utterances are the products of the mind as well as of the
lips.

In the way of the animal world in this act, the brute
view--cunning, pitiless, gross--overcomes and corrupts the
religious sentiments, just as in the comedy of manners,
the flesh-based wit overcomes the heroic and religious pretensions; but there has been a slight symbolic warning:
when the animals (the horses) are loose they kill the young
(the colt).   On the level of moral law as it may be seen
working even in the animal world, he has unloosed the
forces of evil and stands in danger of destruction.   In Act I,
however, it is the animal world, the comic world, that we
see.   The moral implications of Nikita's betrayal of Marina,
the melodramatic implications of Anisya's plan to murder
her husband, the grotesque implications of a union between
Nikita and Akulina are all overcome by the comic.   After

watching the three women--Marina, Anisya, and Akulina--
make advances to Nikita, we can almost sympathize with
his bewilderment.   One almost expects Nikita, like Wycherley's Horner, to complain to the women, "... I cannot
make china for you all, but I will have a roll-waggon for
you, too, another time. "

II

The separation between the first and the second act
is six months in time, but it is an even greater distance in
tone.   In Act I all of the characters are moved to their
sins by sexual desires, but such crimes are comic, animalistic, "like sugar. "   In Act II greed becomes the con-
trolling motive.   No longer is man the animal in search
of physical satisfaction; he is now economic man destroying
human life in the hopes of abstract gain. Nikita could, at
least, imply that in his seduction of Marina he simply
created pleasure for two with no intention of harm for
either, if Marina had simply kept their "sinning" to herself.
Act II deals with the murder of Petr; and Anisya"s first
speech of any length--a soliloquy--puts the struggle on the
level of greed. She is murdering him for his money; and
his own greed--"It's lucky he's afraid to part with it [the
money]. It's still in the house. "--works to her advantage.

Realistic drama has a tendency to involve us in the
problems of society--how to achieve success in some
material or social way.   Ibsen's A Doll House on its most
obvious level is concerned with promotions in business,
hiring and firing, and concealing a crime.   Act II of The
Power of Darkness opens with the problem of the lovers'
ridding themselves of Petr, finding his money, and concealing the crime, and almost every speech in this act is
concerned with this problem.

Religious life and animal life still form the background for much of the conversation, but unlike Act I in
which genuine religious and animal attitudes are expressed,
in Act II, they are subordinated to the workings of a mer-
cantile society.   Money is the single word most used in
this act, and all other matters, both religous and spiritual,
are justified in terms of financial success.

"Money's the root of the whole matter, " Matrena explains to her son, Nikita; and her explanation goes beyond
the simple matter of gaining legal possession of the farm

that prompts her to utter the sentiment.

The longest religious discussions in this act, ironically, belong to the two arch-criminals, Anisya and Matrena; but neither character is concerned with religion. Anisya, who sees that in the natural course of events her husband will soon die anyway and leave her free to marry Nikita, worries about the "sin" involved in poisoning her husband. It is not merely that she fears detection; it is, also, that on the level of the animal world her sin is meaningless. It is the kind of an immoral act that no animal would commit.

In a long discussion with Anisya and a Friend, Matrena asks of Petr, "Well, will you give him extreme unction today?" For her, however, the language of religion is merely a cloak to ask Anisya about the matter of murder. She (and the audience must follow her lead in this scene) is completely unconcerned with the religious life. To her in this act, religion is simply one of the social facts, in fear of which people may be forced to act or restrained from acting. The knowledgable person in the way of the world knows how to use it for his purposes. Matrena, for example, threatens Anisya that she will use the social force of religion against her if they fail to agree. "I'll kiss the cross and say I never gave her powders ...," she tells Anisya.

Nikita, whose animalistic "sins" in Act I set the tragic action in motion, is an unwilling accomplice in this act. He is, on an emotional level, opposed to the women's concern with money, and he feels sorry for the man that he has wronged. His animalistic "joy" in his "sinning" is lost in confusion and resentment as the animal "sin" becomes corrupted to serve a social aim--the acquisition of wealth and power. Until his will is destroyed by his mother, he refuses to become a part of the new crime. "What do I care [about wealth]," he asks; "the money's hers, let her worry about it."

The central figure of this second act is Matrena, and our concern is with the success of her action. As, on one level, we are concerned with how Nora, in A Doll's House, will achieve success--cover her "crime" and retain her home--so we are concerned in Act II of The Power of Darkness with how Matrena will achieve success--get rid of her husband, find his wealth, and secure his property for

her son. It is only on the basis of this concern that we
can respond properly to the "threats" of exposure and delay:
the possibility that Petr's sister will arrive in time to claim
the money, Akulina's reluctance to leave the house so that
Anisya is free to search for the money, the dangers of a
passing visitor, the dangers of Nikita's repentance and his
refusal to take the money and hide it. We must be concerned with the success of Matrena's plan, for the entire
act is structured in terms of it. It is, of course, perfectly
true that from a moral sense, we may find the entire action
horrifying; but from a dramatic sense, we must see Matrena's
plan succeed. Imagine, for example, what havoc would be
done to the play should Nikita persist in opposition in this
act and defeat the plan.

III

Nine months elapse between Act II and Act III, a
proper time for gestation. That which was conceived in
Act II has now been born. The differences in the terms
realism and naturalism are frequently a matter of personal
interpretation, but for this study if we assume that realism
deals with the appearance of things and accepts the laws of
things--economic laws, sociological laws, governmental
laws--as the basis of success or failure, we may call Act
II realistic. In a realistic play, for example, we should
be able to judge whether the protagonist has risen or fallen
in terms of some demonstrable measurement. If he has
risen, he is richer, or healthier, or more popular.
Naturalism takes the "law" of the society and applies it
to a larger context. "Free enterprise" becomes the "law
of the jungle"; the successful protagonist is not the young
man who marries the boss's daughter and gets the job he
wants. Rather he is the gangster who destroys the opposition and then goes to a testimonial dinner held in his
honor by the mayor. If one can, at least for the purposes
of this study, accept this definition, the differences between
Act II and Act III are those implied in the differences between the realistic and naturalistic view. Naturalism then
is what the realistic view finally brings to life, and Act III
is the world of the naturalist.

The third act is, of course, more grim, more sordid,
than is the second. Most noticeably, we see a change in
Nikita from one who appeared to be "gentle" to one who is
now "Rough every kind of way, " as Anisya tells a Friend.

Nikita's change is not fundamental. As the act ends,
for example, we find him weeping and complaining. "Oh,
life is hard for me, awful hard." He is still a man motivated by his animal appetites. Anisya, for example, tells
a Friend that although he pretends to act from concern for
money--"I must go to the bank; ... there's some money
due me," that it is really his concern for Akulina that is
"the cause of all." Unfortunately for Nikita's animal appetites, however, in the world of the naturalist, man as
animal is the beast perverted.

Lust on the animal level carries its own laws. It
is neither moral nor immoral. Once, however, it is subordinated to social law--a law that gives power to money--
it becomes twisted. Money, not physical attraction, becomes the means of achieving physical gratification; and
free animalistic love becomes prostitution. Nikita, who
was once rewarded for his amorous interest, now expects
to pay for his sexual gratification. For to go "on a spree
with some wench" is now possible because "He has money,"
and it is implied that only his money is now attractive.
Anisya, for example, even longs for her dead husband.

There is, in this act, not merely the grimness
that we expect from the naturalistic view, but there is also
the hopelessness. There is no place to go, nothing to hope
for. The comic view asks us to look at life honestly in
terms of our pleasures; the realistic view asks us to be
practical in evaluating how we can achieve those things
that give us pleasure; and the naturalistic view taunts us
with the conclusion that now we have achieved the freedom
of animals, we are animals, or less than animals, beasts.

The frolicking calf of Act I now becomes "a snake"
in Act III, a term that Anisya uses to describe her stepdaughter, Akulina. Anisya is still "a wet hen," but she is
no longer in a natural state. She accepts, for example,
the Friend's suggestion that she has been "bewitched" by
Matrena. She is, moreover, from Akulina's view, " a
prison rat." Nikita is described as being "drunk as a
fish," not quite so startling as Eliot's "pair of ragged
claws," but nevertheless more dehumanized than the calf
of Act I.

Act III, unlike Acts I and II, has no forward movement. In the hell of naturalism--whether in the society of
The Lower Depths or the isolation of Krapp's Last Tape,

people come and go, curse and argue, laugh and cry; but
nothing ever happens, nothing is expected. Nikita offers
his father money; his father refuses. He orders Anisya
from the house, but she does not leave. Akim speaks of
the "ruin" that is coming, but in truth, the ruin is already
there. Only the half-witted Akulina finds any pleasure at
all. For the rest, the present is unendurable, and the
future is unthinkable.

IV

If the author of The Power of Darkness had been
simply a complaining moralist, he might have rested at
the end of Act III convinced that he had demonstrated his
thesis: the power of evil is destruction. There is in
Nikita's curtain line for that act, "Oh, life is hard for me,
awful hard," a kind of finality, a kind of irony that we expect in naturalistic drama. At the conclusion of The Lower
Depths, for example, we are faced with the evidence of
despair. When the Baron announces that "The actor--he's
hanged himself ... ," Gorki allows Satine's epitaph, "Damned
fool--he's ruined the song ..." to be the final word.

But if there is a power to "darkness," there must,
in religious terms, also be a power to light. Tolstoy does
not set his drama in a world without moral laws; rather he
sets it in a world in which the moral laws have been violated. Act IV, in Tolstoy's first version, gives a visual
demonstration of the hell into which his characters have
descended.

The wages of sin [Nikita's "fun" in Anisya's terms]
have come to their most horrible fulfillment. Tolstoy, in
the first version of this act, is not merely satisfied with
the idea of horror--"Don't bury it [Akulina's child]; it's alive.
Don't you hear it? It's alive. There, it's wailing!" He
insists that we witness the horror itself. "How could it
wail?" his mother asks Nikita. "You squashed it into a
pancake. You crushed all its head." And we witness the
absolute act of horror. Even in the variant ending of Act IV,
the action remains the same, but in this version, we receive
the action in narration, rather than in drama.

Tolstoy's intention, however, to make Act IV a scene
of horror, a drama of the grotesque, is still clear enough.
It is true that he removed the macabre act from our sight,
but he adds an episode, unrelated to the action. Mitrich

tells of an experience with a child found by the soldiers, and his account abounds with cruelties--the bogey man, floggings, the tale of the little girl whom the soldiers were "going to smash. "

The variant ending of Act IV, it is true, is more hopeful in that it forecasts the moral restitution that is to come. Mitrich, in the final speech of this act, not only calls upon the saints--St. Nicholas the Martyr and the Holy Virgin Mother of Kazan--but he also forecasts the end of the rule of darkness. "They sure scared you, " he tells Anyutka, Anisya's ten-year-old daughter; but he has some comfort: "... much good may it do 'em. "

In contrast to the original ending--Nikita's cry of despair, "I've ruined my life, ruined it, "--this variant ending seems almost mild. But such a response comes only with a comparison. In either version Act IV is among the most gruesome in drama--more closely akin to the horror scenes in Webster's The Duchess of Malfi or to John Ford's 'Tis Pity She's a Whore than to anything in modern drama.

All that such a scene, such a kind of drama, can do, if taken as seriously as it must be in the context of this play, is to drain the emotions, to put us beyond physical appetite, beyond social desire, even beyond despair. After the horror of the grotesque, there is no place to go in human emotions.

V

Act IV is set in the dark of night, and ends in the pit beyond despair. Act V opens on a pastoral scene: "In the foreground, on the left, a threshing floor, and near it a stack of straw. ... The doors of the shed are open. ... In the background farm buildings can be seen; songs and the tinkling of tambourines are heard. " Even the second scene of Act V, which uses the same basic set as that used for Act I, adds to the impression of lightness and goodness. On the tables are "ikons and bread, " symbols of religious and human life. "The women are singing songs. Anisya is passing wine. "

It is true, of course, that in part Tolstoy uses both of these quiet settings for purposes of contrast. Nikita's torment, Akulina's confession, the continued evil of Anisya and Matrena in their moment of exposure stand out like

black figures before a white wall in these settings.   If in
viewing life from the comic, the realistic, the naturalistic,
and the grotesque, points of view, we have forgotten--or
despaired of ever finding--the good in life, we now see it
clearly before us.   The perverted views of life are only
views; the sun still shines.

Whereas in the earlier acts, the dark deeds and the
evil plotters controlled the world, we have now returned to
the universe of moral law.   As Nikita starts his confession,
for example, the Policeman orders, "Call the elder"; but
Akim, who was pitifully inept in the earlier scenes, is now
in complete control: "Let God's work go on, you know, "
he tells the Policeman, "when it's over, y'see, then you do
your business, y'see. "   And now Akim is the dominant
figure.   At last, in spite of his inability to cope with the
various secular views of the world, Akim has demonstrated
that in the final understanding, the religious view must
prevail.

Other plays exist, of course, in which the same
world, even the same event, is seen from different points
of view, --Pirandello's Right You Are If You Think You Are,
for example.   The Power of Darkness is, however, to my
knowledge the only modern drama that systematically uses
dramatic points of view, not for the purpose of arriving at
a relativist conclusion about the impossibility of truth, but
to demonstrate the supremacy of the moral-religious view.
It has been, it seems to me, the unusualness of this method
of using genre as part of the meaning that has caused some
misgivings about the final accomplishment of The Power of
Darkness as drama; but if a shortcoming does exist, it
seems clear that the fault does not lie with Tolstoy's
ignorance of dramatic conventions, but rather in his critics'
insistence that this play must be interpreted as a faulty
example of the naturalistic drama, only because they have
failed to see that Tolstoy's wide knowledge of dramatic forms
and his understanding of the implications of each form has
made it possible for him to speak through genre.   His "new
dramatic form" uses the conventions of the society about
him to challenge the assumptions inherent in these conventions.

Notes:

1.   (New York, 1956), p. 30.

2.   (New York, 1946), p. 15.

3.   Cited in John Gassner's Treasury of the Theatre
(New York, 1960), p. 175.   All citations to the play are
from the translation by George Rapall Noyes and George Z.
Patrick in this edition.

4.   Shakespeare and Tolstoy   (English Association
Pamphlet No. 88), p. 27.

5.   Tolstoy on Art   (Oxford, 1928), p. 459.

6.   Ibid., p. 457.

2.   About a Department Program

Reviving the Classics

There are two experiences that seem always to
justify themselves in the theater, even when the actual performance itself is below standard--when a new play is performed for the first time and when one of the "great plays"
(the classics) is revived. The reasons for the general
success of both are, oddly enough, contrasting, if not con-
flicting.

Local audiences like "new" plays. They sense in
the first production of a "brand new" drama the excitement
of "being in on the beginning, " of seeing something that
no one else has seen before. There is an added thrill to
watching a play-on-the-stage being created rather than, as
is often the case when a professionally popular play is done
locally, watching a show that is an imitation of another
production.

Local audiences also like to see the standard great
plays of western civilization--Oedipus, Hamlet, Romeo and
Juliet, Doctor Faustus, The Way of the World, She Stoops
to Conquer, The Rivals, Hedda Gabler, Cyrano de Bergerac,
Pygmalion, The Emperor Jones. There is a comfort in
watching a play, assured that the critical judgment as to
its worth has already been rendered. There is the added
comfort--still important to us Americans with our Puritan
suspicions of theater and frivolity--that watching such plays
is an educational experience, something that is "good for us. "

Playmakers, too, find in these two categories of
plays--the great and the new--advantages not found in the
production of the no-so-great and "merely recent" plays.
For the director, doing a new play is as challenging as
writing one. In fact some theater people--even playwrights--
would argue that the director who stages a play for the first
time is indeed a co-author. For the actors a new play means
an opportunity to create character rather than imitate another actor's creation.

In reviving a great play, one of the "classics, " the
director works with materials that he knows contain great
truths that he must make clear to his audience by a fresh

approach. He knows that a "great" play is never done
"perfectly"; and he can find in his production an opportunity
to compare his work with the great productions of the
current and past professional stage.   For a young actor
doing a role that Thomas Betterton did, that Edwin Booth
did, that Richard Burton is doing must be exciting.   When
an actor does a role like Hamlet, he knows he has taken
a part that requires all the talent, all the training, and all
the devotion that he possesses.   And every performer in a
production of a "great" play knows he is doing a role that
some famous actor did with pride.   Even "carrying a spear"
in a Shakespearian production is evidence of one's professional competence.

There are some serious doubts in doing such plays.
Often a "new" play has little to recommend it except its
newness.   It is profitable for the fledgling playwright to
see his work staged, but it is sometimes painful for the
audience, the director and the cast.   It is an educational
experience to see one's first production of Hamlet or
Oedipus, even a weak production; and it is certainly valuable
for the director and cast to work with the "best" drama in
the world.   Unless a production is unusual in some way,
however, it can be tiring to an audience to see "yet another"
ragged performance of a well-known play; and when one is
selecting from the known "great" dramas, he has to assume
that the audience knows the plays, or at least something
about them.

There are some two or three hundred plays in the
history of western civilization that have become so much
a part of our everyday heritage that they are familiar, in
one form or another, to anyone the least bit interested in
drama.   The National Council of Teachers of English, for
example, now has available for classroom use recordings
of medieval mystery plays, expecially an almost complete
production of The Second Shepherd's Play; of a great deal
of Shakespeare, including the complete play of King John,
and All's Well That Ends Well, Hamlet, Julius Caesar,
The Merchant of Venice, A Midsummer Night's Dream,
Romeo and Juliet, Macbeth, The Tempest, in cut versions;
and a full-length production of Oedipus Rex.

The Shakespeare Recording Society, to cite another
example, can now boast that "all of Shakespeare's plays in
consumate full-length performances by the outstanding
dramatic artists of our day" are, or soon will be, available

on record

    The new Greek Festival in Ypsilanti, Michigan, with
the help of such accomplished performers as Judith Ander-
son and Bert Lahr, is putting Greek classics like Aeschylus'
Oresteia trilogy and Aristophanes' The Frogs in the theater
gossip columns of even such non-dramatic newspapers as
Women's Wear Daily. The productions of the college theaters
like the Asolo Theatre of Florida State University are pretty
much covering both the classical and Shakespearian "great"
plays--Sophocles' Oedipus and Shakespeare's Much Ado About
Nothing in the 1966-67 season, for example--and the great
plays of other periods as well--Moliere's The Miser,
Congreve's The Way of the World, Sheridan's The Rivals,
and Ibsen, Shaw, O'Neill.

    Any survey of the various educational theater jour-
nals pretty much demonstrates the uniformity of the selections made from the great plays: all of Shakespeare, even
Henry VI; Oedipus Rex, Antigone, Medea, Oresteia, and
Aristophanes' various comedies--both in translations of the
original and modern French adaptations--for the Greek
drama; Everyman and The Second Shepherd's Play for
medieval drama; Ben Jonson, usually Volpone, and John
Webster, usually The Duchess of Malfi, for the English
Renaissance drama; Moliere and Racine for the French
baroque; Congreve's Way of the World and Wycherley's
Country Wife for the English Restoration; Sheridan's
The Rivals or The School for Scandal for the English
eighteenth century; Schiller's Mary Stuart, Rostand's
Cyrano de Bergerac, Buchner's Woyzeck, Turgenev's
A Month in the Country, Wilde's The Importance of Being
Earnest, about a third of Shaw, half of Ibsen, and all of
Chekhov for the nineteenth century.

    Even with the plays selected for the "curiosity"
value or because they represent an era, there is a sameness in the choices. Among nineteenth-century melodramas,
for example, the choices are usually The Drunkard, Under
Two Flags, or Dracula. For the twentieth-century plays
before World War II Eugene O'Neill is the common choice
for tragedy; Maugham, Shaw, and Noel Coward for comedy;
Peg O' My Heart, Abie's Irish Rose, and Journey's End
for sentimental comedy and melodrama.

Any high school or college theater director who has
done one of these plays--and most of the serious ones have--
has every reason to be a little offended by the inference
here that in doing any of these plays he has done anything
less than a wonderful service.

When a director goes into a school that has given
its audiences nothing but a steady diet of The Hick from
Hicksville, Teen Antics, and Laughing Gas and introduces
Shakespeare or Oedipus or The Cherry Orchard, he has a
right to be annoyed by any suggestion that there is anything
but merit in doing the great plays.

When George Nason, formerly a director for the
Sandia High School theater in Albuquerque and now director
of the San Bernardino, California, High School theater, does
a Shakespearian play, he is certainly not doing "old hat."
He wrote me recently about a production of Romeo and
Juliet that he did in California that suggests some of the
reasons for using the word "great" in describing such plays.

"Last fall," he explained, "the city was disturbed,
racially. What better time to show students and the community that art 'harmonizes all'? Again Mr. Shakespeare
came through and most successfully. We selected Romeo
and Juliet and really rather set it to West Side Story ."

A young couple of Negro students played Romeo and
Juliet, and Lord Capulet was played by a retired professional actor in the community, Chauncey Spenser.
Every theatrical device was used to show the relationship
of the civil disorder of Shakespeare's play to the disorder
of our own time.

It is easy to believe Mr. Nason when he reports,
"What fun it was, and how exciting to see these youngsters--
some of whom had never seen a play--take hold of the
Bard and go! They loved playing it; our audience loved
seeing it."

Even when the production has less imagination and
less daring, the "great" plays in the school theater--even
the most familiar ones--are noble experiments, great
adventures of the spirit. And they do get support. Any
production of Doctor Faustus, for example, probably succeeds
better in pleasing teachers, parents, and school board members than even a superior production of Teen Antics.

High school and college students, however, have a tendency to be suspicious. Macbeth is a great play. But the student who has "studied" it for half a semester in English III, who has listened to records of it, seen it on television and in the movies might well feel, and with some justice, that yet another production of it will offer him few surprises. He might even decide that he has had quite enough of Macbeth in any form for awhile.

To be sure, good productions of any of the great plays can make theater-goers of students as productions of plays like The Hick from Hicksville can never do. It is, however, probably more difficult to get students to support a program of Greek drama, Shakespeare, Chekhov, and O'Neill, until they have developed a taste for drama, than it is to get them out for a teenage play.

In spite of audience resistance, however, school directors can defend their practice of selecting their drama program from the world's "great plays" rather than from a catalogue of easy-to-do plays for the high school theater on several counts.

First, of course, one doing a great play does not need to defend his choice educationally. Productions of such plays as Hamlet, Oedipus and The Doll's House should be as much a part of any educational program as the sports schedule, the science rally, or courses in algebra or chemistry. There are few faculty members, regardless of their field, who would seriously disagree with this argument.

Secondly, the director knows that it is a more valuable experience for the student cast to be involved in a production of Antigone, Julius Caesar, or She Stoops to Conquer than in productions of plays like College Knights, Heavens Above and College Daze. The students learn not only more about life, but more about the craft of the actor, the art of language, the nature of real people.

Finally, it is even less expensive to do a production of some of the "great" plays than to do the average play written for the high school theater. Most of the "great" plays--except for foreign-language plays in modern acting editions--are royalty free, and the stage settings and properties are simpler and thus less expensive. When the director makes a choice between the "great" plays and recent Broadway plays like Critic's Choice, Poor Richard

and It's Never Too Late, this difference in expense can be
large enough to determine whether a school will do one
Broadway play a season or three or four of the non-royalty
"great" plays.

Only the rare high school or college director will
want to do nothing but the established "great" plays. Even
if the paucity of playwrights in every local community means
that one cannot do new plays, even if he wanted to, there
is an excitement in doing a "recent" play--something that
was new on Broadway a few years ago.

To get the balance between tradition and novelty,
between the best and the most recent, most directors want
to do both. It is true, of course, that more school directors
are taking the fair recent plays more often than they are
taking the great older plays; and thus directors who have a
production of Hamlet or Oedipus may well ask the question,
"Why not the best? Those have, it is true, been done
so often in so many media that they are familiar to half
the audience in almost any theater. That's a penalty that
must be paid for greatness, but if one wants 'great' plays,
is there any other choice?"

For the next seven issues of Dramatics, this series
of articles will attempt to answer that question by suggesting
"other" great plays that have the same virtues, the same
educational values, the same curio attractiveness of the
"established" plays, but that also have the added advantage
of being relatively new even for an audience of people who
are familiar with the "best" in the dramatic tradition.

Each article deals with only one play from each of
seven theatrical periods. Euripides' Trojan Women has
been selected from the Classical Greek theater; Abraham
and Isaac from the medieval; Thomas Heywood's A Woman
Killed with Kindness from the English Renaissance; Dryden's
All for Love from the English Restoration; George Farquhar's
Beaux Stratagem from the eighteenth-century English comedy;
"Buffalo Bill" Cody's Life on the Border from the nineteenth-
century American melodrama; and Kaufman and Connelly's
Merton of the Movies for 1920's comedy.

Most directors will agree that these are--at least
in the main--notable dramas, and they will agree, too, that
although most of the titles are familiar, the plays themselves are not often read and seldom performed. Most

directors, to be sure, probably have a dozen or so other candidates for other great plays in each of these periods and a few candidates for periods not mentioned. Last year, for example, the University of Washington brought a fourth-century Indian drama to its campus, The Little Clay Cart. Why not make room for it? Lincoln Center revived George Kaufman's 1920 comedy, The Butter and Egg Man, last year. Why not include it? What about a seventeenth-century French comedy?

It is, of course, to raise such questions that this re-examination of our use of the great dramas has been undertaken. In the process of considering some of the plays that have been neglected, theater directors should become sharply conscious of how wasteful the modern theater has become with its treasures. We are rather like a rich woman with a chest full of precious stones from all nations, who has fallen into the habit of wearing only diamonds. Rubies, pearls and opals have beauty, too.

Although each article concentrates on only one play, some mention will be made of other plays from each of the periods.

3. About One's Specialty

Writing Plays for Children

The market for plays has never been as large as it
is today. Production costs, however, have grown so tre-
mendously that although directors are demanding more and
more plays for the stage, motion pictures, and television,
producers have, also, become increasingly unwilling to
take a chance on unknown writers. New playwrights are
accepted into the profession only after they have shown
their willingness to become professional, full-time theater
men as well. Probably little harm is done by such a
policy--except an unfortunate sameness in the dramatic fare;
but this policy has meant, by and large, that playwriting
has become an art closed to the academic world.

A teacher-novelist, like Professor Jack Farris of
Wyndham College, is encouraged by his publishers to combine teaching and writing. Such a combination helps, they
believe, to keep a freshness in his work and to insure an
artistic integrity that is not always possible for writers who
must sell their wares in order to eat. College and university faculties have probably become our greatest single
source of poets: men like Peter Viereck, Randall Jarrell,
Karl Sharpiro, John Husband, John Holmes, John Ciardi,
and John Z. Bennett, all of whom are professional acade-
micians. The list of teacher-poets can almost be matched
by the list of teacher-novelists: Robert Penn Warren,
Lionel Trilling, Helen White, Caroline Gordon, Wallace
Stegner, and Wilbur Schramm. No such immediate list
comes to mind, however, for the teacher-playwrights; and
it is safe to say that the academic world has given the
American scene few playwrights of any kind and none comparable with its poets and novelists.

I

The reasons for the paucity of teacher-playwrights
are easily seen. The poet and the novelist need publishers;
the playwright needs both a publisher and a producer. The
publishers need only the works; the producers need both the
works and the playwrights. The professor-playwright who
has succeeded in interesting a producer in his play has just
begun his work. He must then be willing to join the comp-

any of the play; and to do this he must leave the campus
and his profession--cease to be a professor--to see the
play through the long months of production.   William Inge
was an instructor in English at Washington University in
St. Louis, but when Come Back, Little Sheba was accepted
for a Broadway production, Inge was forced to leave the
classroom; and he has never returned.

College and civic theaters have done a little to help
the academic playwright.   Generally speaking, however, the
professor-playwright writing for the local theater has found
that the demands made on him by such a theater are almost
as time-consuming and the trials are almost as nerve-
shattering as they are in the professional theater.   The
amateur theater is to be commended for encouraging native
talent, for what it does both for the playwright and for the
theater; but the production of locally-written plays by community theaters is much too rare.   Even if the amateur
theater were more interested in its native playwrights, the
college and community theaters still are not the answer for
the professor-playwright who seeks a regular outlet for his
work.   The Topeka Civic Theater, for example, has a well-
deserved reputation among community theaters for encouraging new playwrights.   In 1958, it announced a playwright-
ing contest.   The deadline for manuscripts was set for
early 1959, and almost four hundred plays were submitted,
presumably a number written by professor-playwrights.
Late in 1959, the screening committee had narrowed the
entries down to about half that number and sent these to
the judges.   By early 1960, the judges had selected about
seventy of these for final consideration; and, as the year
ended, they finally agreed upon one best play, the winning
manuscript.   Playwrights spend more time rewriting than
they do writing, and it is the rare writer who can start a
second play before he knows the destiny of the first, before
he knows, in fact, whether he has finished the first.   Seldom
is a play completely rejected; usually a rejection is simply
the beginning of another rewriting.   Chekov's Uncle Vanya,
is after all, simply The Wood Demon with another rewrite.

If, however, a two-year waiting period stands between the submission of a play and the decision as to its
stage worthiness, the playwright is faced with a long period
of forced inactivity--two years in which he has little in-
centive to practice his craft.   To call attention to this
condition is not to complain about the practices of college
and community theaters.   With the limited facilities of the

amateur theater, two years is a normal time for the careful selection of one play from four hundred. To look at this situation realistically, however, is to admit that the professor-playwright cannot turn to the community theaters as the sole outlet for his plays, if he intends for playwriting to be a habitual discipline for him.

Even such community-academic theaters as Topeka, the University of Arkansas, and the Baton Rouge Little Theater, all of which from time to time encourage new writers to submit plays, are not interested in being a steady market for new playwrights. The majority of their plays will be the time-tested fare of the professional theater. The professor-playwright who hopes to write plays as a regular discipline soon discovers that when the community theater produces one of his plays, the production is a bridal shower, not a marriage. The community theater may be happy to give him his start toward professional theater; it is not willing to make him a permanent part of its theater as a resident playwright from whom it can expect at least one play a year. Edward Devereaux Brown in his doctoral study, A History of the Shreveport Little Theater (The University of Denver, 1958), points out that the Shreveport Little Theater first gained national attention and substantial local support with the production of a locally-written play, Ada Jack Carver's The Cajun, a play that later won the Samuel French Award. Such an event, it would seem, should have encouraged Shreveport to continue the practice of producing local playwrights. The Cajun was the first locally written play produced by the Shreveport Little Theater; and, as of this writing, it was also the last. The director, John Wray Young, has pointed out on many occasions that the community theater charged with giving its audience a season of Broadway-like productions has little time to experiment with unknowns.

II

Playwriting has many values for the professor as a drama teacher. The publish-or-perish edict of many colleges and universities, probably, does not make much sense when used without discrimination for all teachers in all fields. In the field of drama, it does make sense. Whether one is teaching the history of drama, its production, its appreciation, or its composition, quite obviously one has made a commitment to public communication. This, at least, is one field in which those who teach also can do.

Speech, theater, and drama teachers must communicate, and for them communication is an art. They must speak; they must produce plays; and, it seems to me, they must also write plays.

Every drama teacher realizes the necessity of personal experience in the theater. A drama teacher must see plays; he must act in them, direct them, produce them. Only with such personal experience, which gives him the eye of the director and the ear of the actor, can he take the written text and transform it into a living art for his students. He needs to be able to explain from first-hand experience what is possible and what is not possible in any given theatrical medium. Obviously there are advantages if he can also bring to his teaching the awareness of the playwright, an awareness that comes only when one has made it a habit to solve the problems of the playwright in practice. The only meaningful practice is playwriting, and, to make playwriting a habit, the professor-playwright must have an outlet for the products he creates.

The professor-playwright does, of course, use the college and community theaters. He needs, however, something more than a once-every-two-years special event. He needs a constant market, one that is ready to consider his plays whenever he has plays to consider. Only with such a market can the professor be, not a man with an idea for a play, but a man who has disciplined himself to the day-by-day routine of playwriting. He needs to be as regular in the writing of plays as a poet is in the writing of poems; as an artist, in the painting of pictures; as a director, in the direction of plays. If he is to be a professor-playwright, he needs to take his playwriting as seriously as he does his teaching. He needs to make his writing as regular a part of his daily routine as he does his scholarship and his classroom lectures.

III

Fortunately, a constant, accessible market does exist for plays in the United States. Although relatively unknown in the academic profession, this market accepts hundreds of plays a year, and each play accepted is produced thousands of times. The market is the children's theater.

Although the term, "children's theater," is generally
known in the academic world, it means many things to many
people, and, as a result, misunderstandings have occurred.
For some, it is a theater in which the children write, act,
and produce their own plays. Such a theater has many
values, some artistic and some therapeutic. Obviously such
a theater has no market for the adult playwright, but the
danger exists that a new playwright will think this is all of
children's theater and, thus, close his eyes to the entire
field. This theater has as its principal intent self-express-
ion, not the discipline of an age-old art.

At the other end of the scale from such a children's
theater is the theater for children. In the theater for
children, plays written, directed, and acted by adults are
presented to children. During the past forty years, a tremendous growth has occurred in such theaters, both in
professional and amateur theater. The adult theater for
children offers a small market for the professor-playwright,
but a good one. Unlike the Broadway theater, the theater
for children is interested in buying only the play, not the
playwright. Unfortunately, relatively few plays are used.
The Children's Theater Press, perhaps the most active publisher in this field, accepts only about a dozen plays a year.
A few civic organizations, like the Junior League, take one
play a year. In all, probably fewer than twenty-five new
plays a year are used in the entire country.

Few plays are used for the same reason that Broadway
openings are rare. Production costs are high, and risks
are kept to a minimum. A play accepted by the Children's
Theater Press, the Dramatic Publishing Company, Samuel
French, or Baker's Plays has a good chance for wide, ex-
pertly-directed production; but the cost of the production
predisposes the director to select plays that have already
proved their attractiveness to children, adaptions of fairy
tales like The Princess and the Swineherd and of successful
children's books like Tom Sawyer and Huckleberry Finn.

Miss Edna Cahill of Walter H. Baker Company, in
writing of one play recently submitted to her company--a
play based on neither a fairy tale nor a children's novel--
summarized the problem:

> The idea [for the play] is a delightful
> one and handled very competently. ...
> It is the sort of thing this writer would

like to see issued but, frankly,
personal liking for a manuscript
has got to be submerged in dollars
and cents thinking. I honestly
don't think we could find a large
enough market for that sort of
thing to warrant the expense in
which publication would involve
us. The juvenile market is a
poor investment--at best.

This market is probably no more difficult than the
normal commercial and academic markets for novels,
poetry, and critical studies; certainly the encouragement
given new writers and the promptness with which these
publishers handle manuscripts are superior. If the market
were not so small, in fact, one could well agree that here
the professor-playwright had found an outlet for his writing
comparable to that for the professor-poet, the professor-
novelist, and the professor-critic.

Another kind of children's theater, a theater in
which children learn the art of the drama by performing
plays written and directed by adults, however, offers many
of the same advantages as the adult theater for children;
and it has, moreover, a tremendous market. This theater,
existing in every grade and high school in the United States,
is constantly looking for new material; and here the professor-playwright is welcomed. In this theater, moreover, he
will find a steady and rewarding field for a lifetime of work.

IV

Writing plays for children to be performed by children
is a specialized field, and, unfortunately, at the present
time no poetics for this drama exists. Some requirements
for this field are, however, obvious. Plays for this field
need to be both learning tools for the performers and art
experiences for the audience. Edward L. Heuer in a pamphlet, "Pointers to Writers of Amateur Plays," which is sent
to all writers who submit their first works to the Heuer
Company, outlines the problems of the field and calls attention to the most difficult of these problems. High school
audiences are demanding in their entertainment, but the
plays must be within the scope of high school actors. "The
junior class," he says, "is frequently the first acting experience for the cast of the play. The play needs to be within

their scope of understanding. " An examination of some of
the plays published by his company--plays like Deadly
Ernest, Finders Creepers, Desperate Ambrose, and Hillbilly Weddin'--suggests some of the difficulties. They all
belong to the class of the realistic, well-made play. The
human emotions with which they deal seem trivial and
superficial. They are, however, all plays within the scope
of understanding of high school children.

Many directors of high school plays argue for the
standard fare of the adult theater and, with considerable
justice, argue that Our Town and The Importance of Being
Earnest are better, for any audience, than Hillbilly Weddin'
and Deadly Ernest. Their argument is as sound as that of
the college or community theater director who argues for
Oedipus and Lear over Our Town and The Importance of
Being Ernest. A theater can do only those plays which its
actors can perform and its audience can comprehend, and
it seems perfectly clear that all adult plays in their totality
are--or should be--beyond the comprehension of high school
audiences.

What is needed for this theater is neither adult
drama hacked to fit children nor hack children's drama,
but good drama purposefully written for the age group that
will perform it and see it. The drama teacher is uniquely
equipped to write such drama. He has both the skills and
understanding of the professional theater man, and he has
a professional understanding of the learning process. He,
also, has added incentives for writing good plays for
grade school and high school children. It is in their pre-
college training that most people receive their first drama
experiences; and the taste that the professor-playwright is
helping to mold with such work will be the kind of taste
he finds in his own students.

The professor-playwright, by his training, should
understand the difference between adults and children. He
should know, for example, that his plays need not contain
material that is new to himself; most of what he has long
known will yet be unfamiliar to the children. This particular piece of information is, of course, one that every
teacher is made painfully aware of every time he teaches
a class. Yet it is information that A. S. Burack, editor
of Plays, Inc., finds necessary to repeat to his authors
frequently: "The more familiar the material is, the better
the children like it. " The entire dramatic experience in

a formal theater is new for children. They do not need to
be introduced to new emotional problems; they simply ask
for drama that makes their old emotional problems clear
to them. The more familiar they are with the elements
of the drama, the greater will be their enjoyment. This
principle is as old as Aristotle's Poetics. The tremendous
crush of new and varied experiences in the adult world,
however, has meant that in the modern theater this principle
is frequently sacrificed for novelty, and we go to the
theater seeking the new rather than an understanding of
the permanent. In children's theater, the craving for
novelty is satisfied by the freshness of the dramatic experience itself.

Admittedly much writing now being done in this
field is hack work. It is, however, the best that is submitted. The publishers take the best plays available, but
they must be plays for children. A moment's consideration
of the field explains some of its failings. The rewards
for writing children's plays, either in fame or fortune,
are small, even though there is a demand for a considerable number of plays. It might be noted that the rewards
offered the poet in America are also small, but poets are
aware at the start that they will receive little fame and
less money for their work. If they take poetry seriously,
they are satisfied to practice their craft and earn their
bread as bankers, insurance company presidents, or
teachers.

A poet, moreover, does not begin writing poetry
with the expectation of deserting the field for something
more lucrative. Those who write plays for children, on
the other hand, frequently use this field as a place to
learn their craft before moving on to other fields. Betty
Smith, the author of A Tree Grows in Brooklyn, started
with this market and was relatively successful. With her
success in the adult world of letters, however, she wrote
no more plays for children. All her experience was lost
to the field. The professor-playwright looking for a market that will allow him to practice his craft while he remains an active teacher is not apt to follow such a progress, especially if he is conscious that his playwriting
will not only help him to be a better teacher today but
will also help to prepare his students of tomorrow. The
entrance of the professor-playwright into this field, thus,
should improve the standards by giving the field that one
quality which it now most needs--a group of dedicated,

trained practitioners.

Writing plays for children is an individual problem
for the writer. Just as there is no set way to teach a
class, so is there no set way to write a play. Each professor-playwright must simply write the kind of plays which
he thinks will best prepare children for lives in which an
appreciation of the drama will be a regular part of their
cultural wealth. There are classes of plays which sell
more easily than others, of course. Comedies sell better
than tragedies, and realistic prose plays sell better than
symbolic poetic plays. The professor-playwright, however,
is not "economically determined" to write what sells easily
or what makes the best profit. The great demand for new
plays, moreover, means that the chances of a good manuscript being taken are very high. The only final rejection
of a play written by a competent writer in this field is
that which the writer himself makes. The play rejected
by Baker Company, for example, stands a good chance of
being accepted by the next publisher.

V

Since the professor-playwright, even if he has never
published a play, can hardly be considered a newcomer to
the field, perhaps the best service that can be performed
in such an essay as this is simply to review the markets
in this field.

There are a great many markets for plays. Con-
ditions, however, change for various reasons. One publisher does from time to time get more material than he can
handle. However, judging from recent experience, there
are ten markets that I would recommend to the professor-
playwright as a starting list.

Walter H. Baker Company (569 Boylston St., Boston)
is primarily concerned with plays for teen-agers. The
company prefers three-act comedies to all other forms.
The editors answer queries promptly and give each play
submitted serious attention.

The Dramatic Publishing Company (179 N. Michigan
Avenue, Chicago 1) has a wide market for the playwright.
Although the bulk of its business is with the high schools,
the company has been doing increasing business with the
colleges and little theaters.

The Eldridge Publishing Company (Franklin, Ohio) is in the market for both one-act and three-act plays, principally for high schools. It is best to submit material between October and early spring.

Samuel French, Inc. (25 West 45th Street, New York 26) is the best-known publisher of plays in America. The reputation of the company and the fact that much of its business is with Broadway plays make this a somewhat less encouraging market for the new playwright than any of the other markets.

The Grade Teacher (23 Leroy Avenue, Darien, Conn.) is a monthly magazine which publishes three or four plays in each issue. The plays are all for the elementary grades, and the editors are especially interested in plays which combine the drama with a subject-matter learning experience.

Heuer Publishing Company (Dows Bldg., Cedar Rapids, Iowa) has one of the largest listings of one-act and three-act plays for high schools. The editors answer promptly and have made considerable efforts to attract new writers.

The Instructor (F. A. Owen Publishing Company, Dansville, N. Y.) is a monthly journal which publishes about three plays for the elementary grades in each issue. The editors are especially interested in plays which combine drama with an allied art--music, painting, the dance.

Plays: The Drama Magazine for Young People (8 Arlington Street, Boston 16) is a monthly magazine and, in my experience, the best single market for one-act plays for both grade and high schools. All queries are answered promptly, and each play submitted receives uncommonly sensitive criticism.

Row-Peterson Plays (1911 Ridge Ave., Evanston, Ill.) is normally a good market. During the fall of 1960, however, the editors announced they were over-stocked.

The Standard Publishing Foundation (Hamilton Avenue at 1800, Cincinnati, Ohio) is the only publisher in this field, to my knowledge, interested in religious drama. The editors favor dramatizations from the Bible. They are helpful, sometimes even suggesting general subjects for which they have a particular need.

Experiences with various publishers differ with the individual writer and the particular reader for the company, of course. The ten companies listed, however, have consistently shown a desire to encourage new writers and seemingly are interested in long-term associations with such writers as the professor-playwright.

Many other publishers are also in the market for children's plays, and they have reputable records: Children's Digest, Playmate Magazine, Jack and Jill, T. E. Denison and Company, Drama Guild Publishers, Longmans, Green and Company, Northwestern Press, Banner Play Bureau, Gillum Book Company, World Publishing Company, Random House, Follett Publishing Company, Children's Theater Press, and the Sterling Publishing Company, all of whom have indicated an interest in new plays for children. The Writer's Handbook (ed. A. S. Burack, 8 Arlington Street, Boston 16) is probably the best single guidebook for all markets in this field.

Generally speaking, after a year of writing and querying, each playwright usually finds that there are four or five markets for which his work seems best suited. Which markets these are will frequently be determined by temperament and lucky timing. Anyone new to the field should decide, however, that until he is established, every play he thinks worthy of publication should be sent out until it is accepted. Quite often the play rejected by one publisher is not only taken by the next but becomes the means by which the writer establishes a long-term association with that publisher. The important point is not that different publishers have different and changing demands; it is, rather, that there is a constant demand. This is a field to which the professor-playwright may give serious long-term interest.

Writing plays for children is a twice-rewarding activity for the professor-playwright. It gives him the opportunity to practice the art of playwright and, at the same time, to extend his influence as a teacher beyond the classroom of today to the students he may have tomorrow.

Shop Talk 79

4. About the General Problems of Education

A Problem in Qualifications:
The Faculty for the New Graduate School

Central University recently announced that it will
start offering doctor's degrees in selected disciplines. The
announcement was greeted with something less than unan-
imous approval, but the need for more holders of the doctorate and the general opinion that a graduate school would
improve the intellectual environment of the campus won
Board assent. For better or for worse, Central University
will soon be one of the institutions meeting the demands
of "a complex industrial society ... for highly trained
personnel."

There is little argument about the need for more
graduate schools. Dr. Oliver C. Carmichael's summary
of the need is accepted as gospel: "The Doctor of Philosophy degree in the United States has a unique status. For
the profession of college teaching it is the union card.
With rare exceptions a teacher cannot rise to the top without
it. But government, business, and industry also hold it in
high esteem and employ almost half of those produced by
the universities each year. They could use more if they
were available; indeed, much of the research they require
is done by professors in the universities."[1]

Some of the faculty at Central have, indeed, argued
that the problem in recruiting new teachers with the doctorate is, in itself, evidence that the school must join in the
education of graduate students. They can demonstrate that
Central alone would willingly employ all the doctoral gradu-
ates produced in the entire state each year; and Central
is only one of fifteen colleges and universities in the state
needing new faculty annually. The immediate problem for
Central, it is agreed, is an adequate faculty for a responsible graduate program.

Twenty years ago, when the end of World War II
brought a boom to the campus, Central was an all-purpose
state college with an enrollment of fifteen hundred students.
Its main concern was with a general, four year liberal arts
program, with secondary interest in teacher training, prelaw,
premedical, and pre-engineering programs. Two thirds of

its course offerings were on the junior college level. Here
and there, a Central College faculty member was doing a
little research, publishing an occasional article.

Such scholarly activity was not openly discouraged,
but with teaching loads of fifteen hours a semester and 150
students for each teacher, such activity was suspect. Any
publication was viewed as evidence that the author was neglecting his students. If one did have time and energy after
his classroom duties, the sponsoring of undergraduates--the
pep squad, the debate team, dances--was judged to be a
more worthy expense of spirit.

Today, Central is a budding university with an enrollment of almost ten thousand students and the frightening
expectation of increasing this enrollment at the rate of two
thousand students a year for the next ten years. The liberal
arts offerings are now the business of a liberal arts college
within the university, and the preprofessional programs now
have their own colleges: engineering, business and commerce,
education, nursing, agriculture, and the newest college, the
graduate school.

For the past five or six years, Central University
has been offering the master's degree in various disciplines,
starting first with education and then developing liberal arts,
science, and engineering master's degree programs. The
average class load has been cut to twelve hours for those
faculty members at all associated with the graduate program.
Publications are now viewed as "necessary evils"; and perhaps as many as one in ten of the faculty will publish something each year. The faculty now has nearly five hundred
members, including the teaching fellows, and last year its
total publications included four books and editions, and over
150 articles, reviews, notes, abstracts. Two departments,
history and English, are responsible for more than half the
publications, but members of other departments argue that
publication is more difficult in the sciences.

There is more concern on the new Central faculty
with "scholarly activities." More go to scholarly meetings;
more are publishing; more doing "research." Almost all
of the faculty are anxious to establish themselves as "teaching scholars," thus insuring a place on the graduate school
faculty, for such appointments mean smaller teaching loads,
better opportunities for academic advancement, prestige,
higher pay.

The demand for graduate work at Central is still
relatively slight, and there are more volunteers to teach
graduate courses than there is need. The faculty and administration realize that something must be done about the problem of determining qualifications for appointments to the
graduate faculty. Ten years ago, when the first graduate
courses were being offered, a graduate program was an
experiment, carrying with it no rewards for success and
the risk of failure. Now, the graduate school--and its
position of power--is a fact.

"Qualifications" are not easy to determine. For
Central College, faculty members were selected on the basis
of personality, with the recognition that the accrediting association to which Central belonged demanded that a "proper
number" of the faculty hold terminal degrees. No one on
the Central faculty is "clearly" a scholar with "a national
reputation, " although a few--with a book or two published--
will argue their own merits. Many, however, argue that
their records give them claims to a place on the graduate
faculty. Some taught the first graduate courses offered,
even planned the programs. All who hold the Ph. D. argue
that the degree is, in itself, evidence that they are trained
scholars.

The problem of qualifications has become the concern
of the separate departments, and the various departments
have developed policies of "exclusion. " Such policies are
useful in excluding those who are obviously not qualified to
offer graduate work: teaching fellows, of course; new young
faculty members without the terminal degree; older faculty
members who have never taught courses beyond the sophomore
level. Such policies serve to exclude about two-thirds of
the Central faculty.

The one-third remaining, however, presents problems.
The group is still larger than the present need, and yet it
does not constitute the kind of graduate faculty envisioned
by those who hope to build the Harvards of the South and
the Princetons of the West. Some departments will have
fifteen to twenty "qualified" faculty members, but they have
not been selected with any plan. The English department,
for example, has twenty on its graduate faculty, but twelve
consider themselves American literature specialists and four
others are eighteenth century English literature specialists.
The department needs at least one Old English specialist,
a linguist, a seventeenth century English specialist. The

history department, too, has the same problem--too many
American history specialists and obvious gaps in other areas.

New faculty members will be needed for the graduate
program, and for the first time, Central University must
select its new faculty for their scholarly qualifications as
graduate school professors. In the process of making such
judgments about applicants for the new positions, the old
Central faculty is coming to the realization that "graduate
school qualifications" are being established for all faculty
members, old and new.

The first assumptions used in appointing faculty members to the graduate faculty were, to a large degree, personal: long service to Central, a general "reputation" of
being a "good teacher," the possession of a terminal degree
in one's field, experience in teaching graduate courses and
directing theses. When the graduate program was an experiment, such assumptions were easy enough to make.
Since teaching graduate courses carried with it no special
rewards, no need existed to examine any method that worked. But now, appointment to the graduate faculty is judged
to be a basic necessity for survival.

All of the graduate faculty of Central have either
completed the doctorate or all course work and examinations,
"except the dissertation." Some will probably receive the
degree in a year or two; some never will. For some of
those who have the doctor's degree safely tucked away in
their files, the degree assumes great importance. It, and
it alone, should determine what people are qualified to
offer graduate work.

Unfortunately for such an argument, some of those
who do not hold the degree have been the most active in
publications, thesis direction, and participation in scholarly
organizations. They argue that a book--any book--or four
articles in the past five years should be considered "the
equivalent" of a terminal degree, and some of them argue
further that holding a doctor's degree followed by ten years
of no scholarly activity is evidence that Dr. _____
is intellectually bankrupt.

Some of the faculty argue in terms of the status quo.
They have been teaching the graduate courses at Central
longer than Central has been offering graduate work, since
many of the present graduate courses are undergraduate

courses renumbered. They argue their "qualifications" in
terms of experience in the classroom and "squatter's rights. "

In search of a list of qualifications that will support
their various claims, all turn to such statements as The
Doctor of Philosophy Degree, " a pamphlet of 16 pages
issued by the Association of Graduate Schools in the Association of American Universities and the Council of Graduate
Schools in the United States.   The title of the organization
suggests that the statement will be, fortunately or unfortunately, broad enough to support a variety of claims:

> Excellence of the Professors. Of highest import-
> ance in the establishment of a sound program lead-
> ing to the Ph. D. degree is the quality of the gradu-
> ate faculty involved.   Each of these professors
> is a scholar with proved creative and teaching
> capacity; and each has usually earned the Doctor
> of Philosophy degree or its equivalent in scholarly
> activities in his field and is personally engaged
> in creative research which is published in pro-
> fessional journals so that his contributions may
> be appraised by his peers.   And each teaches
> and assists students in the doctoral program.

In selecting new faculty members for the graduate
program at Central, there is no problem in interpreting
these "qualifications. "   The candidate must hold a doctor's
degree, must have some teaching experience in the graduate
program, must have published a book or several articles,
must belong to and attend the annual meetings of the national
and regional scholarly organizations in his discipline, and
must have directed graduate work.   In brief, Central is
now looking for the conventionally trained teacher-scholar.

But the present faculty at Central was not selected
on such a basis, and, in general, those Central faculty
members who meet such qualifications made errors in
judgment in accepting positions on the Central faculty of
the past.   Why should an Old English scholar teach in a
college which does not offer Old English, has a library
that gives little opportunity for research in Old English,
and a general faculty that equates "good teaching" with an
interest in the volleyball team?

And yet the present faculty must supply the majority
of the graduate faculty.   Bringing in an entirely new faculty

for the graduate school would not be economically possible,
even if the present faculty would cooperate in such a program. Some recruitment is needed, of course; but the
central problem is the selection of a graduate faculty from
the existing undergraduate faculty. The selection must pay
homage to past services rendered, and at the same time
it must develop a graduate faculty that will make possible
"the establishment of a sound program. ...."

Central University does not exist, of course; but
its history is like that of a hundred or so institutions that
have started to offer graduate work in the past twenty years
and now are moving to doctoral programs. And this fiction-
al problem for Central is a real problem for a multitude
of new state universities.

It is a particularly uncomfortable problem since it
involves judgments that must be made of one's fellow faculty
members, one's friends. It is uncomfortable, moreover,
because there is no fair way to make such judgments.
These new graduate schools in their first experiments used
their old faculty. Now to deal ruthlessly with these professors, as some will do, not only endangers general faculty
morale, but also weakens the undergraduate program. Undergraduate courses should not be the limbo into which are
thrown those not "good enough" for the graduate program.
At the same time, however, to make a graduate school
appointment a reward for service is to create a monster,
a fraud. "A sound program leading to the Ph. D. degree"
cannot be built except with a faculty that has demonstrated
"creative and teaching capacity."

The new graduate schools are attempting to solve
the problem in various ways. One school, for example,
immediately established "minimum standards" for its
graduate faculty: the doctor's degree, at least one book
or four articles published in the past five years, active
participation (a paper read or an office held) in one scholarly organization; and it was also announced that the qualifications would be reexamined every five years. In one
department, with a faculty of thirty-one members with the
rank of assistant professor and above, only four members
teach all the graduate courses that may be counted toward
the doctor's degree and direct the theses. (Some of the
others are allowed to teach courses on the master's level.)
The department has three students working toward the doctorate and is now trying to find "qualified faculty members"

to offer the required courses in the program. The chairman of the department admits that the first candidates are likely to find the program monotonous and long, but he argues that such sacrifices at the start will insure a "sound program" in the shortest possible time. He admits there is discontent among the excluded faculty members; some of them are leaving and others are working to establish their "qualifications" so they may leave for "better" schools.

Another of the new graduate schools "certified" all of its present faculty who had in any way worked with the graduate program. In one department with twenty on its graduate faculty, seven have not yet completed the doctorate. Only three have published books; only nine have any publications of any kind--including reviews and notes. The program here is much larger; the course offerings are varied; the students have more choices, both as to courses and teachers. There is, however, a general uneasiness that the graduate program may become a "degree mill," lacking any real standards of scholarly excellence. It is admitted by the chairman of the department that the present system places too much emphasis upon the popularity of the teacher with the students. Nevertheless, morale in the department is high, and the school is judged to be a good place for young faculty members who "want to work up."

Obviously, neither of these extremes is being argued as a solution. The graduate program at the first school may well cease to exist, and it is an expensive one, not only in that four faculty members for three students is expensive, but in the general discontent of the entire university. The faculty members who were excluded can either leave, attempt to upgrade their qualifications, or stay on the undergraduate faculty, convinced that they are either the victims of prejudice or inadequate.

The second school offers a pleasant life for both the students and the faculty, but if the present system is followed, the graduate program there is likely to become weaker each year. There is no need for excellence, for a full professor on the graduate faculty has every reason to believe that he has already demonstrated his worth and has no need to do more than meet classes.

Obviously in an undergraduate school developing a graduate program, the current faculty is the primary source for teachers. The present faculty must be used just as the

present campus, the present library, the present administration are used; but the new needs must be recognized.
The buildings used for undergraduate instruction can be
used for the graduate school, but changes need to be made.
For one thing, graduate professors need more office space,
and private office space, for their work. So, too, must
the faculty member be stimulated, not merely by what is
done for him--more office space, more secretarial help,
more books in the library, fewer classes, and fewer
students--but also by what is expected of him. The working scholar, who has delayed finishing his dissertation, can
delay no longer. The non-scholarly teacher who holds the
doctorate should use his degree only as his license to work,
not his ticket to semi-retirement. The scholar who gave
up research when he joined an undergraduate faculty must
start that research again. The promising scholar must
stop promising and start producing.

The new graduate school needs to admit, too, that
there is less real argument about the evidence for determining "excellence of the professor" than has been pretended.
Certainly, all can cite examples to challenge the evidence.
All know of a brilliant scholar who never took a formal
degree, of another who publishes only once in every twenty-
five years, usually a short study of revolutionary proportions.
The new graduate school faculty should admit, however,
that even if no standards of "excellence of the professors"
were established, the exceptional scholar is not likely to
make his home there anyway. Schools like Central do not
have--do not yet have--the environment, the tools of scholarship, needed by the exceptions.

It seems both necessary and desirable, therefore,
for the new graduate schools to establish "minimum standards, " mechanically: the terminal degree, publications,
other scholarly activity, teaching experience. It probably
would be wise, however, to set these standards as goals
to be achieved. In justice to past services and in recognition of present needs, the new graduate school should give
a liberal interpretation to such qualifying phrases as "or
its equivalent" and make generous judgments of what con-
stitutes a "scholarly contribution. " With concern for its
future and respect for the standards of its profession, the
new graduate school should also inform its graduate faculty
that all of the mechanical standards must be met within a
reasonable length of time, three years, four years, five
years, and that permanent appointment to the graduate

faculty depends upon meeting the standards.

There are, of course, weaknesses in this suggestion. Some, in fact, will argue that with such choices necessary, the new universities probably should not offer graduate work. The problem, however, is not whether the new graduate schools are going to come into being or not, but rather how these graduate schools will build their faculties and how they will use the undergraduate school that is supporting the program. It is a problem, obviously, that needs some "creative research" now.

Notes:

1. Jane Graham, ed., A Guide to Graduate Study: Programs Leading to the Ph. D. Degree (Washington, D. C., 1965), p. 3.

IV

As One Adult to Another

All professional people, and perhaps especially teachers, stand in danger of two misunderstandings about the
relationship of their professional knowledge and the general
adult public. On the one hand, there is the assumption
that the knowledge held by any profession--law, medicine,
education--is the most important information in civilization,
a kind of information without which society cannot exist,
or at least not well. On the other hand, there is a general
assumption made by a great many professional people that
no one could possibly understand this knowledge unless it
were delivered in professional tones. As a result, teachers
are frequently apologetic and defensive when they are talking about the subject matter of the classroom to "lay"
listeners. Certainly no adult wants to be "lectured to"
by another adult in a common social situation, but certainly,
too, adults want information from informed sources.

The five selections for this chapter are all directed
toward a non-student adult audience, and the content of
each of these essays came from the normal preparation
that Nolan made for his work as a teacher in the classroom.
The first, an account of a piece of theatrical history, was
first published in Real West, IX (September 1966), pages 26-
28 and 46-48, a popular journal for Western history readers.
The second, an account of the way in which a state university library found a dramatic manuscript, was first published
in the Baton Rouge (Louisiana) Sunday Advocate Magazine,
the Sunday feature section of the state newspaper, October
29, 1967, section 3E. The third, a discussion of two
modern popular plays, Williams' The Glass Menagerie and
Miller's After the Fall, was first published in a general
literary journal, The McNeese Review, XVII (1966), pages
27-38. The fourth, a review of an academic book, was
first published in the Journal of Southern History, XXXI
(November 1965), page 357; although the journal is a
scholarly one for historians, Nolan's review essentially
is designed for the generally well-educated adult, rather

than the historian.   The last selection, a chapter taken
from Nolan's book, Writing the One-Act Play for the Amateur Stage (Pioneer Drama Service, 1964), is in the general
format of an academic textbook; but, quite obviously, it is
the kind of self-help textbook that the non-student adult
takes to read at home, rather than the kind used in the
classroom.   It is worth noting, I think, that the first
institution to adopt Writing the One-Act Play was San Quentin
Prison.   A group of inmates there wanted a self-help book-
let to introduce them to some of the problems in writing.

    In all of these selections, Nolan is using the materi-
als of his academic field.   Even if he never wrote a word,
he would need to know almost everything that is in these
selections for normal classroom performance.   In none of
these selections, with the possible exception of the last
one, does he make his appeal as a professional teacher;
in all of them he is using the techniques of the teacher to
communicate his information.

1. About a Generally Interesting Event

Buffalo Bill's Secret Life

The tall man with the full dress suit, flowing hair, and western-style Stetson watched nervously as the curtain at Niblo's Garden in New York was being drawn. He had been to the theater there often, so often, in fact, that the managers, Jarrett and Palmer, had given him a pass to see their most popular play, The Black Crook, as often as he pleased. But this night was different.

The theater was playing a five-act melodrama, Buffalo Bill: The King of the Border Men by Fred C. Meader, adapted from the stories by Ned Buntline; and the tall man was William F. Cody himself, "Buffalo Bill" of Buntline's stories.

The play opens in Buffalo Bill's cottage. On stage: Mrs. Cody and her daughter, Lottie, "feeding a bird in a cage hanging on a tree. An air of contentment and quietude reigns around, so as to form a contrast to subsequent scenes."

> Mrs. Cody: Lottie, has not Lillie returned yet?
> Lottie: No, mother, let us hope by her absence, she received a letter.
> Mrs. Cody: My dear Son--I presume he writes as regularly as he can, but it's hard to bear such suspense.
> Lottie: Here is Lillie, Mother!
> Lillie: News! News! The war is begun. The Confederates are fortifying all over the South, and threaten Washington from Manassas--and ah! Mamma, brother is coming home! He says he will be here before the Sun sets on the 25th.
> Mrs. Cody: Today is the 25th, is it not?
> Lillie: To be sure it is, and he will be here. Our William is wild, but is too proud to tell a falsehood.

In a few minutes, Buffalo Bill--"Our William"--and his friend, Wild Bill, burst on stage; and for the next two hours little of this opening "air of contentment, and quietude, reigns." Among the scenes which caught the attention of the dramatic critic of the New York Herald, who watched the play, was one in which Buffalo Bill, "finding himself surrounded by Indians, ... slipped like a snake into a hollow log; which log

the redskins presently added as fuel to the campfire; but
the trapper soon found it grew uncomfortably hot, so he
threw his powder horn into the fire.   There was a grand
explosion and the Indians went yelling skyward, while the
hero escaped unscathed. "

Henry Blackman Sell and Victor Weybright in writing
about Buffalo Bill and the Wild West try to read Cody's
mind during his viewing of this performance.   "What might
have been in Buffalo Bill's mind as he saw himself portray-
ed on the stage?   It must, " they decided, "at first have
seemed like an incredible nightmare that such a distorted
version of his life should be the subject of a play and that
such a drama would appeal to New York audiences. "   Sell
and Weybright conclude that it was only his need for financial assistance that finally led him into the theater as a
professional actor and playwright.

The idea that William F. Cody was a man of action
who was trapped into becoming a popular performer now
has almost universal acceptance; and even during his own
lifetime, it was generally accepted that not only was Cody
a poor actor and a worse writer, but that he hated the
stage and probably never wrote the words to which his
name was signed.

His enemies shouted these charges.   In 1894, for
example, when he and one of his former co-stars, John
W. "Capt. Jack" Crawford, were feuding, Crawford wrote
him a stinging letter: " ... you know very well that you
yourself never wrote a paragraph for publication in your
life and that you are not in reality the author of your book
or any other dime novel supposed to have been written by
you. "

Cody and his friends suggested that Buffalo Bill's
lack of concern with authorship was a part of his charm,
an evidence that he was not really a stage hero at all,
but the "real thing, " caught for a moment on stage between
Indian wars.   In such "autobiographical" accounts as The
Life of the Honorable William F. Cody (1879), Buffalo Bill's
Own Story (1920), The Story of the Wild West and Campfire
Chats (1888), Life and Adventures of Buffalo Bill (1917),
Cody frequently suggested that he did little of the writing
and was therefore not completely responsible for the "lies
and bloodshed of the author. "   It was all a kind of game,
played by a fun-loving, action-seeking man.

The only similarity between Cody and Shakespeare--
Buffalo Bill, his enemies, and his friends would all agree--
is that they were both named William.

Cody, however, was neither as indifferent to the
stage nor as opposed to writing as his friends and critics
pretended. After he started his Wild West show in the
1880's, it is true that it became almost official policy to
make fun of the early melodramas in which he had appeared; but the Wild West show was trying to sell a new kind
of drama to the American who frequented such theaters
as Niblo's to see such plays as Buffalo Bill: The King of
the Border Men. When Cody left the stage for the circus
arena, others were still writing the western stage melodramas; and other scouts, like Capt. Jack Crawford and
Texas Jack Omohundro, were anxious to pick up Cody's
audience. It was only good business to make fun of such
drama, and the easiest way for Cody and his company to
do it was to make fun of their own.

Over and over again, Cody would tell colorful
stories, about how bad these plays were. In telling his
readers, in The Story of the Wild West, about the critical
reception of Buntline's Scouts of the Plains, the first play
in which Cody appeared as an actor, for example, he wrote,
with obvious glee: "The next morning [after the opening
performance] there appeared in the Chicago papers some
funny criticisms of our first performance. The papers
gave us a better send-off than I expected, for they did not
criticize us as actors. The Chicago Times said that if
Buntline had actually spent four hours in writing the play,
it was difficult for anyone to see what he was doing all the
time. Buntline, as 'Cale Durg,' was killed in the second
act, after a long temperance speech; and the Inter-Ocean
said that it was to be regretted that he had not been killed
in the first act. The company, however, was very good,
and M'dlle Morlacchi [who later married Texas Jack], as
'Pale Dove,' particularly fine; while Miss Cafarno 'spouted'
a poem of some seven hundred and three verses, more or
less, of which the reader will be glad to know that I only
recall the words 'I was born in March'."

In describing the composition of Life on the Border,
the first play to which he signed his name as author, Cody
gave credit for "arranging it for the stage" to J. V. Arlington, an actor. He described the play in terms that would
have made even the most severe critics speechless. "It

was," wrote Cody, "a five-act play, without head or tail,
and it made no difference at which act we commenced the
performance.   Before we had finished the season several
newspaper critics, I have been told, went crazy in trying
to follow the plot.   It afforded us, however, ample opportunity to give a noisy, rattling, gunpowder entertainment, and
to present a succession of scenes in the late Indian war,
all of which seemed to give general satisfaction."

      The stories that demonstrated the inability (and un-
willingness) of the "real" scouts to be happy as stage actors
became a part of the legend.   Wild Bill Hickok, in particular, supplied many of the stories.   At one performance,
for example, the action of the play, Buntline's Scouts of the
Plains, called for Wild Bill to tell a story as the scouts
sat around the fire, "passing a whiskey bottle."   Wild Bill
took a swig of the stage whiskey (cold tea) and then threw
the bottle into the audience.   "You think I'm the worst fool
east of the Rockies," he shouted.   "I can tell whiskey from
cold tea.   I can't tell my story unless I get real whiskey."

      Probably some of the old scouts really did object
to stage work.   Wild Bill not only quit the stage, but he,
also, chased an actor off the stage for using the name of
"Wild Bill Hickok" without his permission.   But the scout-
actors also know that the audience loved it when they
kicked up their heels and made fun of the dramas in which
they were appearing.   Cody brought his son, Kit Carson
Cody, to his performances, for the audience loved it when
the little boy would shout to nim, "Good house, Papa."
And early in his career as an actor, Cody discovered that
shouting "Oh, I'm a bad actor, Mama" to his wife, Louisa,
was good for a round of applause.

      Such stories and such "unscheduled" performances,
however, do not obscure the fact that for over ten years
Buffalo Bill was not only a playwright and actor, but that
he was one of the most successful actor-playwrights on the
American stage, even out-drawing the famous Edwin Booth
in Hamlet.   While the other "frontier heroes" came and
went, Buffalo Bill lived on; and anyone in show business
will admit that ten years' success in the highly competitive
race for audience approval is not won except through hard
work, talent, and careful planning.

      One of the reasons that Cody's career as an actor
and playwright has been viewed as a kind of short-run

joke is that the Wild West show was so spectacular, so
successful that it overshadowed his early work on the
conventional stage.   But even if the Wild West show had
never come into being, Buffalo Bill would still have a big
place in the history of the American theater for his work
in the 1870's.

Cody's playwriting activity has received even less
notice than his work as a legitimate actor.   First, there
is a general notion that he had nothing to do with the writing.   Secondly, the general belief that such plays as Life on
the Border, May Cody, or Lost and Won, and the Red Right
Hand, or Buffalo Bill's First Scalp for Custer are, in Cody's
own words, plays "without head or tail" make even his most
ardent biographers willing to accept the judgments of the
most critical (and satirical) of the newspaper reviews as
fact.

For some reason, Cody never allowed any of his
plays to be published.   Until recently it was impossible
for anyone to give anything more than a second-hand judgment as to the real nature of a Buffalo Bill melodrama.
It seems, in fact, that Cody intentionally destroyed every
copy of his plays when he left the stage for the Wild West
show, or, at least, that he tried.   Even if critics doubted
that the judgments made by the newspapers of the times
were accurate, there was little that could be done with all
of the plays gone.

Not only have copies of all of the plays written by
Cody disappeared, but even copies of plays about Buffalo
Bill are rare.   Meader's Buffalo Bill: The King of the
Border Men, for example, now exists in only one hand-
written copy, owned by the rare book room of the Harvard
University Library.   This copy, once owned by William E.
Coleman, a prompter at the Capital Theatre in Albany,
New York, is in poor condition.   Parts are crossed out
and added; there are errors in both the writing and order
of the story.   But it is still so rare and valuable, that
Harvard University will not permit an edition to be made
or even a photostatic copy to be generally distributed.

In the spring of 1964, however, a great-granddaugh-
ter of Capt. Jack Crawford, Mrs. Buford Richardson, found
a copy of Life on the Border, Cody's first play.   Capt. Jack
joined Cody's company after the Sioux War of 1876, and
Cody gave him the leading role of "Buffalo Bill" in the play.

He also gave Crawford a handsome handwritten copy of the
play, which Crawford kept for the rest of his life and then
passed on as a legacy to his family.

This copy of Life on the Border, seemingly the only
copy of any of Buffalo Bill's plays still in existence, is
going to force a few revisions in the story of Buffalo Bill
as a playwright.   In fact, this play suggests that if Cody
had not been so successful in a life-time career of playing
Buffalo Bill on stage, in the arena, and off-stage, he might
well have developed into a competent writer of melodrama.
While it is probably true that nothing he ever wrote was
staged or published without corrections and revisions by
ghost writers and editors, it is also pretty clear from a
comparison of Maeder's play and Cody's first play that Cody
brought more to the play than a lazy charm and a handsome
exterior.

When Cody went east in 1872 to become lionized by
New York society, he came in contact with the theater.
Even before he thought of the stage as a career, he was
stage-struck.   His frequent appearances at Niblo's occurred
before he saw Maeder's Buffalo Bill, not after.   His introduction to theater, in fact, convinced him that "as yet I had
seen but a small portion of the world. "   And he was pleased with this "new world" in which everything was "new and
startling. "

He was, it is true, uneasy when he first saw himself as a character on the stage.   "The audience, " he
remembered "upon learning that the real 'Buffalo Bill' was
present, gave several cheers between the acts, and I was
called on to come out on the stage and make a speech.
Mr. Freleigh, the manager, insisted that I should be introduced to Mr. Studly (the actor playing the role of Buffalo
Bill).   I finally consented, and the next moment I found
myself standing behind the footlights and in front of an
audience for the first time in my life.   I looked up, then
down, then on each side, and everywhere I saw a sea of
human faces, and thousands of eyes all staring at me.   I
confess that I felt much embarrassed--never more so in my
life--and I knew not what to say.   I made a desperate
effort, and a few words escaped me, but what they were
I could not for the life of me tell, nor could any one else
in the house.   My utterances were inaudible even to the
leader of the orchestra, Mr. Dean, who was sitting only
a few feet in front of me.   Bowing to the audience, I beat

a hasty retreat into one of the canyons of the stage.   I
never felt more relieved in my life than when I got out
of the view of that immense crowd. "

After this experience--which would have dismayed
even a Richard Burton--Cody turned down an offer by Freleigh to take over the role of Buffalo Bill at five hundred
dollars a week. "I told him, " Cody said, "that it would
be useless for me to attempt anything of the kind, for I
never could talk to a crowd of people like that, even if it
was to save my neck, and that he might as well try to make
an actor out of a government mule. "

Cody, however, had nothing but praise for the play
itself.   J. B. Studley, he said, was "an excellent actor, ...
in the character of 'Buffalo Bill, ' and Mrs. W. G. Jones,
a fine actress, taking the part of my sister, a leading
role. " The drama, itself, he concluded, "was played
smoothly and created a great deal of enthusiasm. "

In less than a year, in the fall of 1872, Cody changed
his mind about his acting capabilities.   He accepted an offer
from Ned Buntline to star in a play, Scouts of the Plains,
and took his friend, Texas Jack (J. B.) Omohundro with him
to play a supporting role.

The preparations for that play were terrible.   Buntline not only did not have the arrangements made--the
theater rented, the actors hired, the scenery prepared--but
he had not even written the play.   In a burst of energy,
Buntline threw together a play in four hours, but Cody
and Omohundro were unable to learn the parts.   In spite
of these difficulties, however, the play went on; and at
least for the audience--and the box office--the debut for
Buffalo Bill in Scouts of the Plains was a success.   The
newspaper critics thought the play and Buntline's performance were so bad that it almost made the show worth seeing for the unintentional comedy.   Cody, however, impro-
vised his role as he went along playing the role of the
"hero of the West" with tongue-in-cheek; and even the reviewers liked him.

For a year, Cody toured with Buntline, but when
the profits were distributed and Cody got the mouses's
share while Buntline played the lion, Buffalo Bill decided
that he would run his own company.   Buntline let him keep
Scouts of the Plains, and in addition to the changes that Cody

had made in the play for his own performance, further
changes were now made, including the cutting of a long
prohibition lecture by Ned Buntline; and an important character, Wild Bill Hickok, was added.

Cody toured with this play for almost four years,
and during these years, he not only made a small fortune
and became a national hero, but he also developed ideas
about what a play should be. In 1876, with the aid of an
actor, J. V. Arlington, he wrote his first play.

Cody's first play shows a remarkable improvement
over Maeder's Buffalo Bill. Although in public, Cody joked
that the play had neither "head nor tail," in the privacy of
the writer's study, he made a play that is tight in its
construction and consistent throughout.

Life on the Border deals with the young Buffalo
Bill in the early years after the Civil War had ended.
There is one principal villain, Captain Huntley, a self-
appointed head of local law enforcement, a counterfeiter,
an Indian-rouser, and murderer. He and Buffalo Bill are
opposed in every activity, even in their rivalry for Emma
Reynolds. In the course of the drama, Buffalo Bill out-
shoots the Indians, out-wrestles a bear, and out-draws
Huntley; but throughout the play, all his actions are limited
by some notion of the possible. He does not blow himself
up to frighten away the Indians, as the hero did in Maeder's
Buffalo Bill.

Then, too, although he is the "heroic man" of the
West, brave, strong, and honest, he is also a modest
fellow with a sharp sense of humor. Both heroes and
villains hate the Indians, but Bill holds a "moderate view."
He recognizes that the Indians are a threat, but he also
recognizes that they have cause to hate the white settlers.
Nor is he a part of a prohibition campaign, as he was in
Buntline's Scouts of the Plains. True, he turns down
a drink offered him by General Duncan, but his refusal
was caused by a lack of time, not a lack of taste. Finally,
although his friends and enemies, Longtrailer, Old Sloat,
Grasshopper Jim, Toothpick Ben, sing (or curse) his praises,
the stage character of Buffalo Bill, as created by Cody,
does not pose as an heroic man. He would rather trick the
enemy than out-talk them or out-shoot them.

The results of these changes in plot and characterization were remarkable in the final product, the play itself;
and if Life on the Border does not make Cody as good a
playwright as Shakespeare, at least he compares well with
the writers of Gunsmoke and Bonanza.

After one season's success with his own play, Cody
became a perennial playwright. In 1877-1878 he drama-
tized a story about himself, May Cody, or Lost and Won,
written by Major A. S. Burt, one of the better known dime
novelists. This play proved to be an even bigger stage
success than Life on the Border. That same year,
capitalizing on the publicity of his fight with Yellow Hand,
he wrote the Red Right Hand, or Buffalo Bill's First Scalp
for Custer. Critics, it is true, still made fun of the plays.
One critic, for example, wrote that he couldn't decide if
one of the characters in the Red Right Hand, Land-Wha-
Hoo, played by the Irish comic, Dennis O'Gaff, was supposed to be an Indian or a Chinese; but no longer were the
entire reviews written as one long joke, as the critics had
treated the first performances of Scouts of the Plains.

There can be no doubt that Cody played the leading
role in all of his plays, but many of Buffalo Bill's biographers have serious doubts about how much actual writing
Cody was doing. They complain, too, that all of his plays
followed a "tried-and-true formula." By 1888, however,
Cody had written, in part or whole, at least a half dozen
plays. In addition to Life on the Border, Red Right Hand,
and May Cody, these plays included Knights of the
Plains, Buffalo Bill at Bay; or The Pearl of the Prairie,
White Beaver, and the Prairie Waif. Although no
copies of these plays remain for comparison, judging from
the reviews one would conclude that the longer Cody wrote,
the smoother the plays became, the more the character
of Buffalo Bill became realistic and believable, and the
closer the plots came to real life.

With the success of the Wild West Show in the mid-
1880's, Cody not only left the stage and destroyed his plays,
but he also started a systematic campaign to mock the old
Western melodramas as such. If this campaign did not
succeed in ending the western melodrama, as the later
success of Tom Mix, Buck Jones, Hoot Gibson, and Matt
Dillon proves it did not, it seems at least to have ended
Cody's reputation as a playwright.

In passing, it is interesting to note that another
Bill--Shakespeare--after a playwriting career of about the
same length and success, also threw away his plays and
fled the stage.   Fortunately for Shakespeare's reputation
as a playwright, his fellow actors gathered together the
manuscripts of the discarded plays into a single volume.
When Cody left the theater, however, he took half of his
actors with him to the new Wild West show; and the other
half--Capt. Jack and Texas Jack--stayed on the stage,
borrowed some of Cody's ideas and play techniques and
hoped their audiences would forget there ever was a
Buffalo Bill.

Bibliography

In addition to the original manuscripts of Buffalo
Bill plays--Fred Maeder's Buffalo Bill [in the Harvard
University Library] and William F. Cody's Life on the
Border [published by the Pioneer Drama Service] and
newspaper reviews of the plays, the following printed
sources were especially useful: W. F. Cody's Story of the
Wild West and Camp Fire Chats, 1902; and Henry Blackman
Sell and Victor Weybright's Buffalo Bill and the Wild West,
New York, 1955.   Those interested in the western stage
melodrama may also find additional information about
Buffalo Bill as an actor and playwright in my two academic
articles: "When the Curtains Rise, Scouts Fall Out,"
Southern Speech Journal, XXIX (Spring 1964), 175-186,
especially useful for its notes on unpublished materials,
and "Buffalo Bill's Life on the Border," Dime Novel Round-
Up, XXXIII (August 15, 1964), 68-69.

2.   About a Local Piece of Scholarship

Jack Whisler:
Louisiana Sojourner Finds a Home

The Archives of the University of Southwestern
Louisiana is richer by one package of original dramatic
manuscripts.

This fact, in itself, is not surprising. For the
past 10 years, the Lafayette university has been building
one of the best collections of Southern regional drama in
the United States.   It now has, for example, the most
complete set of dramatic manuscripts by Espy Williams,
the most successful nineteenth-century Louisiana professional playwright.   It has a larger collection of plays by nineteenth-century Mississippi and Arkansas playwrights than
the combined library resources of those two states.   It
has the most complete set of the plays of Marc Connelly
in the United States.

What may be a little surprising, however, is the
way in which the new discovery of dramatic manuscripts
found its way to the USL collection.

Ernest J. Whisler, who wrote under the name of
Jack Whisler, had only a sojourner's relationship with
Louisiana.   For 20 years, before and after World War I,
he was a public relations man for the Southern Pacific
Railroad.   Part of his job was to follow the route of the
Southern Pacific, taking color photographs of special interest
for West, the Southern Pacific magazine.

In one issue of West, Whisler told his readers of
his first visit to Louisiana: "I went to old New Orleans
for a day that stretched into a week, and then headed
west on Southern Pacific's Sunset Route ... west across
Louisiana's bayou country.... " That first visit led to
dozens of others, and thereafter Louisiana became one of
Whisler's favorite scenes.

His photographs of Canal Street, of the Pontalba
Apartments, of St. Louis Cathedral, of Pirates' Alley, of
a maiden in the Evangeline Country made public relations
history for the Southern Pacific, and many of his camera

studies may still be seen on the dining cars of the Southern
Pacific.

Doing public relations was Whisler's way of earning
his living, but his first love was the theater.   Back in Ro-
chester, Pennsylvania, where he was born in the 1870's,
Whisler established a reputation as a playwright for the
campus.   One of his early plays, "His Brother," was produced by Beaver College, a women's college in Pennsylvania.
It drew such favorable attention that Whisler was encouraged
to write for publication.

Two of his plays--"A Trick Dollar" and "Lexington"--
were published by the T. S. Denison Company, one of the
leading play-publishing companies in the midwest at the time.
Another, "Alias Brown," was published by the Walter H.
Baker Company of Boston

Whisler, then just turning 20, had every reason to
expect a successful career as a nationwide dramatist.

At the turn of the century, however, his parents
had to move west for their health.   Jack and his baby sister,
Lois, went along.   When the Whislers settled in Tucson,
Arizona, Jack was doing something more than moving away
from the stage markets he had developed.   He also gave up
any chance to get a college education.

"Next only to the theater," his sister Lois says,
"my brother loved education.   But he needed to go to work,
fulltime, to help our parents."

Arizona was about as far from Broadway as a
writer could get at the turn of the century.   Tucson did
start a small college soon after Jack arrived, but it would
be many years before it would even offer a drama course.

For about 20 years, however, Whisler, in spite of
the burden of family responsibilities, did yeoman service in
helping Tucson become drama-minded.   He wrote, directed,
and starred in a variety of plays and musical comedies for
both the college and town; and much of what he wrote was
good enough that the national play publishers still wanted it.
The Baker Company, for example, published his "Private
Tutor" in 1907 and his "Tommy's Brides" in 1924.

These plays, and others that he did, were produced

in schools and community theaters all over the country.
But then as now, the only way to first-rate professional
success in the theater was through successful Broadway
productions.   Whisler did not feel that he could chance his
family's security, but he was ready when the right chance
came.

In 1924, Victor Herbert, then at the height of his
popularity, vacationed in Arizona, saw some of Whisler's
musical productions, and offered him that one-chance-in-a-
lifetime that every regional playwright dreams about.   Herbert wanted Jack to do the book for a new musical for him.

After 24 years of delaying his life's ambition, the
big chance was here.   That same year, however, Victor
Herbert died.   Whisler was left with half a book that he
had finished for their musical and the feeling that another
such chance would never come.

For the next 10 years, Whisler continued to write.
According to his sister, Lois, however, he no longer wrote
with any hope that he would be "discovered."   After the
death of their parents, Jack and his sister moved to California.   Here he had one play, "Curtain Call," produced by
the Padua Playhouse.   When the production was over, however, Whisler was so certain that the play had no future
that he was using it for kindling--until his sister Lois took
the manuscript away from him.

During this time, too, Whisler turned to fiction,
writing at least two folk stories of the Old West.   One of
these, "Hopeless Tubbs and the Trade Ants," was published
early this year by the Charleton Publishing Company.   The
editor there, Edward T. LeBlanc, was so pleased with the
work that he has nominated it for the Cowboy Hall of Fame
award.   The other fiction manuscript, a novella titled "The
Parson and the Dance Hall Lady," is still in manuscript,
never having been submitted for publication.

"After coming so close," his sister Lois said, "my
brother never wrote with any hopes of success--but he continued to give his work the same careful attention that he
had in the days when success was just around the corner."

In August 1958, Whisler died of a heart attack at
his home in Burlingame, California.   His sister, Lois, is
still an active newspaper woman in California.

Whisler never became the writer he wanted to be. He was, however, the first successful playwright in Arizona, and for the first twenty years of that state's modern existence, he was far-and-away the best talent it had. For a man who had a close brush with national attention, this fact was probably unobserved.

At the University of Southwestern Louisiana, however, for the past ten years, a number of the faculty have been making an effort to discover the regional playwrights, "Across the South." Arizona was one of the eleven states selected for examination, and any examination of Arizona drama, of course, threw the spotlight on Jack Whisler.

The results of a preliminary investigation were published in Arizona Teacher, and the Arizona Sun editor commented editorially on the neglect shown one of the "favorite sons." No one in the state had ever bothered to notice Whisler's work, and even the college at which some of the plays had first been produced did not have copies.

Miss Whisler was pleased that her brother's work was finally getting some attention. She wrote to the Southwestern Louisiana researchers, "I am most appreciative of all the painstaking research work you have done in regard to my brother's plays. How surprised and delighted he would have been."

She, also, offered to send all of the materials that she had kept--an unpublished full-length play, the two western stories, programs, news clippings, some published plays. "I have all of his possessions," she wrote, "but I am appalled at how little he kept."

It was from this material that the university researchers arranged the publication of one of Whisler's unpublished stories, "Hopeless Tubbs and the Trade Ants." Negotiations are in progress for publication of others.

In the spring of 1967, Miss Whisler made a tour of Louisiana and visited the University of Southwestern Louisiana library. She was pleased with what she saw, and made the university a gift of the entire collection. Later, she wrote, "I would feel honored to know that they were being permanently preserved."

Dr. Henry Dethloff, director of the Archives, in commenting on the collection, called attention to the many uses which such materials offer to scholars.

"All of our ideas of the past are based on records we have kept. When a discovery of new material like this is made, it is important to note that the value it has comes not merely because we have added some new manuscripts to our collection. It is, rather, that we have a new opportunity to learn more of the truth about where we have been and what we are. Research is not a process of shuffling the old and familiar evidence; it is discovering what has been overlooked."

Dr. Dethloff's opinion is shared, begrudgingly, by at least one other archivist. After the attention given to Whisler by the Southwestern Louisiana researchers, one of the Arizona state librarians wrote and asked Miss Whisler if she would like to give her brother's literary remains to the Arizona collection.

"I was able to tell them, quite happily," Miss Whisler said, "that Jack's manuscripts had found a home."

3.   About Modern Events in One's Specialty

Two Memory Plays:
The Glass Menagerie and After the Fall

For the past seventy-five years or more, playwrights
have attempted to move beyond the traditional scope of the
drama--to show an action--to deal directly with the source
of action itself, the mind. The soliloquy of drama, once
an embellishment, an aside, has become the basis of the
entire play in such forms as the "dream play" and "expressionistic drama." An interesting and important achieve-
ment in this search to stage directly the mind of man is
the "memory play," a term that has been in use by dramatic critics for only about twenty years. It is now common-
place to describe such plays as The Glass Menagerie[1] and
After the Fall[2] by the term "memory plays"; but no critic,
to my knowledge, has yet suggested that this is a separate
form, built upon a different set of assumptions from the
traditional drama-of-action and different, too, from such
mind-searching plays as Strindberg's Dream Play or Kaufman and Connelly's Beggar on Horseback. The new "memory
play," unlike the dream play and expressionistic drama, is
a projection of the conscious mind; and, unlike the traditional
drama-of-action, it is concerned only with that action that
is understood and retained in the mind of the protagonist.

The memory of a character has, of course, always
been a part of drama. It is the memory of the Chorus
that informs the audience of the events leading to the final
catastrophe of Aeschylus' Agamemnon. A single actor's
memory, moreover, has long been a part of drama. Hamlet's soliloquies are essentially his statements of his memory of the past. The memory of Willy Loman in Death of a
Salesman is projected into a character that may be seen by
the audience; Uncle Ben, as he is seen in the play, is
Willy's memory of him--not a character created from the
person himself.

There is, however, a difference between "memories
in drama," either recalled or projected, and a "memory
play." In plays that merely use memory as part of the
drama, the world of the drama is rooted in some kind of
real world beyond the characters themselves, a world shown
or suggested, against which the audience must evaluate the

truth or falsity, accuracy or distortion of every act, speech, and memory.

In the memory play as a particular form, the world of the drama is the memory of a single character, the narrator-protagonist. Tom Wingfield in The Glass Menagerie and Quentin in After the Fall show the audience their memories, and that memory is all the world there is. The memory play is set in the conscious mind of the protagonist, and it stands aloof from outside testimony. If the play is true, the memory is true.

Tom Wingfield assumes the "truth" of his memory, but he recognizes that the world of his memory is full of distortions. He promises, in his opening speech, "truth in the pleasant guise of illusion," but as he continues his opening narration, it becomes obvious that he is speaking of the relationship of the play to his memory, not of his memory to any fact beyond the theater. The play, he suggests, has a "social background," Depression America; but beyond the fact that Tom's memory was formed in turbulent times, the background is meaningless to the play.

"The play is memory," Tom tells his audience. "Being a memory play, it is dimly lighted, it is sentimental, it is not realistic." One of the characters in the play, he suggests, came into his memory and remained there without distortion, "the gentleman caller who appears in the final scenes." "He is," says Tom, "the most realistic character in the play, being an emissary from a world of reality that we were somehow set apart from." The other characters in the play--the narrator himself; Amanda, his mother; Laura, his sister; and "the larger-than-life-size photograph" of "our father"--clearly are characters of the memory. Even the character of the gentlemen caller, Tom qualifies, is not wholly realistic; "But since I have a poet's weaknesses for symbols, I am using this character also as a symbol; he is the long awaited but always expected something that we live for."

In the list of "Characters" Williams gives his "objective evaluations" of the characters: "Amanda ... much to admire in Amanda, and as much to love and pity as there is to laugh at ... Laura ... too exquisitely fragile to move from the shelf. Tom ... not remorseless, but to escape from a trap he has to act without pity. Jim ... a nice, ordinary, young man." It would be a mistake, however, to

confuse these evaluations with the characters of the memory.
"Laura's situation, " for example, is described in the list
of "Characters" as being "even graver" than Amanda's; but
in the world of Tom's memory, she is stronger, not merely
than Amanda but than Tom, too. Tom might have said,
"Oh Laura, I tried to leave you behind, but [you are stronger, rather than] I am more faithful than I intended to be!"
And Tom, himself, does not escape "his trap, " no matter
what the "Character" notes say. This is not to suggest
that Williams' character notes may not be helpful to the
actors playing the roles; it is, however, to argue that
finally we must accept the characters as they appear in
Tom's memory or not at all. Amanda, whatever a person
like such a character may be in life, is a monster in
Tom's memory, and the monster is all the Amanda there
is in The Glass Menagerie.

Any audience has the right, of course, to ask what
are the relationships between the world of the play and the
world outside the play that is being mirrored. When that
world is one that we can see about us in time or in space,
we can, by our own standards, evaluate the truthfulness of
the play-world by comparing it with our concept of the world-
outside that it reflects. But in a memory play, the world
outside the play is the memory of the narrator, and our only
access to that world is through the memory of the narrator-
protagonist in the play. As a social comment, we may, of
course, complain that the memory of the narrator is a
distortion of an outside world that it remembers; but this
is simply to observe that a subjective memory of a person
and an event is not an objective recording, a fact of dramatic composition that the playwright, by using the form of
the memory play, has insisted upon from the first.

The narrator in the memory play promises his
audience only that he will show the people, the events, the
cause-effect relationships that make up his memory. In
After the Fall, it is suggested that in the process the
audience will be shown how the character of the narrator-
protagonist came to accept his memory and live with it;
and in The Glass Menagerie, it is suggested that in the
process the audience will be shown why the narrator-protagonist is taking leave of his memory--"Blow out your
candles, Laura. " But in both plays, once the audience has
accepted the world of the memory, all objective criticism
in terms of economic theory, psychological realism, or
philosophical logic becomes impossible, or at least fruitless.

The advantage to the playwright of the memory play
is quite clearly that he can unroll his memory--the real
history of his character--without having it edited, corrected,
challenged. The reviewer for The Village Voice, who insisted that there is a one-for-one relationship between
Quentin and Arthur Miller, saw After the Fall as a public
confession of the playwright: "Quentin, at all times, remains
Arthur Miller, questing among his moral flash-cards, mus-
cling his way toward the perfect analysis."[3] Undoubtedly, the
writer of the "memory play" will create a narrator-protagonist whose history closely suggests his own. Miller and
Quentin both married three times; both had, for a second
wife, a public performer who took her own life. Williams
and Tom Wingfield both had fathers who, in one way or
another, "deserted"; both had Southern-belle mothers
and "psychologically crippled" sisters. To acknowledge
these similarities, however, is to do no more than to say
that a playwright must mirror the world that he sees; and
the author of a memory play must work in terms of his
own memory. He can see no other.

The difference between Miller and Williams and the
rest of us is not that they unburden the memory of their
private lives on others and we do not, it is rather that they
wrote The Glass Menagerie and After the Fall and we did
not. Newspaper reviewers, like John Chamberlain and
Russell Kirk, who complain on Monday of Miller's lack of
taste and on Tuesday take their readers into intimate con-
fidences about their own private family affairs, are not
merely being inconsistent; they are also confusing what they
read into a playwright's personal life with a play. The
author of the successful memory play should, of course, be
aware that such a play--even more than most plays--will
be an invitation to the critic to go prowling around in the
facts of his private life. Edward Albee in dedicating The
Sand Box to his grandmother seems intentionally to have
thumbed his nose at such criticism. Perhaps, as one re-
veiwer commented, such investigations go "with the territory",[4] and the playwright should cooperate in the game.

But it is an error to think that a memory play will
succeed because of the private memories of the playwright.
The memory play pleases for the same reason any other
play pleases; it offers its audience an involvement in a
world that seems more real (or more attractive) than its
own. The audience must judge whether or not to be concerned with the characters and their problems; but, unlike

the audience of a play that pictures an objective world, the
audience of a memory play is really unable to measure the
subject against the portrait.

The narrator-protagonist in a memory play tells the
audience that he is the result of his memory. He offers
to show this memory in the form in which it exists at the
moment of the play. Arthur Ganz complains that After the
Fall is "not a memory play--but a Chronicle History" and
argues that after the first quarter of the play the memory
technique is abandoned as a meaningful structure. [5] It would
be fairer to suggest that Quentin's memory deals with
episodes first thematically, then chronologically. The Glass
Menagerie, it should be noted, follows a chronological order
throughout. Admittedly, there is something frustrating
about a critical examination of a memory play, especially
for a critic whose first concern is with "ideas." One cannot carp that "people are not like that," the "economy
is not like that," and "things do not happen that way," if
the whole form of the play proclaims, "Perhaps not, but
this is the way in which my memory has stored them."

One whose primary concern is with ideas can, however, take comfort that there is no need for such judgments
of a memory play. In such a play, the narrator-protagonist will tell his audience that he is in the midst of a problem, a problem created by a memory that is hard to bear.
He will then unroll that memory, not selecting those details that would most meaningfully dramatize his problem
but rather dramatizing those details which have been selected for storage in the memory. Since it is suggested
that it is the memory that is the man, it is, of course,
further suggested that an open examination of the whole
memory will lead to an understanding of that man, perhaps
implying that when the man comes to an understanding of
himself (his memory), he will be able to act. It is probably further suggested that as the memory becomes more
detailed, better ordered, and more objective, the narrator-
protagonist is moving toward understanding.

The characters in the memory play exist only in
relationship to the narrator-protagonist. They may appear
to him to be weak or strong, heroes or villains; but the
point of their interest is not what they are but what they
are to the narrator. Amanda, for Tom, is so monstrous a
character that he is made ill by her mere mundane comments. It is really not important, although we may note

it in passing, that she was for the playwright a woman of
some courage.

In retrospect, of course, the critic may ask what
relationship there is between the memory and the reality
that gave it its nature; but the focus in the memory play,
it seems to me, should be on the narrator-protagonist,
the owner of the memory, how he came into possession
of it, in what form it possesses him, and, finally, what
will result from it.

I

When the curtain rises on The Glass Menagerie,
the audience meets Tom Wingfield, the narrator-protagonist,
"dressed as a merchant sailor," entering "from an alley,"
performing an amateur trick of magic. He comes as a
self-proclaimed philosopher: "I give you truth." The
truth, somehow, is associated with the past decade--the
age of depression, "when the huge middle class of America
was matriculating in a school for the blind." But the
immediate truth has to do with Tom and his associations
with "other characters ... my mother ... my sister ... and
a gentlemen caller. ... There is a fifth character ... our
father." The elder Wingfield has deserted his family, for
what exact cause we never learn; but in Tom's memory,
"He was a telephone man who fell in love with long distance;
he gave up his job with the telephone company and skipped
the light fantastic out of town. ... The last we heard from
him was a picture post-card ... containing a message of
two words--'Hello--Goodbye!'--and no address." For Tom,
this cryptic message is all the memory there is, and Tom's
final words in the play, "... and so good-bye ...," are a
conscious echo of the father. After a long reflection, one
may wonder if Tom in following his "father's footsteps,"
attempting to find in "motion what was lost in space," ever
had doubts concerning his father's wisdom. Such a concern,
however, is beyond the scope of the play. Tom's memory,
the play itself, does not move forward from the opening
speech. The play is dramatic in that the memory is revealed like an action, but the memory itself is static.
The character of Tom is not affected by revelation.

As a memory play, The Glass Menagerie is not
essentially about other people, but rather about Tom's
memory of other people. Even in the most tense conflicts
between Amanda and Laura, the audience is aware of Tom's

standing in the wings waiting; and after a scene is over, he
will by a comment or gesture--"TOM motions to the fiddles
in the wings"--remind the audience that it is unimportant as
to what effect the scene has for them.   It is only important
what effect it had on him.

   In the simplest terms, The Glass Menagerie sets
forth Tom's "reasons" for his renunciation of the conventional goals of the society in which he lives.   The play
is his memory, and his memory--not a rational analysis
of it--is his evidence.   It is not necessary to accept the
memory as a valid artifact of the deed.   It is necessary
that one accept the memory itself as a fact, the one fact
of Tom's existence.   Tom's world--from a distance "lit
by lightning," the war in Europe--is his description, not
his defense.   The world beyond, in rags and at war, is
beyond his responsibility, beyond his memory.

                                  II

   The Glass Menagerie has a purity of genre that
does not exist in After the Fall.   Miller's first directions
inform that "The action takes place in the mind, thought,
and memory" of Quentin; and the addition of "mind" and
"thought" marks the difference in the plays themselves.

   After the Fall takes place in the mind of Quentin,
but unlike Tom, Quentin does not accept his memory as
the only truth that exists for him.   Tom offers the memory
of a single, trivial episode (set in a terrible, shadowy
world which he acknowledges only faintly) as truth.   Quentin
brings a broader memory--one that encompasses the lives
of others, one that tries to reconcile the "blasted stone
tower of a German concentration camp" with personal fears
that he is sacrificing his career, perhaps "trying to destroy
myself"--as one piece of evidence which he intends to
examine with his mind and reason (thought).   Tom is a
poet who finds truth in a symbol; Quentin is a lawyer who
finds meaning in the law.   Both characters escape from
intolerable situations; but Tom is eager to escape, certain
that he can trust the symbols of his memory.   Quentin can
leave only with the most profound regrets and feelings of
guilt for his lack of regret.   Tom feels no responsibility
even for the immediate world in which he lives; Quentin
feels a responsibility even for the world beyond his control,
beyond his understanding.   He feels responsibility for the
Nazi terror: "Who can be innocent again on this mountain

of skulls?" He feels responsibility for all the deaths he
knows, a personal responsibility: "... I loved them all,
all! And gave them willingly to failure and to death that
I might live."

Tom has control of his memory. The Glass
Menagerie has the simple cause-effect action of the well-
made play. As anything else but a memory play, it would
be a pathetic little sentimental piece, not even as large
as Thornton Wilder's Happy Journey to Camden and Trenton.
The Glass Menagerie, in fact, suggests a larger world by
the mere fact that Tom, willfully, discards from this memory everything beyond his physical senses. He can see
the lightning of World War II, but he cannot see the world
that is lit by it. Tom has complete faith in his memory,
but this memory is as rigorously controlled in its selection of details as is Amanda's memory of her youth; and
he is as devoted to the movies, the casual companion, and
the symbol out of context as Amanda is to the D. A. R. , the
genteel social amenities, and the wonderful new serial by
Bessie Mae Harper.

Quentin has no such control of his memory. The
play sprawls like a novel by Tolstoy. Allan Lewis argues
that in After the Fall, Miller's real problem is "original
sin, " from the fall of man to the horror of post-war Europe;
his real audience is not, as Tom Wingfield's is, his slightly inferior contemporaries, but rather the maker of all
truth. The opening lines, "Hello! God, it's good to see
you again!", according to Lewis, should be punctuated,
"Hello, God. It's good to see you again. "[6] Quentin brings
his memories and his beliefs to the listener, and in a
series of agonizing sessions, he asks to have these memories fitted to his beliefs or to have his beliefs altered to
fit his memories. Standing between the belief and the memory is the questioning mind, doubting itself, to be sure,
weary with failure, but never really abdicating--not to the
memory, not to the old beliefs, not to a new philosophy
of despair.

Both The Glass Menagerie and After the Fall have
autobiographical elements in them. Maggie is a memory
of Marilyn Monroe, perhaps Arthur Miller's memory, perhaps only the audience's hopes or fears that this is a personal memory since it seems to agree with its own. Laura
is a memory of Tennessee Williams' sister. Critics have,
however, complained only about Miller's use of such personal

history and, at that, only such personal history as relates
to Marilyn Monroe (Maggie), although, in truth, Maggie is
a good deal more attractive character than are Mother,
Father, or Louise--all of whom are, seemingly, also characterizations of people close to Miller.   The reason for
this complaint is, I think, not merely the general feeling
of guilt that many Americans have about the death of Marilyn
Monroe, but it is that After the Fall is a memory play that
is a part of our world.   The Glass Menagerie, on the other
hand, is a memory play of a world that is "somehow set
apart. "

    The world of After the Fall is full of people striving,
no matter how foolishly, for goals that are important.   It
is a world, moreover, of size and power.   There is no
value judgment intended in this observation, but it is obvious
that while Tom Wingfield is a boy running away from his
small world, Quentin is a man trying to make complex
choices, trying to live in a very large world.   Beyond a
few flippant comments, there is no world in The Glass
Menagerie beyond the physical reach of Tom Wingfield.
Quentin's world, by contrast, is so large that even with
"memory, mind and thought, " Quentin's problem is essentially finding some means of coming to workable terms
with that world.

    Historically, the world of After the Fall is modern
western civilization from World War I to the early 1960's.
The central historical fact of this world is the Nazi reign
of terror and the discovery of the crimes of the concentration camp.   "Dominating" not only the stage but the
world of the play as well "is the blasted stone tower of a
German concentration camp. "   Critics who felt that After
the Fall is primarily a play about Marilyn Monroe must
have been somewhat disappointed that Miller followed this
play with An Incident at Vichy, rather than with The Further
Adventures of Maggie.

    The Nazi terror is, however, only the central fact;
and its lasting horror is that it is symbolic of the whole
history of the world of the play, on both the public and
private levels.   This history starts a little before World
War I with a personalized picture of American immigration
history, when children were shipped from Europe to America
with tags around their necks, as Quentin's father was,
"like a package in the bottom of the boat. "   It includes
World War I, the boom that followed, the Crash, the De-

pression, the Confusion, the Japanese invasion of Manchuria,
World War II, the bombing of Hiroshima, the discrimination
problems of America, the post-war European boom, the new
affluence of America, the McCarthy investigations, the anti-
Communist witch hunts, the church investigations. A collection of the footnotes that might one day be needed to
"explain" the historical references in the play could run
several times the length of the play, and such a collection
might serve as a good running commentary on the history
of America and Europe from 1915 to the 1960's.

The characters within this wider world have more
active, more classically dramatic, lives than the characters
of The Glass Menagerie, who could summarize their lives
briefly: tried one small thing once, feebly; failed, and re-
signed. But a dozen of the characters in After the Fall
and perhaps two who do not appear on stage--Maggie's
Judge Cruse and Mother's Dr. Strauss--have biographies
in the play, complete enough to make them the central
characters in dramas of their own.

The play is Quentin's "spiritual autobiography" to
be sure; but within his autobiography are the complete lives
of Rose, his mother; his father; Dan, his brother; Quentin's
"women"--Louise, Maggie, Holga, Felice, Elsie, Lou, Mickey; and the Rev. Harley Barnes. Miller uses characters
both to show Quentin's problems and to suggest the multiplicity of personal dramas taking place within the central action.
Such a use is not a violation of the memory-play principle
of After the Fall, but rather it serves to explain the reason that Quentin, after so many falls, cannot give himself
up to despair. Unlike Tom Wingfield, Quentin holds a
memory that includes a great deal of sympathy for the
memories of others.

Tom Wingfield avoids all real contact with the other
characters of the play, and he has genuine sympathy for
only one, his sister Laura. Quentin, however, in spite of
his first wife's complaints, is in close association with
others. He is, to be sure, often in a struggle with them,
but in each of his encounters--with Maggie, Louise, Rose,
Felice, Lou, Mickey, Elsie, Barnes--he gives them his
understanding and takes responsibility for their defeats. He
is aware, of course, that he can fail others (as he does his
father) without causing a defeat and he is, also, aware that
he can try to help others (as he tries with Maggie) without
insuring a success. But it is through his review of his

relationships with his women--Louise, Maggie, and Holga--
that Quentin is able to come to a workable conclusion:
"... not certainty, I don't feel that.   But it does seem
feasible. "   As Quentin is able to verbalize his problems
and their solutions, he speaks of man, "after the fall, "
and he concludes that man must know his limitations, must
be able to forgive others and himself.   In his relationship
with Louise, his first wife, he was aware only of his
negative virtues.   His love for her, his affection for her,
should have been clear to her by his restraint.   It was
not; in fact, she did not even accept the fact of his negative virtue.   From this relationship, he learned that what
one does not do is less important than what one does; and
in his relationships with Maggie, he is guided by the lessons
of his first marriage.

     He greets each of Maggie's confessions of her past--
even of two lovers in one day--with learned tolerance.   He
forgives too much, too soon, too many times.   In fact,
the only time that Maggie's "past" stands between him and
his love for her, she is not "guilty. "   He renounces his
love for her--"The only one I will ever love is my daughter. "
--because he is suspicious that among the grinning men who
"chewed" her up and "spat" her out are his house guests,
and he is in error.   He cannot reassure her of his love
because in no positive act--not even in twice stopping her
from suicide--is there evidence of his negative virtue.
Maggie has more need of what he does not do than what
he does do.   She must know that he does not laugh at her
and that he does not wish to be rid of her.   It is not at
all odd that Quentin confuses her with his mother, that he
finds himself trying to kill her.   The only thing positive
in an act of death is murder, and in trying to formalize
a philosophy from his memory of his marriage to Louise,
Quentin has chosen the positive act of love.   It is obvious
that he speaks with more terms of endearment -- "darling, "
"dear, " "sweetheart" -- to Maggie than to Louise.   It is
obvious, too, that Maggie does not have Louise's complaint
that he touches her, "Silent, cold. "

     The memory of these two loves and the lessons
learned--not to be negative in one's acts nor to be positive
in one's absolutes--gives Quentin hope that Holga will "know
what I mean. " 'Burning cities" have taught her what Quentin's memories have taught him--that man is dangerous,
that the memory is for examination, that the mind is for
tempering, that thoughts are the principles that hang between

the memory (the emotion) and the mind (the rational judgment).

In After the Fall, Quentin's memory does not have the absolute quality that Tom's memory has for him in The Glass Menagerie. After the Fall is a memory play, but it is a memory that the narrator accepts as a responsibility, not as a final authority.

III

The memory play as a kind of drama has so many advantages that it seems likely that there will be more of them. The danger of this genre is that it can give the playwright a sense of omniscience and that from the humble act of admitting or implying that all the world he knows is the one he remembers, he can leap to the assumption, or presumption, that the world of his memory is all the world there is. Williams, it seems, avoids such a leap in The Glass Menagerie on the narrowest grounds by making both the protagonist (Tom) and the antagonist (Amanda) morally inferior to the victim (Laura).

A second danger of this form is that it can lead to an abdication of responsibility with the assumption that memory is caused by events beyond the narrator's control. Critics who took Quentin's memory of Maggie as a biographical account of Miller's memory of Marilyn were offended and accused Miller of trying to "whitewash" himself in that relationship. Miller, it seems to me, does not "excuse or defend" his protagonist, but rather he makes Quentin responsible for his memory, not that it was formed, but responsible for what it will mean. When all is said and done, the audience for After the Fall has more sympathy for Maggie than Quentin has--but the audience's sympathy is a product of Miller's craftsmanship, not a denial of it.

One may easily identify the mechanical devices of a "memory play"--a single protagonist who serves as narrator; a sequence of actions selected from his memory to show his problem or demonstrate his nature; antagonists and supporting characters who exist only in relationship to the protagonist; a staging that borrows techniques from the expressionistic theater; a method of dialogue, half-narrative in nature, personal in tone. These devices, however, are only the trappings of the form. The heart of

the memory play is the dramatist's insistence that the most
meaningful part of life is what is remembered, not what is
done; and as such it is probably closer to romantic lyric
poetry than to objective drama. It is a musing to be shared,
not a debate to be judged.

Notes:

1.   All citations from The Glass Menagerie are from
the edition in Haskell M. Block and Robert G. Shedd's
Masters of Modern Drama (New York, 1962), p. 989-1017.

2.   All citations from this play are from Arthur
Miller's After the Fall (New York, 1964).

3.   Michael Smith, "Review: 'After the Fall,'" The
Village Voice, January 30, 1964.

4.   Tom Prideaux,"Marilyn's Ghost Takes the Stage,"
Life, LVI (Feb. 7, 1964), 64D. In the same issue, Miller
attempts to answer the criticism (65): "With respect for
her agony, but with love" he calls his use of Marilyn's
"Ghost"; and he argues, moreover, that the "game of Find
the Author" is "one of the more diverting, if minor, pas-
times of literary life."

5.   "Arthur Miller: After the Silence," Drama
Survey, IV (Fall, 1964), 520-30.

6.   American Plays and Playwrights of the Contemporary Theatre (New York, 1965), p. 37.

4. <u>About Another Man's Work</u>

<u>The Theater in Colonial America</u>, by Hugh F. Rankin.
(Chapel Hill: University of North Carolina Press, 1965.)

"The basic elements of theater," Professor Rankin
informs his readers, "are play, actors, and audience, held
together by a bond of interest." In this gracefully written,
carefully documented account of theatrical activities in
America from 1526 to 1775, Dr. Rankin sifts the evidence
and gives a detailed analysis of two of these elements--act-
ors and audience.

Undoubtedly, <u>Theater in Colonial America</u> will be
standard work on American theater before the Revolution
for a long time to come. Its value to historians of colonial America lies both in the mass of detail and in the
composite picture of what, Dr. Rankin admits, was a
narrow artistic activity. "The limitations of the colonial
theater are obvious," he concludes: "It was derivative in
nature; it produced practically no playwrights; and its
stylized acting ignored the more natural innovations introduced to the English stage by David Garrick."

The limitations of the book are inherent in the
material, and Dr. Rankin--perhaps wisely--does not strain
against them. The modest claims of the book are a part
of its grace; but this reviewer, at least, would have liked
more concern with the native plays--the thirty-some extant
dramatic compositions--belonging to this period, even at
the risk of strain.

On the matter of the first English-language play
published in America, <u>Androboros</u>, for example, Dr. Rankin
is content with a general comment--"a clever, but rude,
satire on the actions of the Assembly and Lieutenant Govern-
or Francis Nicholson. ..." Such a comment, though it
be standard treatment of the play in the theater histories
of American drama, seems to me to be inadequate for
this play. While it is true that the particular targets of
satire in <u>Androboros</u> are minor figures, the central theme
of the play lies in a conflict in theories of government,
royalist and republican; and such a theme should be worth
more careful scrutiny in a historical treatment of the pre-
revolutionary period of a republic.

Then, too, while Dr. Rankin carefully lists the
popular British plays performed in America--Cato, Douglas,
The Recruiting Officer, and various Shakespearean tragedies,
he is concerned with them only for their theatrical form
and not for their ideational content.   One may, of course,
make too much of the popularity of plays with political content; but, from this reviewer's point of view, some attention
should at least be given to the possibility that the popularity
of Cato in America, for example, might have been related
to the political sentiments of the audience.   Dr. Rankin is
not much concerned with relating the theater to the political
activities of the day, and, in all fairness to his neglect,
such an approach might have produced nothing but some
interesting speculation of doubtful worth; but the absence
of all such speculation tends to make the book seem unrelated to the political life of the times.   One would find
it difficult to believe that the world of The Theater in
Colonial America could ever erupt into revolution.

There are only two quibbles that need to be made
about the style and scholarship of the book.   Dr. Rankin
used the spelling theater throughout, although it was spelled
theatre during the period, as is evident in the quotations
in the book.   Since theatre has again become the preferred
spelling, at least with drama critics, there seems to be
little reason for the double spellings throughout.   And,
finally, there is one rather serious typographical error on
page 77--the date "1763" is given for "1753," an error
that is merely an annoyance since the correct date is clear
in the context.

But quibbles aside, The Theater in Colonial America
is a carefully conceived, sanely written account of a neglected aspect of early American history, an account that
most readers will wish were longer.

University of Southwestern Louisiana   Paul T. Nolan

5.   About the Uses of One's Special Knowledge

Chapter VI, "Dialogue"
From the Book
Writing the One-Act Play for the Amateur Stage

Dialogue in a play serves four purposes.   It is
narrative in that it is the means by which the story is
told; it is dramatic in that it is the means by which the
action is performed; it is artistic in that it is, in the final
analysis, that element in the play that most commands the
immediate attention of the audience, making the play an
exciting or dull experience.   And it also serves a sub-
ordinate function in that it is the best means of understanding the nature of the characters.

1.   Dialogue as Narration

Although drama shows someone doing something, it
is only through dialogue, (except in silent movies and panto-
mine), that the viewer knows who the someone is and what
it is that he is doing or trying to do.   Any information
that the audience is to receive about the events of the story,
except those few events that he may see from the physical
on-stage action, he must get through the dialogue.

In Strindberg's Miss Julie, for example, Miss Julie
narrates for both John and the audience the details of her
mother's life and her own youth.   The primitive selves in
"Overtones" tell the apparent selves--and the audience--the
history of their marriages.   There is, it must be remembered, no author in a play; there is only the playwright outside
the play.   Thornton Wilder in such a play as Our Town
may create the character of the Stage Manager, a character
who can speak directly to the audience and give information
the playwright judges necessary, but the Stage Manager is
still a character; he is not Wilder.   Any character can
finally tell the audience only what he knows as a character,
not what the playwright knows.   He can, moreover, speak
only of such matters as the occasion demands.

The playwright usually faces the immediate problem
of informing his audience about certain basic "facts" concerning his characters and the actions they are to perform.
The Greek playwrights could, and sometimes did, use the

Chorus for this purpose. With no apology, the Chorus or
a god simply came on stage and explained what had happened and, sometimes, even told what was going to happen.
Euripides' Hippolytus, for example, opens with a long speech
by Aphrodite, in which she expains that Hippolytus' past
behavior in ignoring the demands of love is going to be
punished. When the character, Hippolytus, makes his appearance, the audience already knows him and his problem.

Shakespeare used minor characters to open an action.
Hamlet, for example, opens with a discussion of ghosts and
the state of affairs in Denmark. Before Hamlet is ever
brought on stage, the audience knows he is a prince, that
his father recently died, that his mother has married his
father's brother, and that something is wrong. It is aware,
too, that Hamlet will have to take some action.

Such narrative devices as the chorus and talkative
servants, like the soliloquy are now out of fashion, and
the playwright--especially one who works with the one-act
play--has generally to rely on his main characters to tell
their own stories. They cannot, however, with any psychological soundness, simply tell a story with no motive for
the telling. For example, although it may be necessary
that the audience know that two characters are secretly
married, it is unrealistic to have one tell the other this
secret, since normally both parties to a marriage are aware
of the fact.

The playwright, therefore, does well to start with
two assumptions. First, he should assume that the whole
story from which he builds his play is not important to his
drama, but just that part of it that is revealed naturally
in the acting out of the play. Secondly, he should assume
that his audience is not only capable of creating a full
picture from a few suggestions, but that part of the pleasure in watching drama is in deducing more than is shown.
Thus, in creating the means of telling the story, the playwright should remember that a play is not a piece of fiction
spoken aloud. It is, rather, an action that is seen through
speech.

2.   Dialogue is Conflict

Dialogue, it should be repeated, is the only means
open to the playwright to tell what is happening, but dialogue
is not primarily narrative. It is the means of action, as

Aristotle pointed out; it is, in fact, the action itself.

Soap operas have their faults, but they are a useful
form of the drama for the beginning playwright to study,
especially in the use made of dialogue as conflict.   It would
almost seem that no piece of dialogue is allowed in a soap
opera that is not charged with tension.   Take a typical, (or
burlesqued), soap opera episode.   The wife in the drama
has decided that her husband is chasing after other women.
She is wrong.   In truth, he is secretly seeing his widowed
mother, who also happens to be an exotic dancer in a night
club.   He has not told his wife about his mother for fear
that it would make her unhappy since she herself, the wife,
has never been able to dance a step.   The audience has
this information as the program opens, and this day's
episode is going to deal only with the discovery by the wife
that her husband was seen lunching with a "strange woman"
that day, and the crisis that comes when the husband learns
that the wife has this information.   As the scene opens,
the husband enters:

HUSBAND: Hello, dear.   Did you have a good day?

WIFE: Why do you ask?

H: I've asked that same question every day during the seven years we have been married.   Why
shouldn't I ask it now?

W: You asked it somehow differently today, as
though you really wanted to know what I was doing today.

H: Is that wrong?

W: No.   No, not wrong, exactly.   Married people
should know about each other, all about each other.
Don't you think so?

H: Why, yes, I suppose I do think so.   Why do
you ask?

W: Do you really think so?

H: Of course I do.   Why do you doubt me?

W: Do I doubt you?

H: Don't you?

W: Did you have a good day today?

And so forth until he finally admits his luncheon engagement, and the episode ends for another day.

Anyone watching such a scene for a minute or two is aware that there is conflict, that each word is a sword thrust. Unfortunately, of course, this constant exchange finally is wearing, rather than dramatic, and we begin to wonder if such characters could even say "Good morning" to each other without facing a third degree.

An exchange of words--a conversation, the dialogue-- between two characters should be an agon, a conflict, but the playwright should conceive of his words as a professional heavyweight conceives of a blow, not as an amateur fly- weight does. A constant barrage of small glancing blows doesn't make a good fight. Constant bickering, moreover, is principally useful for showing that the conflict between the two characters will admit of no solution; it is merely indicative of a basic disagreement. Williams' The Glass Menagerie, for example, uses a pattern of constant bicker- ing between Tom Wingfield and his mother to show that they can never be reconciled. If a playwright, however, expects understanding to come from the dialogue, quite obviously he cannot show us people who cannot exchange words without crossing swords.

Conflict in drama, moreover, is only partially a surface battle between opposing characters. It is, in the best drama, a much deeper conflict within the character himself or between a character and the world, (or society), in which he lives. Hamlet in his few brief agons with Claudius does little more than bicker with his uncle. But few think of these scenes as being the most dramatic of the play. Rather it is when Hamlet crosses words with himself--"To be or not to be"--and when he crosses words with those whom he loves, like his mother, and trusts, like Horatio, that the agon becomes a battle rather than a quibble. In an odd sort of way, a dialogue is often more dramatic-- shows more conflict--when the character is battling against a condition, through an exchange with another character, rather than doing battle with the other character himself.

3.   Dialogue as a Key to Character

Dialogue, in addition to giving information and being
the means of the conflict, has another most important function in building a play: it reveals character.

William Congreve, one of the masters of dramatic
dialogue, wrote a short essay, "Concerning Humour in
Comedy, " in 1694, which is still a primary document in
character creation for the playwright.   Let the playwright,
Congreve argued, select characters by occupations and
geographical regions, if he wants to make the job of dis-
tinguishing character by dialogue easy.   A sailor who speaks
like a sailor is easy to distinguish from a Scotsman who
speaks like a Scotsman, and so forth.   Such practice,
though easy, should, however, be avoided, Congreve main-
tained, because the result is not distinctive characterization
but stock characterization achieved through cliches.

To create character the right way, rather than the
easy way, Congreve argued, the playwright should take pains
to distinguish each character from all others, not merely
by the choice of words, (the vocabulary), and accent, but
by his entire method of speaking.   Even the grammar and
rhythm of the speech should be as unique to the characters
as are his own fingerprints.   If a playwright is perfectly
successful, it would be possible for one to distinguish each
character in the play--even the minor characters--from all
others with an examination of any single speech.   Congreve's
own Way of the World is as good an example of distinctive
dialogue as exists in drama.   But even Congreve admitted
that such a goal can only be achieved with some of the
characters in any drama.

Unless the playwright makes distinctive characterization his primary aim--and this practice is not to be
recommended--he needs to create the dialogue from the
quality of the character rather than to create characters
who will serve distinctive methods of speaking.

The beginning playwright must observe a few obvious
qualities in his characters when creating dialogue for them.
A character's education is usually reflected in his speech.
An educated man does not normally clutter his speech with
"ain'ts and "gollies, " but some educated men do--either
because of an affectation, (a desire to be "one of the boys"),
or because his formal education was unable to correct,

(or merely alter), an earlier pattern of speech.

4.   Dialogue as the Music of Drama

Some critics during the past century have complained
that when drama gave up poetry, it also gave up being an
art form, that the playwright who restricted his dialogue
to prose is little more than a chronicler, a journalist, a
man with a tape recorder. The complaint is an exagger-
ation, but it is undoubtedly true that some modern plays
do exist without a single speech that is distinguished by
its music.

One listening to the music and lyrics of My Fair
Lady, for example, can readily understand what is lost
to dialogue when the music is stilled. Not a single one
of the lyrics to that musical play--as clever and as charm-
ing as many of them are--means quite the same--perhaps
not half the same--without the music. And yet the music,
without the words, is not particularly striking. The two
together serve as an excellent example of the right thing
said in the right way.

Music created by non-human instruments or sung by
the human voice is, however, only one kind of music.
There is another music that comes when words are put together so that the sound of the words and their relative
positions to each other give us a kind of pleasure that is
akin to the pleasure that comes from poetry, and this pleasure can be achieved with prose as well--or perhaps only
almost as well--as with formal poetry.

In The Way of the World, for example, the antagonist,
Fainall, tells the protagonist, Mirabell, that he has been
misused by the heroine, Mistress Millamant. Mirabell
agrees that Millamant has some personality quirks that
would "try the patience of a stoic." Fainall then accuses
Mirabell of being a cold lover, too observant of his mistress' faults. Here is a reasonable music-less translation
of Mirabell's answer--a translation that gives (1) all the
information needed for the plot, and (2) is consistent with
the character of Mirabell:

> MIRABELL: It is true that I am critical, but I
> must also be in love. Although I have examined
> all her faults and I am aware of them, I love her
> anyway. She has faults that I can even feel a

certain amount of affection for, just as I do my
own faults.

Congreve, however, is aware that the audience has
ears as well as minds and eyes, and the speech Mirabell
does speak is a delight to those ears:

MIRABELL: And for a discerning, (critical), man,
somewhat too passionate a lover, for I like her
with all her faults, nay, like her for her faults.
Her follies are so natural, or so artful, that they
become her; and those affectations which in another
woman would be odious, serve but to make her
more agreeable. I'll tell thee, Fainall, who once
used me with that insolence, that in revenge I
took her to pieces, sifted her, and separated her
failings; I studied 'em and got 'em by rote. The
catalogue was so large that I was not without
hopes one day or other to hate her heartily: to
which end I so used myself to think of 'em that
at length, contrary to my design and expectation,
they gave me every hour less and less disturbance; till in a few days it became habitual to me
to remember 'em without being displeased. They
are now grown as familiar to me as my own
frailties; and in all probability, in a little time
longer, I shall like them as well. "

This speech not only describes a situation, but it
also presents the situation with dramatic structure, being
climaxed with a final statement: "... I shall like them as
well, " that is ironically opposed to the whole movement of
the speech to that point, a kind of "reversal of fortune, "
that the audience understands through the experience of
following the progress, rather than by merely listening to
a narration. In the first sentence, for example, the word
"fault"--the strongest word in the sentence--is repeated,
thus placing an emphasis on Millamant's short-comings.
In the second sentence, words like "follies, " "affectations, "
and "odious, " a continuation of the character of the word
"fault, " are set in conflict with--and overcome by--contrary
words, "natural, " "artful, " and "agreeable. " If one could
conceive of these words as characters, this single speech
offers a kind of morality drama in which the evil forces
are overcome by the virtues through a paradox that the
man who pursues evil with too much moral indignation will
finally find the fault in his own actions.

This piece of dialogue, moreover, draws heavily on the formal techniques of poetry: balance and metaphor. Mirabell, for example, pictures Millamant as an object that may be taken "to pieces" and studied as one analyzes a flower. But since this is a human relationship, a question of a quality rather than a quantity, the metaphor itself forecasts the final conclusion--failure in his plan--even before he admits it in a prose statement. The balance of the piece resides partially in the formal structure, the setting of one word against another and one sentence against another in similar grammatical formations. It also resides, however, in the balancing of one idea against another. In fact, this separate speech could be made into a formal self-contained poem, like one of Shakespeare's sonnets, with only minor alterations.

A simple test for the musicality of a speech is this: after hearing a speech, does the auditor attempt to reproduce it <u>exactly</u>, or does an approximation do as well?

A play in which every speech can stand alone as a separate work of art, always seems to have a precious, a "bookish," cast to it. Critics, for example, complain about such plays as <u>Romeo and Juliet</u> and <u>The Lady's Not for Burning</u> in such terms. Louis B. Wright and Virginia A. LaMar, in their edition of <u>Romeo and Juliet</u>, argue that "At times the lyrical poet runs away with the play and inserts lines of sheer poetic exuberance." While not necessarily agreeing with such a judgment of this play, one can always remember plays in which the separate lines-- full of beauty and brilliance--have seemed to distract the audience from the total design.

In the one-act play, however--perhaps because its brevity allows greater concentration--if the playwright does not sacrifice the <u>function</u> of dialogue to tell the story, show the action, and reveal the character, he seldom needs to worry about writing "too fine". We expect more music in a one-act play, just as we expect more lyricism, (perhaps all lyricism), in a sonnet than we do in an epic or a long narrative poem.

Exercises for Dialogue

    1.   Using the accounts that you have been writing in the other exercises, now tell the stories solely by the <u>conversations</u> of the characters.

2.   Revise these conversations, taking into account
particular qualities of each character; and be sure that
each speech is justified by the circumstances.

3.   Set these speeches in a pattern so that they
show conflict between the characters, between the two
selves in a single character, between what a character
believes to be so and what is really so.

4.   Now revise each of the speeches so that it is
as musical as you can make it, but do not sacrifice the
informational content, the conflict, or the truth of the
speech to the character in making your revisions.

5.   Now put your finished accounts into a mechanical
form for actors.   You should now have three plays--one
based on historical materials, one on mythical materials,
and one based on an episode of your own observation or
invention.

Reading Suggestions

Cerf, Bennett and Van H. Cartmell.   Thirty Famous One-
Plays. New York, 1943.

James, Henry.   The Scenic Art.   New Brunswick, 1948.

Nelson, Robert J. Play Within a Play; The Dramatist's
Conception of His Art: Shakespeare to Anouilh.   New York,
1959.

Peacock, Ronald.   The Art of the Drama.   London, 1956.

Rowe, Kenneth Thorpe.   Write That Play.   New York, 1939.

Speaight, Robert.   Christian Theatre.   New York, 1960.

Stein, Jack.   Richard Wagner and the Synthesis of the Arts.
Detroit, 1960.

V

The Teacher as Performer

All teachers will admit that they are performing, but it is not unusual for many teachers to think of their performing duties as being limited to teaching. A teacher should be able to perform as a teacher, they will agree, but does a teacher also need to perform in terms of his subject matter? Does an engineering teacher need to perform as an engineer as well as a teacher? Does the philosophy teacher need to perform as a philosopher? The mathematics teacher as a mathematician? Professor Nolan, in the opening essay in this collection, argues that "teachers should at least be able to do what they expect of their students."

It should be understood, of course, that history teachers do not make history nor do political scientists win elections. It should be further noted that not all performances can, or should, be done in print. Professor Nolan as a teacher of dramatic literature is, obviously, in an academic discipline that lends itself well to offering opportunities for the teacher to perform outside the classroom. Anyone who teaches how literature is written should be prepared to demonstrate his preaching by his practice. Moreover, in one respect, the classroom situation itself is a kind of drama in which the professor takes a leading role and creates a kind of dialogue (or monologue) for the purpose of communicating information that leads to intended conclusions.

In selecting four of Nolan's plays to demonstrate the ways in which he has put his classroom preaching into practice, I do not mean to suggest that all English teachers, or even all drama teachers, should write plays; but, obviously, those who teach people to write plays should. In his classes in modern drama, in the history and development of drama, and even in freshman and sophomore surveys of English literature, Professor Nolan often assumes that one way to understand a play and the problems of play-

131

writing is to become actively engaged in it. His students,
as one of the requirements of these courses, are expected
to "produce" plays in the classroom; and production sometimes means writing, sometimes adapting, sometimes
arranging.

To make such an assumption, the teacher must
demonstrate that any normal, intelligent person who tries
can do the work. If the work that results is judged, in
some editor's opinion, to be worth publication, so much
the better. If not, the teacher is still performing what
he preaches. The four plays in this collection, selected
from the more than fifty that Dr. Nolan has had published
in the past ten years, demonstrate some of the educational
uses to which he has put his work as performer.

The first, If Wishes Were Horses, started with a
classroom problem. While teaching Chaucer's Canterbury
Tales to a group of elementary school education majors,
he was challenged to show how Chaucer could be used in
the primary grades. This play, an adaptation of Chaucer's
Knight's Tale, was the demonstration; and it proved popular
enough so that Nolan developed the idea of adapting Chaucer
to an elementary school situation into a full-length program.
This work, titled Chaucer for Children: An Evening's
Entertainment from the Canterbury Tales, was published
by the Little Red Schoolhouse Press in 1964, and it is
now being distributed to children's theater directors through
the Eldridge Publishing Company, Franklin, Ohio.

The second play, A Lass Unparalleled, is also an
adaptation. Nolan's work with this play started in a class
in which he taught the original, Anton Chekhov's Swan Song.
"I liked the play," he says, "and I was disappointed that
it was not performed more often. A college-theater director said the play had two problems from his point of view.
First, it has no feminine roles; and secondly the theatrical
references of Chekhov's plays are unfamiliar to young people
today." Nolan's adaptation follows Chekhov as closely as
possible except for two rather extensive changes. The male
characters were changed to women, and the situation is up-
dated. "With every change I made, the play lost something," Nolan says, "for I'm not Chekhov. But as I viewed
the situation, the question was not whether students would
do Chekhov or my version of him, but whether they would
do my version or not do the play at all." This play was
published by Pioneer Drama Service in 1966.

The third selection, the full-length play, Last Week
I Was Ninety-Five, belongs to a group of performances that
Nolan has been making during the past twenty years that
are campus-centered, rather than classroom-centered. In
1947, while teaching at the State College of Arkansas, he
wrote a play, Turn of the Moon, for the College Theatre.
The play was popular on the Arkansas campus, and the
players then took it to a neighboring college, Henderson
State College, for another performance. "There were
several million better-written plays available to them,"
Nolan says, "but they had a chance in working with this
play to create something new. They could suggest changes;
they could interpret; they could watch it come to life."
From Nolan's point of view, at least, writing a play for
a local group is an interesting educational experience; and
every three or four years, he writes another. One, Two
Gentlemen from the House, performed at Centenary College
in 1950, was written specifically for a group of students,
all of whom needed a leading role to complete the requirements of their major in speech. Another, A Writer in Our
Midst, produced by the Shreveport Writers Club in 1953,
was written as a money-making project to finance a Town-
Gown summer writers' conference. Another, There's Death
for the Lonely, produced first by the Burlington (Iowa) Little
Theatre, won the Players Workshop Award in 1964. Last
Week I was Ninety-Five was written for a faculty group at
the University of Southwestern Louisiana, and every role
was taken by a faculty member or wife. "It was my
intention in this play," says Nolan, "to create an entertainment that puts all the focus on the on-stage performers.
The set has no 'formal' scenery; the roles are divided
more-or-less equally among all the players, so there is
no 'star'; and curtains were ignored." The play was produced in March 1966, by the Lafayette Little Theatre for
one run and by the Louisiana Civic Theatre for another.
Publication in the present volume represents its first appearance in print, and all rights to this play, including professional and amateur productions, are controlled by the author.

The last play, Justice for Andy Jackson, was written
for one specific purpose--to encourage elementary-school
children to learn to read plays. When Dr. Marguerite Bondy
Bougere, Professor of Education of Tulane University, told
Dr. Nolan that she was preparing a reader about Louisiana
for elementary schools, he expressed the hope that a play
would be included. She asked him to submit one. Nolan
went to Louisiana history, found an episode that seemed to

lend itself to dramatic treatment, and wrote a play that
could be performed in the classroom.   The play was first
published in Dr. Bougere's Louisiana Stories for Boys
and Girls (Baton Rouge: Louisiana State University Press,
1966) and is now reprinted with the permission of that
press and the author.

1. Solving a Classroom Problem

"If Wishes Were Horses"

CHARACTERS:

ARCITE
PALAMON . . . . Two Young Knights

JUNO . . . . The Jailor's Wife

EMILY . . . . A Princess

THESEUS . . . . The King

EGEUS . . . . The King's Father

HIPPOLYTA . . . . The Queen

VENUS
DIANA . . . . Three Invisible Powers
MARS

HISTORICAL SETTING: This play is set in the reign of
the legendary-historical hero of Athens, Theseus; but this
account of his adventures was told some two thousand years
later.   Thus the setting is a mixture of Ancient Greece
and Chaucerian England, and both ages are pictured with
a great deal of the "fairy story" touch.

THE STAGE SETTING, therefore, should reflect only one
thing--an age of romance and chivalry, an age when a
Knight, either like Chaucer's Knight or Homer's Odysseus,
would feel comfortable in defending fair maidens and pur-
suing two-headed dragons.   The costumes, too, need only
reflect that the characters are creatures from this world.
The actual stage setting should be intentionally artificial.
On stage left there is one wall, facing stage center, that
represents a jail.   A sign above the wall reads "Ye Olde
Prison Tower. " No attempt should be made to disguise
the fact that this is simply a paper wall.   Stage right is
a field.   In the background are trees, and about the stage
there are clumps of bushes.

AS THE CURTAIN RISES, The two young knights are sitting

on a bench left on the jail wall.   They face downstage.

ARCITE: It is spring again, Palamon.
PALAMON: Ah, me.
ARCITE: If we were back in Thebes, we would be going
to the games.
PALAMON: Ah, me.
ARCITE: Well, don't take it so hard.   We are prisoners
here the rest of our life, and we might as well make the
best of it.
PALAMON: I suppose.
ARCITE: After all, we are friends, cousins, blood brothers.
Nothing can be too bad if we share it with each other.
PALAMON: I suppose.
ARCITE: Though I must admit, life would seem better if
you could manage to say something more than "Ah me" and
"I suppose. "
PALAMON: (Sighing,) Ah, me. I suppose. I am sorry,
Arcite. I won't say either again. I am not a coward, you
know. I wouldn't mind dying in battle. But to sit here
day after day for the rest of our lives does seem hard to
me. Hard and rather boring. Ah, me.
ARCITE: I suppose.   There, now you have me saying it.
       (Enter Juno from stage left, carrying two bowls of
       mush.)
JUNO: Here's your breakfast, Boys.
PALAMON: Mush again, I'll bet.
JUNO: What do you expect King Theseus to feed jailbirds?
Strawberries and cream?
       (She hands them the bowls.)
PALAMON: (Getting up and going to the barred window on
the wall, a window that faces on stage right.) I wish ... I
wish that just for a day I might roam free in the hills and
meadows.
JUNO: If wishes were horses, boy, beggars would ride and
old crones like me would be Queen of the May. (Laughing
to herself, she exits off stage left.)
PALAMON: Just for a day ... (Looking longingly out of
jail window, then stops and stares as Emily comes on stage
right. She is collecting flowers in a basket which she
carries. Arcite does not observe her, but continues to eat
his mush.)
ARCITE: (Eating.) You know, Palamon, this mush isn't
bad. Of course, it is mush. And when one eats mush
three times a day, three hundred and sixty-five days a year,
one sometimes wishes for a piece of toast ... a piece of
toast with butter on it ... or even marmalade ... but as

the Old Woman says, if wishes were horses ...
PALAMON: (With great agony.) Ah, me.
ARCITE: (Looking at him.) Now buck up and be a man.
After all, in this life, we face what we must face, and
there's no sense in moaning about it. (Seeing Palamon
staring out the window.) What's the matter? (He goes to
the window and looks out. He sees Emily.) Well, look
at that. There's the girl for me.
PALAMON: (Coming out of his trance.) Traitor, I saw
her first.
ARCITE: But I spoke first.
PALAMON: But I'm your blood brother.
ARCITE: But I'm your cousin.
PALAMON: We have been friends since birth, Arcite, but
if you try to steal my girl ...
ARCITE: Why are we being so silly? We will both be
here until we die, and the beautiful princess in the field
will never even know we are alive.
PALAMON: I suppose. Ah, me.
    (They both return to the bench and sit glumly.)
ARCITE: Aren't you going to eat your mush?
PALAMON: No.
ARCITE: Would you like me to eat it for you?
PALAMON: I suppose.
ARCITE: (Taking the bowl and starting to eat.) It isn't
particularly good mush, but one must keep his strength up.
PALAMON: If we were both free ...
ARCITE: If ... if ... if ... if, and ah, me. No one
knows which way the next wind blows.
    (Juno enters from stage left.)
JUNO: All right, Arcite, pack up your things. You're
leaving.
ARCITE: I'm leaving?
JUNO: You're being set free. But you must return to
Thebes, and if you ever come back to Athens, your life
will be the forfeit. That's what the King says, and Theseus
means what he says.
ARCITE: But my friend? But what of Palamon?
JUNO: He stays.
ARCITE: Then I stay, too.
PALAMON: No, Arcite, you go.
JUNO: You might as well. You can't do him any good
here.
ARCITE: That's true. Maybe when I return to Thebes, I
can find some way to free you, Palamon.
PALAMON: I suppose.
    (Emily disappears off stage right.)

ARCITE: And eat your mush, Palamon.   You must keep up your strength.

JUNO: (Picking up the two empty bowls.)   He seems to be doing all right.   These bowls are licked clean.

PALAMON: He ate them.

JUNO: (Stepping downstage, "out of the jail," with Arcite.) Well, all right, boy.   You're free.   But you'd better keep moving.   If Athens' sun sets on your head, this day will be your last.

ARCITE: I'm going.

> (He starts across stage right, and stops at the edge of the stage.   Emily enters again, and he hides behind a bush.   Juno exits off stage left, and Palamon again goes to the window and stands there saying "ah me."   Then Emily goes up stage into the trees.

PALAMON: There she is again.   And now Arcite is free. True, he is banned from Athens, but what does that mean to a smart fellow like him?   Look how he ate all my mush. He'll find a way to return and win my girl.   I've got to get out of this place.   (He turns downstage, and stands there thinking.)

ARCITE: (Coming from behind the bush.) There she is again.   I must win her as my bride.   If I don't, Palamon will.   True, he's in jail.   But what's jail to a smart fellow like him.   Look how he got me to eat all that terrible mush. I must stay and win her even if it means my life.   (He starts upstage.)   Young lady, may I help you?   (He disappears into the trees.)

PALAMON: I'll just break out.   That's what I'll do.   It doesn't seem quite proper, but I'm not going to let Arcite steal my girl.   (He steps out of the jail downstage.)   Now, that's done.   (He starts toward stage center, as Arcite and Emily come down center from the trees.)

ARCITE: So your name is Emily?   A pretty name if I may so so.

EMILY: You may say so.

ARCITE: A pretty name.

PALAMON: (Seeing them and rushing to them.)   You traitor, you are trying to steal my girl.   (He grabs Arcite by the throat.)

EMILY: Who is he?

ARCITE: This is my friend, Palamon.   We were in that jail together.   (To Palamon.)   Her name is Emily.

PALAMON: (Turning toward her and nodding his head.) How do you do, Emily?

EMILY: Very well, thank you.

ARCITE: (Who now has Palamon's throat too.) He saw you

first, but I spoke first.
PALAMON: We were blood brothers.
ARCITE: And cousins.
PALAMON: But now he is trying to steal my girl.
ARCITE: You are trying to steal mine.
          (Enter Theseus, Egeus, and Hippolyta.)
THESEUS: Here. Here. What's going on here?
          (Arcite and Palamon stop choking each other.)
EMILY: They are Arcite and Palamon, Your Majesty.
THESEUS: The two prisoners in the Tower?
ARCITE: I have been pardoned, Your Majesty.
PALAMON: But on pain of death if he did not leave Athens,
and he's still here.
THESEUS: And what are you doing out of jail?
PALAMON: I broke out, Your Majesty.
THESEUS: Well, I'm going to have you both put to death.
You can't just go around breaking the King's law and jails.
Not here in Athens, you can't. This is a law-abiding place.
EMILY: They are both in love with me.
HIPPOLYTA: How romantic. I suppose it was because
of you, they were fighting.
EMILY: I suppose.
PALAMON: I saw Emily first.
ARCITE: But I spoke for her first.
PALAMON: And he is my blood brother.
ARCITE: And he is my cousin.
THESEUS: Quiet, both of you. So you're both in love with
Emily. Well, this does present a problem.
PALAMON: I saw her first, Your Majesty.
ARCITE: I spoke to her first, Your Majesty.
THESEUS: (To Egeus.) Father, what do you think?
HIPPOLYTA: Well, you just can't put them both to death.
That's obvious. No girl can afford to lose two boy friends
in one day.
EGEUS: That's true, my son. The Queen is right. You
can't put them both to death. Suitors don't grow on trees,
you know.
HIPPOLYTA: And they both have a claim. Of sorts.
EGEUS: Palamon saw her first.
HIPPOLYTA: But Arcite spoke first.
EGEUS: There's no question about it, Son. You have a
problem.
THESEUS: I suppose.
ARCITE: I wish everyone would stop saying, "I suppose."
The whole matter is really simple enough. We'll have a
duel.
PALAMON: That suits me.

THESEUS: If it suits both of you, it suits me.

HIPPOLYTA: A duel for the hand of my little sister, Emily. How romantic. Isn't it, Emily?

EMILY: I suppose.

THESEUS: All right, Egeus. You get two swords ... with blunted tips. The winner gets Emily, and the loser must depart the land of Athens forever. There is nothing like a rejected suitor for stirring up trouble.

EGEUS: That sounds like the only solution, Son. (He goes off right.)

THESEUS: And as for us, My Queen, we might as well inspect the jail. I suppose it will need repairs. I do wish the prisoners would have more respect for other people's property.

> (Theseus and Hippolyta go over to jail. The three Powers come on stage. Venus goes to Palamon; Mars to Arcite; and Diana to Emily.)

PALAMON: I wish ... I hope I win Emily this day.

VENUS: (Touching him on the arm.) You will, Palamon.

PALAMON: Oh, my goodness. Who are you?

VENUS: I am Venus. And I can grant you any wish you want.

PALAMON: Well, that's the wish I want. I want to win Emily, more than anything else in the world.

VENUS: She shall be won by you before the day is through.

PALAMON: Thank you, Venus. Thank you. But hadn't you better go now before someone sees you. It might not look quite right if I win by a wish.

VENUS: Have no fear. I am invisible to all but you. Just stand as though in deep concern.

> (Palamon and Venus stand in similar poses of deep thought.)

ARCITE: I wish ... I hope I beat Palamon today.

MARS: (Touching him on the arm.) You will, Arcite. You will.

ARCITE: By Zeus, who are you?

MARS: I am Mars, and I can grant you any wish you please.

ARCITE: Well, that's the wish I please. And I think it only fair because although he saw her first, I spoke first. And besides all is fair in love and war.

MARS: Your wish shall be done. Today you will defeat Palamon in the duel.

ARCITE: I rather hate to do it--having been his blood brother and all--but Emily is really my girl. Why, I was the one who introduced them.

MARS: Have no fear. Your wish will come true. You shall be the victor today.

ARCITE: I certainly do thank you, Mars.   But don't you
think you'd better run along now before someone sees you.
MARS: Don't worry about that.   I am visible only to you.'
Now stand as though you were thinking.   Today, you win.
       (Mars and Arcite stand in similar poses of deep
       thought.)
EMILY: They're both nice boys, but I wish ... I wish that
I could make my own choice instead of being won like a
turkey in a raffle.   I don't know which one I prefer.   But
I wish I could be asked instead of won.
DIANA: (Touching her on the arm.)   You will, Emily.
You will.
EMILY: Well, of all things.   Who are you?
DIANA: I am Diana, and I can grant you any wish you
please.
EMILY: Well, that's the wish I please.   And I think it's
only fair, because I am of the Amazon race where women
pick their husbands themselves.   I'd like to have the right
to say "Yes" or "No" ... or even "Maybe" or "We'll see. "
That's every woman's right, it seems to me.
DIANA: Today your wish will be answered.
EMILY: Oh, thank you, Diana.   Thank you.   But now,
hadn't you better go?   There's bound to be some trouble
if I am to get my wish, and if you are seen, others will
know.
DIANA: Don't worry your pretty little head.   No one but
you can see me.   Now stand as though you were thinking.
       (Diana and Emily stand in similar poses of deep
       thought.)
EGEUS: (Entering from right, carrying two huge swords.)
Ah, all in deep thought.   That speaks well for the younger
generation.   Although it seems to me that young folks don't
think the way they used to when I was a boy.
THESEUS: (Coming to stage center with Hippolyta.)   But
now the time for thought is over, and the time for action
is begun.   Here, give me the swords.   (He takes the swords
from Egeus and puts them on the ground, points facing each
other.)   Now, Palamon, you stand there.   (Pointing to a
position five paces left to the swords.)
PALAMON: Gladly, Your Majesty, for today's the day that
Emily will be mine.
THESEUS: And you, Arcite, stand there.   (Points to a
position five paces to the right of the swords.)
ARCITE: And gladly for me, too.   For I know that today
I will win.
THESEUS: All right, Now when I yell, "Go, " you both will
race to the swords, take the sword facing you, and the battle

will begin.   The first one to force the other to yield wins
the duel and the fair Emily.
EMILY: I don't want to be won.
THESEUS: What did you say, Emily?
EMILY: I said, where shall I stand?
THESEUS: Out of harm's way. Ready. Let the battle
begin.   Go!
   (Arcite and Palamon race to the swords. Palamon
   reaches his first, but he is unable to lift it off the
   ground. Arcite takes his sword and puts it against
   Palamon's throat.)
ARCITE: Yield!
THESEUS: The battle is done, and Arcite has won.
EMILY: (To Diana.) But you told me, I wouldn't be won.
DIANA: Patience. The day is not yet ended.
ARCITE: That's what comes from not eating your mush,
Palamon. You didn't have strength to lift the sword.
PALAMON: (Turning to Venus.) What about my wish?
You said I would win.
VENUS: Patience. The day is not yet ended.
PALAMON: No, but I am.
ARCITE: (To Mars.) Well, thanks, old fellow. You kept
your word.
MARS: Yes, I've kept my word. And now I must leave.
You got your wish.
ARCITE: I did. I did. I won.
MARS: But take your victory with a humble heart, Son.
Fortune loves to trip the proud. (He exits off stage right.)
THESEUS: Well, that's settled. So we might as well have
the wedding tomorrow. Is that all right with you, Arcite?
ARCITE: The sooner the better I say. But, your Majesty,
may I have permission to go now and send a message to my
kinsmen to come to the celebration?
THESEUS: You may, my son.
ARCITE: You will, of course, be my best man, won't you,
Palamon? You owe me that as my blood brother.
PALAMON: I suppose.
ARCITE: (Running off right, carrying the sword in the air.)
I won. I won. Today I won.
HIPPOLYTA: I think he could have said something to Emily.
THESEUS: Oh, he was just excited.
HIPPOLYTA: Amazon women don't like being treated like
something won in a raffle.
THESEUS: I know my dear. And if he lives long enough,
he'll learn. (Arcite screams off right, and Egeus goes off
right.)
HIPPOLYTA: What was that?

EMILY: It sounded like a scream.
PALAMON: It sounded like Arcite.
EGEUS: (Returning, carrying the sword.) It was Arcite.
Running without thought, he tripped and fell upon his sword.
THESEUS: Is he hurt?
EGEUS: He will never be hurt. He's dead.
DIANA: (To Emily.) You see. Today you will not be won.
EMILY: But I didn't want him to die. I didn't mean for
it to happen this way.
DIANA: You should have thought of that before you wished.
      (Diana exits off stage right.)
VENUS: Now, there is only you, Palamon. If you ask her,
today you will win a bride.
PALAMON: But I didn't want it to happen this way. He
was my friend.
VENUS: Oh, don't be silly. All's fair in love.
PALAMON: But he was my friend. I wish I had never
wished.
VENUS: It's a little late to be thinking about that. But
I kept my word, and so good-bye.
      (Venus exits off stage left.)
EGEUS: Well, this has been an unusual end to the day's
events. But come, stop moping. Arcite died victorious.
I wish we all could do the same. But you two, Palamon
and Emily, you have your lives before you.
PALAMON: He was my friend, and I killed him.
THESEUS: He killed himself.
PALAMON: But if I had not wished to win Emily. ...
EMILY: And if I had not wished to be asked instead of
won. ...
EGEUS: And I wonder what Arcite wished.
PALAMON: Wishes! The old woman told us that if wishes
were horses, beggars would ride. But it isn't true.
EGEUS: No, it isn't, Palamon. If wishes were horses,
we would all be trampled to death by a wild herd. But
come, enough of this. We'll all mourn Arcite's passing.
He was a good and clever lad. But then, tomorrow, we'll
go right on living and loving and wishing.
HIPPOLYTA: And all in all--day by day--dreams and dis-
appointments--it's not bad. Life's not bad.

CURTAIN

PRODUCTION NOTES:

Characters: 5 male and 5 female.
Setting: One set with one wall of the jail on one side and

a forest green on the other.

Costumes: Venus should carry a stuffed dove; Diana a bow and arrow; and Mars should wear a helmet.   The other characters wear the tunics of Greece and Rome.

Properties: For Juno, two bowls of mush; for Emily, a basket of flowers; for Egeus, two large wooden swords.

Lighting: No special effects are necessary, but for an elaborate performance, spots may be placed on the main action and dimmed and raised as the action shifts from one part of the stage to another.

2. Adapting to Different Times

A Lass Unparalleled
A One-Act Play
Adapted from Anton Chekhov's Swan Song

CHARACTERS

LOLA MONTEZ...... a once famous stage and movie star.
HEDDA.... the cleaning woman, in her middle sixties.

SCENE

The scene is set on the stage of a community theater,
at night, after the play. To the RIGHT, the flats are stacked
against the wall. To the LEFT, a part of a stage setting still stands. The furniture is piled in the UP STAGE
left corner, ready to be moved. In the MIDDLE of the
STAGE is an overturned rocking chair and stool. Lights
from BACK STAGE cast shadows across the STAGE.

LOLA: (Enters from Down Stage Right with a flashlight in
her hand. She is still a handsome woman, a beautiful woman, but she looks old, tired, and a little
tight. She is wearing a dressing robe and a white
towel around her hair.) Gone. All gone. This is
a fine joke. I must have fallen asleep in my dressing room when the play was over and there I was
gently dreaming after everyone else had left the
theater. (Goes to rocking chair, sets it upright and
sits in it.) Ah, I'm a foolish old woman, a poor,
lonely creature. I shouldn't have drunk that champagne. It always makes me sleepy. And a little
fat. What a fool am I, what a bloody fool. (Stands
up and calls aloud.) George. Edgar. Eddie.
Where the devil are you? (Pause.) They've gone.
They've left me. Alone. Alone. All, all alone.
(Looks around suspiciously.) There's not a sound.
They've all gone. I gave them my car to go to the
party and they've gone without me. They've probably
locked up the theater and I shall die here. (In Lady
Macbeth pose, she holds the flashlight pointing to her
face.) Out, damned spot. (She turns off light and
holds it in front of her like a candle.) Out, I say.

One, two. Why, then, 'tis time to do it. Hell is
murky. Fie, my lord, fie, a soldier and afraid?
What need we fear who knows it, when none can call
our power to account? Yet who would have thought
the old man to have so much blood in him. (She sits
down in the rocking chair again quietly, then rocks
back and forth furiously.) A horse! A horse! My
kingdom for a horse. (She stops abruptly.) I was a
fool to take this tour. "You've got to make America
love you again," that fool agent told me. "Look at
Bette Davis. Look at Joan Crawford," he told me.
(Stands up and looks from her feet up.) Well, look
at me. I've drunk too much champagne. (Feeling
her face.) Good heavens, my body is burning all
over. I've got twenty tongues in my mouth. It's
horrid. It's idiotic. This was to be my chance for
a come-back. And here I am, alone, deserted, and
I don't even know what I'm doing here. (Goes to
stool and leans on it.) My head is splitting. I
am shivering all over. I feel as dark and cold as
if I were in a cellar. Even if I don't care about my
health I should have remembered my figure. Flo
Ziegfeld himself told me my figure was my fortune.
(Examing her hips.) It has expanded. I wonder
if my banker knows. And at my age, too. I'll
never get my figure back. At my age I should know
better. I'm sixty. ... I'm almost sixty. Well, at
least I'm past fifty. I must admit that. One cannot
be a star with Barrymore, with Leslie Howard, with
... what were their names? Where have they gone?
I'm old. Face it, Lola, you are old and you are a
fool. (Goes back to rocking chair, sits huddled.)
The time has come for me to play a mummy, whether
I like it or not. It's strange... but I feel... I feel
death here on this stage. I've been an actress for
forty-five years and for the first time I feel as
though I'm playing a walk-on for death. (Rises and
walks slowly down stage center.) How dark it is
here. I can't see a thing. The wind blows through
this empty theater like a train in a midnight subway.
What a place for ghosts. George! Eddie! Edgar!
Where the devil are you all? The shivers are running down my back. What on earth makes me think
of such things. I must give up drinking. I must
exercise. And no more rich foods. I'm an old
woman. I won't live much longer. At my age, people go to church and prepare for death. Here I am,

an old fool, still playing at games on a miserable
stage. And look at me, I'm a fright. I must get
out of here. I shall die of fright. (Starts off stage,
sees Hedda, steps back and shrieks.) Who are you?
What do you want? You're death and you've come to
take me.

HEDDA: I'm just Hedda, Miss Montez. (A spot goes on
over chair.)

LOLA: Hedda Gabler! You are a ghost.

HEDDA: No, Miss Montez. Hedda Strang. I clean the
the theater.

LOLA: Oh--Hedda, the cleaning woman. (Turns back and
returns to rocking chair.) What are you doing here
at this hour?

HEDDA: I clean after the play is over, Miss Montez.

LOLA: But I've seen you here during rehearsals and during the performances.

HEDDA: I like to watch. Only please be kind and not tell
Mr. Burleigh, Miss Montez. He might not like it.

LOLA: You watch all the rehearsals?

HEDDA: I have no family at home. It is something to do,
and I have always loved the theater.

LOLA: Oh. (Rises.) Did you like the performance tonight?.

HEDDA: It was wonderful, Miss Montez. Just wonderful.
I have seen you in a hundred plays and movies but
tonight you were better than I have ever seen you
before. (Laughs.) But I say that to myself each
time I see you.

LOLA: Perhaps it was merely the play. "Elizabeth the
Queen" is a fine play, a great play. Maxwell did
very well with it. I told him so at the time he
wrote it.

HEDDA: It is a fine play. But it was not the play, Miss
Montez. It was you.

LOLA: I got sixteen curtain calls. They brought me three
wreaths and lots of other things, too. They were
wild with enthusiasm. (Turning away.) And yet,
when the play was over, not a single person waited
to take this tired old lady home. (Turns back.)
And I am a tired old woman, Hedda. I am over
six... I am almost sixty years old. (Goes to
stool and leans on it.) And I am ill. I haven't the
heart to go on. (Goes to Hedda and weeps on her
shoulder.) Don't leave me, Hedda. Don't leave me.
I am old and helpless, and I feel it is time for me
to die. I would die now, but there's one more part

I want to do. Lear! It's never been done by a
woman, you know. But I could do it. I know how
that great king felt. (Going into Lear pose.) "Oh,
my poor fool is hang'd! No, no, no life! Why
should a dog, a horse, a rat, have life, and thou no
breath at all? Thou'lt come no more, never, never,
never, never, never! (Turns to Hedda.) Pray you
undo this button. Thank you, sir. Do you see this?
Look on her! Look! Her lips! Look there, look
there." (Lola staggers to stool and falls gracefully
over it so that she is draped in a kneeling pose.)

HEDDA: (Going to her and falling into the character of
Edgar.) He faints! My lord, my lord!

LOLA: (Rising with speed and anger.) What did you say?

HEDDA: I... I just gave the next line, Miss Montez.

LOLA: I am the actress on this stage, and don't you forget it.

HEDDA: I am sorry, Miss Montez. I meant no harm.

LOLA: (Starts to weep again and falls on Hedda.) There,
I have done it again. I turn upon my friends. I
lose control of myself. Don't go away, Hedda. I
am old and hopeless, and I feel it is time for me to
die. It is dreadful, Hedda, dreadful.

HEDDA: (Tenderly, almost in tears.) Please, please, Miss
Montez. Don't cry. It's time for you to go home.

LOLA: (Drawing herself away tragically.) I won't go home.
I have no home - none! - none! - none!

HEDDA: Oh, dear, have you forgotten where you live?

LOLA: I won't go to that place in New York again. I won't!
I am all alone there.

HEDDA: But your home in California? I have seen
pictures. ...

LOLA: I won't go there, either. I have nobody, Hedda!
No husband--no children. I am like the wind blow-
ing across the hills of Montana. I shall die and no
one will remember me. It is awful to be alone--no
one to cheer me up, no one to caress me, no one to
bring me breakfast in bed. Whom do I belong to?
Who needs me? Who loves me? Not a soul, Hedda.

HEDDA: (Now weeping.) Your fans love you. Miss Montez.

LOLA: My audience has gone home. They are all asleep,
and I have been forgotten. They have forgotten their
make-believe queen. I am as dead as Essex. No,
nobody needs me, nobody loves me. I have no husband, no children.

HEDDA: Please, Miss Montez, do not be so unhappy.

LOLA: But I am still a woman. I am still alive. Warm,

red blood is tingling in my veins, the blood of noble
ancestors. I am an aristocrat, Hedda. I am really
an aristocrat. It was not just publicity. In these
veins flows the blood of the conquerors of California.
And I was beautiful once, and gay and desirable.
But now look at me. What has become of the old
days? There's the pit that has swallowed them all!
(Pointing to the audience.) I remember it all now.
Forty-five years of my life lie buried here on this
stage, and what a life, Hedda. What a life! I can
see it as clearly as I see your face--the ecstasy
of youth, passion, the crowds, the love of men...
men, Hedda!

HEDDA: It is time you went to sleep, Miss Montez.

LOLA: I was a lass unparalleled. John Barrymore himself
told me that. Do you know what he meant?

HEDDA: That you were like Cleopatra? I--I recognized
the line.

LOLA: You read too much, Hedda. You should get out
and live.

HEDDA: I am sorry, Miss Montez.

LOLA: You should have lived, Hedda, as I lived. When
I first went on the stage, in the first glow of passionate youth, I remember a young man who loved me
for my acting. He was beautiful, graceful as a
poplar, young, shy, pure, and radiant as a summer
dawn. His smile would charm away the darkest
night. I remember I stood before him once, as I
am now standing before you. He had never seemed
so handsome to me as he did then. He wanted me
to marry him. He would have given me everything.
He was rich, the heir to one of the largest fortunes
in America. But he wanted me to give up the stage.
Give up the stage, do you understand? He could
love an actress, but marry her--never. I was in
a play that day... a gay, happy play by Noel Coward
--"I'll Leave It To You," I think. The play was a
failure but Noel was wonderful and I was happy to
give him his start. But my lover--he wanted me
to give up the stage. I sent him away and the next
week I was doing Roxane in "Cyrano." Then, right
in the middle of the last scene, I felt my eyes being
opened. I saw that the worship of my art that I had
held so sacred was a delusion--an empty dream.
I knew at that moment that I was a fool, the plaything of the idleness of strangers. I understood my
audience, my fans, at last. I have not, since that

day, believed in their applause, their cheers, their
expressions of love. They don't know me. Not the
real me. I am as the dirt beneath their feet. They
want to meet me, to hold my hand, to get my auto-
graph. But they think all actresses are monsters,
and they feel sorry for any friend who marries one
of us. I have no faith in them (Sinks into the rocking chair.), no faith in them at all.

HEDDA: You look so pale, so dreadfully pale. You frighten
me to death. Please go home. If not for your sake,
then for mine.

LOLA: I saw through it all that day, Hedda. After that I
wandered aimlessly about, living from day to day
without looking ahead. I took parts that had no art
in them--cardboard figures of tinsel. I had done
all the great parts ... Cleopatra, Joan, Nora, Juliet.
I had been a great artist once, but little by little
I threw away my talent. I gave Hollywood my throat
and they choked the life out of me. I, who had played
with Barrymore, had become the plaything of the
Marx brothers, the girl back home for Gary Cooper,
the other woman in a Warner Baxter triangle. I lost
the power to express myself. I lost my looks. I
lost my figure. (Stands up and points out to the
audience.) I have been swallowed up in that great
black pit. I never felt it before, but tonight when I
woke up I looked back and there behind me lay sixty-
eight... almost sixty years. I have just found out
what it is to be old. (Sinks back in chair.) It is
all over (Sobs.) ... all over.

HEDDA: Miss Montez, please, you need your friends. Let
me call them for you.

LOLA: Yes, call them. Call their names--Eddie, Edgar,
George.

HEDDA: I meant I could call them on the phone for you.

LOLA: No, call them here.

HEDDA: Miss Montez....

LOLA: Call them, I said. Scream their names. (Rises.)

HEDDA: All right, Miss Montez, all right. Don't disturb
yourself. I'll call them. Eddie. Edgar. George.

LOLA: Louder. You won't be heard in the balcony.

HEDDA: (Cupping her lips and calling into audience.) Eddie!
Edgar! George!

LOLA: What are you screaming about? They're gone.
(Sinks back into chair.) They're gone and I'm alone.

HEDDA: Please, Miss Montez. Let me call a taxi for you.

LOLA: But what a genius I was. You cannot imagine what

power I had, what eloquence. How graceful I was,
how tender. (Putting both hands to her throat.) It
chokes me to think of it. Listen, now. Wait, let
me catch my breath. There. Now listen to this.
Here's something from "Cleopatra." Barrymore
loved me in this role. (In character.) "Give me
my robe, put on my crown. I have immortal long-
ings in me. Now no more the juice of Egypt's grape
shall moist this lip. Yare. Yare, good Iras, quick.
Methinks I hear Antony call. I see him rouse himself to praise my noble act. I hear him mock the
luck of Caesar, which the gods give men to excuse
their after wrath. Husband, I come--" (Breaks out
of character.) But I have no husband. Every woman
in the world, be she ever so ugly, ever so dreary,
every woman in the world has a husband except me.

HEDDA: I have no husband, Miss Montez.

LOLA: Every woman in the world has children.

HEDDA: I have no children, Miss Montez.

LOLA: There was a part once that was made for me--
Juliet. Like Juliet I should have followed my lover.
You remember the scene. She awakes in her tomb
and there finds her lover dead. Friar Laurence
would have her leave, but she sends him away.
(Takes off towel around her hair, letting it fall down
around her shoulders. She sinks to the floor and
goes into Juliet pose.) "Get thee hence, for I will
not away. (Pauses and pantomimes picking up a cup.)
What's here? A cup, closed in my true love's hand?
Poison, I see, hath been his timeless end. O, churl!
drunk all, but left no friendly drop to help me after?
I will kiss thy lips. Perhaps some poison yet doth
hang on them to make me die with a restorative.
(Pantomimes kissing the Romeo in her lap.) Thy
lips are warm." (To Hedda.) Quickly, my next cue.

HEDDA: (Hesitating for a moment.) Lead, boy. Which
way?

LOLA: (Back in character of Juliet.) Yea, noise? Then
I'll be brief. O happy dagger. (Pantomimes finding
a dagger and raising it.) This is thy sheath. There
rest and let me die. (Pantomimes plunging the dagger
into her breast and falls in heap, gracefully.)

HEDDA: (Applauding and almost weeping.) Beautiful.
Beautiful. Beautiful.

LOLA: (Rises and Bows, then back into character of tired
old actress.) Yes, beautiful. But who is there to
play Romeo to that Juliet? Burton? He's too old

and pudgy.   All the great ones are gone.   (But pleased.)
Yet that was a good performance, was it not?
Where is there old age in that?   It is true that I
may be close to fifty, but actresses have done
Juliet in their forties before.   This is all foolishness.
I am not old.   Some of the younger playwrights are
doing roles for women my age--women in the full
bloom of their maturity.   I might do "Who's Afraid
of Virginia Woolf?" next season.   I have the figure
for it.   I shall have to diet, of course, but I feel
better when I diet.   It makes me more spiritual.

MALE VOICES OFF STAGE: Lola!   Lola, where are you?
Lola, where are you darling?

LOLA: (Startled.)   What's that?

HEDDA: It is only your friends, Miss Montez.   I knew
they would come back for you.   (Calls off.)   She is
coming.

LOLA: Of course they would come back for me.   I am
Lola Montez.   Come, come, old woman, don't
stare.   I must get dressed for my party.   (Hugs
Hedda.)   There, there, don't look sad.   I am all
right now.   I am always sad, always full of remorse
when a play is over.   I think about death and old
age.   But no more now.   Where there is art and
genius and beauty there can never be such things as
old age or loneliness or sickness, or death.   (Then,
sadly.)   No, Hedda, it is all over for us.   I'm
like a squeezed lemon, a cracked bottle.   And you,
you dear Hedda, you are an old rat in the theater.
A stage-struck clean-up woman.   But come on.
Come with me.   We shall go to the party together.
Tomorrow we shall be old again, but tonight, dear
Bette, dear Joan, great Ethel, tonight we shall be
the toast of the town.   Tonight we shall be all the
heroines I play and you dream--Elizabeth the Queen
and Joan of Arc and ...   (Laughs) and you, dear
Hedda, shall be Cleopatra.   I give you the role.   But
I shall keep Juliet.

MALE VOICES OFF: Lola, hurry, dear.   The party will
be over before the star gets there.

LOLA: We're coming.   We're coming.   (To Hedda.)   Come,
Cleopatra, we go to join the Antonys.   (They start
off, Hedda first.)   So fare thee well.   Now boast
thee, death, in thy possession lies a lass unparalleled.
Downy windows, close; and golden Phoebus never be-
held of eyes again so royal.   (The spotlight goes out.)

CURTAIN

Note: Permission to produce this play must be secured
by writing Pioneer Drama Service, Cody, Wyoming.

3. In the Academic Community

Last Week I Was Ninety-Five

CAST: (In order of appearance)

JACK BURLINGTON: Director of the Life Players.
CLARENCE: A Young Actor.
BUD: Another Young Actor.
CYNTHIA: A Young Actress.
TOM DOGGET: An Older Actor.
GEORGE BELLOWS: Another Older Actor.
MRS. FRANCINE EGGERS: An Older Actress.
ZIGGY: A Ninety-Five-Year-Old Man.
NOD: His Ninety-Four-Year-Old Companion.

SETTING: The action takes place on an undressed stage.
          Upstage left is a raised platform upon which is set
          a white wrought-iron garden bench. This is area
          No. 1, and is lighted by a single spot. Downstage
          right is another raised platform, but not as high as
          the one in area No. 1, on which is set a davenport,
          a bridge table, and four folding chairs. This is
          area No. 2 and also lighted by a single spot. Up-
          stage right, set in an angle from the upstage wall
          to wall right, is a large sign which serves as an
          archway. It reads "Welcome Miss America."
          Downstage left is a director's table and chair and
          a lectern.

ACT ONE

AS THE AUDIENCE ARRIVES, the house lights are on,
          the stage lights are off, and the curtain is open.
          As the play begins, BURLINGTON comes onstage
          from upstage center. He is followed by CLARENCE
          and BUD, each of whom is carrying white wrought-
          iron chairs, which they set in position on Platform
          No. 1. BURLINGTON comes downstage to his desk,
          reading a sheaf of notes. He sits and looks at them.
          CLARENCE and BUD sit in the chairs they have
          carried on stage. CYNTHIA comes onstage from up
          center, carrying a small bird bath. She stops and
          looks at BUD and CLARENCE, but when they make
          no move to help her, she carries the bird bath to

Platform No. 1, sets it in position on Platform No.
1, then sits down on the edge of the platform.
Music starts off-stage, too loud at first, then too
soft, then at a wrong tempo, then a little loud again.
DOGGET comes on stage from up left, listening to
the music from various spots on the stage.

WHEN THE AUDIENCE IS ALL SEATED, DOGGET goes
off-stage, and the music stops. BURLINGTON rises,
clears his throat, and starts his little speech to the
actors, with a mixture of apology and arrogance.

BURLINGTON: Well, I guess the Life Players are ready.
Or at least as ready as we ever are. I think we'll
call the first act the proposal.
DOGGET: (Who has returned to the stage in the middle of
Burlington's speech.) Jack, do you mind if I close
the curtains?
BURLINGTON: Yes, I mind.
DOGGET: Oh. (Shrugs.)
BURLINGTON: Now some of you may disagree, but in a
way, I see this story as starting with the proposal.
DOGGET: Can we, at least, turn off the house lights.
It's depressing looking at all those upturned, empty
seats. I feel like a latrine orderly in a deserted
barracks.
BURLINGTON: All right, Tom, if it will make you happy,
we'll turn off the house lights. Get them, will you,
Clarence?
CLARENCE: Sure thing, Mr. Burlington. (He bounds off
up right.)
BURLINGTON: Now as I was saying, I think we'll call
the first act, "The Proposal." That's really the
first big thing in the old man's life.
BUD: As the old man tells it, it is. But I don't know how
far we can trust him.
BURLINGTON: As he tells it is the way it is, or at least
the way we are going to do it. I warned you all
last week that we won't be able to get anybody to
come here and let us act out his life unless we have
a little respect for people.
DOGGET: I find it very difficult to have any respect for
anyone who wants to watch people act out his life.
It's perverted, that's what it is. Sick.
BURLINGTON: We're all a little sick, Tom.
DOGGET: I may vomit once in a while, Jack, but I don't
play in it after I do.

BURLINGTON: A human life is not vomit. We might as
        well get it straight once again before they get here.
        The Life Players was not created to insult people.
        That's not our purpose.
CYNTHIA: I wish we were doing regular plays about normal
        people, like "Tiny Alice" or "The Beard" or some-
        thing like that.

        (The house lights go out and the theater is in dark-
        ness.)

BURLINGTON: Who turned out the lights? What the hell's
        happened?
CLARENCE: (Off-stage.) You told me to turn them off,
        Mr. Burlington.
BURLINGTON: Turn on the stage lights, you idiot.
CLARENCE: (Off.) Okay, whatever you say. (The stage
        lights come on.)
DOGGET: I don't know why you fool around with that kid.
        He's an idiot.
BURLINGTON: Clarence is all right. At least, he has a
        little charity. Now where the hell was I?
CYNTHIA: You were calling the first act "The Proposal."
BURLINGTON: Oh, yes, "The Proposal."
CLARENCE: (Coming back on stage.) Is this guy really
        ninety-five years old?
BURLINGTON: Ziggy? Yes, he's ninety-five, give or
        take fifteen minutes.
BUD: How does a man that age get around?
TOM: In a wheelchair. He gets around in a wheelchair.
        Nod pushes him around just the way Bud pushes you
        around.
BUD: Is that the same Nod in the story we're doing to-
        night?
TOM: The same one. How many Nods do you think there
        are in this town?
BUD: But he must be....
TOM: He's ninety-four.
BURLINGTON: It's all in the synopsis. You all have read
        the synopsis, haven't you? I gave you all your
        copies two weeks ago.
BUD: I looked at it, generally.
CLARENCE: I meant to look at it, but I lost my copy.
CYNTHIA: I read it, and there's not a good part in it
        for me. I wish we could do "Cat on a Hot Tin Roof."
        I'd like to do Maggie. I could do that part without
        a bit of trouble.

BURLINGTON: That I can believe. But the Life Players
    are not doing "Cat on a Hot Tin Roof," and we are
    not doing "Tiny Alice." We are the Life Players.
    We do life!

CYNTHIA: Well, life's all right. But a little liberty and
    pursuit of happiness wouldn't be so bad.

CLARENCE: Why can't we do regular plays?

BURLINGTON: Tom, where are George and Francine?

TOM: I saw them both today. George said he would be
    a little late, but Francine said she would be here
    on time. I judge you want separate reports because
    I don't like to gossip.

BURLINGTON: Just once. Just once, I'd like the whole
    cast to be here on time, to have read the synopsis,
    and be ready to go to work. Just once, I say.
    Just once.

CYNTHIA: What difference does it make whether we come
    prepared or not? We don't even have an audience.

BURLINGTON: We have the best audience in the world,
    the people whose lives we are dramatizing, the
    censure of which must outweigh a whole theater of
    others.

TOM: Did you want some violin music? That's just crap.

BURLINGTON: All right, just look at the facts. You take
    the normal play. How is it made? Well, I'll tell
    you how it's made. A playwright gets a wild idea
    and invents a lot of impossible people and gives
    them a lot of nonsense to speak. "To be or not to
    be" and "It is a far, far better thing I do than I
    have ever done."

CLARENCE: That's a Tale of Two Cities. I know that one.

CYNTHIA: But it's not a play.

BURLINGTON: All right, all right. It's not a play. But
    you take any play, and what do you have? A wild
    idea, impossible characters, and more impossible
    dialogue. The playwright and the actors may think
    this is all great stuff, but do you know what the
    audience thinks? He looks at the play, and the best
    he ever thinks is, "So that's the way they live."
    And he may think that Shakespeare knew a lot of
    crazy people, and he's glad he doesn't live in the
    same neighborhood with Tennessee Williams. But
    he knows one damned thing. Those characters on
    stage aren't him or anybody he knows, except maybe
    some in-laws. Your average theater-goer visits the
    theater the way he goes to the zoo--to see the animals
    at feeding time, to feel superior to the flea-bitten

monkeys and sorry for the dumb hippos.   But theater
is nothing to him.   He's way out there in the dark,
scratching himself and worried about whether his
supper is going to digest all right in a cramped
seat.   The play is way up here.   The guy out in
the audience never asks himself if the play is true.
The gas he's got, that's true.   The gas on the stage,
that's just to take his mind off the real gas.   The
play is a kind of half-assed lie, and the design--the
structure--that's just a kind of clock to tell him how
much longer he has to watch before it is all over
and he can go home.

TOM: If I could go home a little early tonight, I could
watch the late news.   I hate to miss the news.   It's
real, you know, Jack.

BURLINGTON: But take our group, the Life Players.   We
don't tell lies, and we don't fake.   We play the life
of our audience, and that audience is right up here
on stage with us, checking us every minute, commenting, judging.   The guy we play knows the truth.

BUD: Maybe he does, maybe he doesn't.   But he doesn't
always tell it.   Now you take Mrs. Compton last
week, trying to tell us how happy her life has been
with old Boozy.   Everybody in town knows the only
happy day she ever had with him was the day she
poured him into his grave.

BURLINGTON: That's what the town thinks!   Maybe that is
the way every other woman in town would feel, but
that's not necessarily the way she felt.   She's not
a statistic, she's a person.   And that means we
don't know how she feels.

BUD: Well, that's the way she should feel.

BURLINGTON: Now, you're talking like a damned playwright.

TOM: I agree with you, Jack.   I agree with you.   I think
maybe we gave Mrs. Compton a better shake than
the playwrights would have.   But she just got mad
anyway.   So what's the sense.

BURLINGTON: Sure, she got mad.   You'd get mad, too,
if the actor who was playing the person you loved
made him look like a freak.

CLARENCE: She'd have gotten mad anyway.   She didn't
want to see her life as it really is.

TOM: He's right there, Jack.   He's right, you know.
People don't want to see the truth about themselves.
People come to the theater to be flattered, to be
told that from a distance their lives look better than

they do close-up. All we have ever done with this
Life Theater is make people mad.

BURLINGTON: All right, I'll admit that. Some of the
people are going to get mad. But that's all right.
When you lie to people, you've got to make them
happy. We'd have nothing else to offer, but we can
make our audience angry. That's all right. We
don't charge them anything, so they can't get their
money back.

CYNTHIA: Well, they certainly make a lot of noise.

BURLINGTON: All right, but the noise is real. When our
audience gets angry or cries or laughs, it's real.
They really care. It's not just a bunch of characters
sitting out there--half of them dragged here by their
wives. The only time that group out there moves
is to test their own reflexes to be sure they are still
alive.

BUD: They laugh and applaud.

BURLINGTON: Sure, they do. Sure, they do. They laugh
to stop from belching, and applaud to cover up the
rumbling of their big, fat stomachs. Say what you
want about the Life Players, but our audience cares.

GEORGE: (Making an entrance upstage right.) I see I've
just missed the opening prayer. But it's all right,
Rev. Burlington, I'll stay for benediction. (Coming
downstage and flopping on the davenport on platform
No. 2.)

BURLINGTON: George, can't you make it on time, just
once?

GEORGE: I almost didn't make it at all. This is the day
that shouldn't have been. Tom told you I'd be late,
didn't he, Jack?

BURLINGTON: He told me.

GEORGE: It was really most prophetic of me, because when
I told him I was going to be late I really expected
to be here on time, I really did. Really, really,
really.

BURLINGTON: It's all right, George.

GEORGE: But I was nearly killed--three times. You know
dirty old man Whitten? Well, he's running for some
office. Governor or something. And he cornered
me in my office, puffing a huge, black cigar, breath-
ing cancer germs all over me.

BURLINGTON: George, could we take a rain check?

CYNTHIA: Besides there's no such thing as a cancer germ.
Cancer isn't a germ.

GEORGE: All right, all right, I stand corrected. You are

absolutely, positively right.   I wasn't nearly killed
three times today--only twice.   Does that make you
feel better, Cynthia?   Your scientific mind has destroyed another of my poetic visions.   I had finally
come to accept the germ theory--poetically, of
course.   And you tell me there are no germs.
You've taken one-third the romance out of life for
me.   But at dinner tonight, my wife tried to poison
me.   And don't tell me that I am mistaken.   I know
damned well there's poison.   Ethel's mother was
there, and she said that Ethel was trying to poison
me, too.   And my mother-in-law speaks the truth.
It's her only virtue.

BURLINGTON: Damn it, George, you talk too much.

GEORGE: All right, all right.   It probably isn't good show
to reveal in public that one's wife is a poisoner.
All right, all right, I'll lie about it.   I wasn't poisoned.   But anyone who tasted that roast tonight would
admit that Ethel did something criminal.   But I'll
let it pass.   I wasn't germed and I wasn't poisoned,
but all of you will admit that the third attempt on my
life was real.   I passed Ziggy and Nod on the road--
on the road, mind you, in a car.   They aimed that
instrument at me, but fortunately Nod is blind so he
missed.   Honestly, there should be a law against
allowing old fools to drive cars on a public highway.

BURLINGTON: George, are you quite finished now?

GEORGE: No, not quite.   But I nearly was.   Do you know
what it is like to find yourself in the sights of two
hold-overs from the Spanish-American war?   Incidentally, Ziggy and Nod ought to be here in a few
minutes.   If they don't crash when they come in for
a landing.

BURLINGTON: I wish Francine was here.   It's awkward
when the cast gets here after the audience.

GEORGE: Francine!   I had forgotten about her.   She tried
to kill me today, too.   Insisted upon riding up on
the elevator with me.   Fortunately, we had a very
thin elevator boy.   And talk, talk, talk every moment.   The weight of her words alone will one day
throw the earth off-kilter and send us whirling into
the sun.   Honestly, Jack, why does a person talk
so much?

BURLINGTON: I wish the hell I knew.

GEORGE: Please, don't swear at me, Jack.   You're not
my wife.   You're not even my mother-in-law.   And
I know what you mean.   I can tell.   You think _I_ talk

too much. All right, I'm through. I'll not say
another word. I heard the best story--positively
scandalous--about you today, but I'm not going to
tell it to you. I'm just going to sit here and think
about it. I may chuckle a bit, even laugh, but I'm
not going to say a single word. So don't beg me.

CYNTHIA: Mr. Burlington, if we would do real plays, you
wouldn't have to listen to this. It's always a mistake to encourage actors to make up their own lines.
Everybody knows that.

GEORGE: She's just hateful, Jack, just hateful, and getting
fat too.

TOM: All right, George, you've given the ghost of Noel
Coward one more rousing shake. Now let's give
Jack a chance. He is the director, so let him
direct.

BURLINGTON: Thanks, Tom.

TOM: And then maybe I can get home to watch the news.

BURLINGTON: If George is right, we've only got a few
minutes before they get here. You all know the
story of Ziggy and Nod. Next to them, Damon and
Pythias were just a couple of casual acquaintances.
For over ninety years--ninety years, mind you--Ziggy
and Nod have been friends. Seventy years ago, when
Ziggy married Faith, a lot of people here in town
thought it was going to be the end of that friendship.

GEORGE: I had a friend before I married Ethel. A man
always loses a friend when he marries.

BURLINGTON: But the marriage wasn't the end of the
friendship between Ziggy and Nod.

GEORGE: It was the end of the friendship between me and
Ethel.

BURLINGTON: George, will you shut up!

GEORGE: I'm shut.

BURLINGTON: It really gets annoying after awhile, George.
It really does.

GEORGE: I'm sorry. I'm sorry.

BURLINGTON: The friendship between Ziggy and Nod didn't
die at the altar. If anything, it grew closer, but
now there were three--Ziggy, Faith, and Nod. Faith
found in Nod as good a friend as her husband had
found. The first scene that we'll do tonight is the
proposal scene. Bud, you'll play the part of Ziggy.
Cynthia, you'll do Faith, of course. And, Clarence,
you'll do Nod. Now, look at the synopsis and get
the action straight. If we decide we need any more
characters, Tom, you and George can handle them.

I don't think we need more. I rather see this scene
with just three characters, but, of course, we never
know where we're going to end when we start.

CYNTHIA: Where are we going to do the scene?

BURLINGTON: (Moving to Platform No. 1.) We'll do it
up here. This is a garden scene. Do you kids want
to take your places? Cynthia, you and Bud sit on
the bench. (They go up on Platform and sit on bench.)
Let's see how that looks. All right. Not so close
together. This is an old formal garden in 1895, not
a modern drive-in movie. And, Clarence, you sit
in one of those chairs up there.

CLARENCE: Mr. Burlington, would I be there--I mean was
Nod there--for the proposal? I know they are great
friends and all that, but I don't think I'd take Bud
with me to propose. I mean, after all, this isn't
a hippy honeymoon, is it?

BURLINGTON: They were both there. It's in the synopsis,
Clarence.

CYNTHIA: Don't we need costumes or make-up or something?

BURLINGTON: This is a Life Theatre, Cynthia, not a
museum. Stop thinking of the past as something
dead. Just think of 1895 as today.

BUD: Well, I'll try. But it's not easy to play a man of
ninety-five, you know. Not at my age.

TOM: There he goes with that age business again. I don't
know what makes young people think they have accomplished something because they are young. Everybody's young once, but only the smart ones get old.

BURLINGTON: Ziggy wasn't ninety-five on the day he proposed, Bud. In fact, he was just about your age--
maybe a little younger.

CLARENCE: What about the way we talk? They used Old
English or something, didn't they?

GEORGE: He's ninety-five, Clarence, not nine hundred and
fifty. What do they teach you kids in school these
days?

CYNTHIA: They teach us that cancer isn't a germ.

BURLINGTON: All right, all right. Let's get back to the
scene.

TOM: Everybody pay attention to the director.

BURLINGTON: All right. Here's the scene. It's a May
afternoon in the year 1895 in Faith's garden. The
flowers are blooming, the birds are singing, and
everyone's in love. Even Nod.

(There is a crash upstage off.)

ZIGGY: (Upstage off.)   You did that on purpose, Nod.
         You're a thoughtless, stupid, old bag of garbage.
         You pushed me into that can on purpose.   You're
         stupid, stupid, stupid.
GEORGE: Well, here come Damon and Phythias.
         (Ziggy comes onstage in a wheelchair, pushed by Nod.
         They are both old men, but Ziggy appears to have
         fallen apart.   He looks unkempt and disorderly and
         he waves his cane with wild abandon.   Nod, in spite
         of the fact that he needs a cane to walk, has an al-
         most military bearing.)
BURLINGTON: (Going upstage to help them.)   I wish the
         devil Francine were here.   She's the only one around
         who can talk to them easily.   They were her sugges-
         tion.
GEORGE: Why not?   She's of the same generation.
ZIGGY: Nod, what's that fool talking about?
NOD: It's Mr. Burlington, Ziggy.   He's the director here.
ZIGGY: He's a damned fool, that's what he is.
BURLINGTON: Now, Mr. Ziggy, you don't mean that.
ZIGGY: Lot you know what I mean.
BURLINGTON: (To Nod.)   What did I do?
NOD: Ziggy doesn't like people to talk about him as though
         he's not here, unless he's not here.
BURLINGTON: Oh, I'm sorry.   Was I doing that?
ZIGGY: Damned fool, that's what he is.   Whispers about
         the blind and makes faces at the dead.
BURLINGTON: Well, well, perhaps you're right.
ZIGGY: I'm always right.   Remember the first Dempsey-
         Tunney fight, Nod.   You remember I was the only
         one who knew that Tunney would win.   It was a
         Wednesday afternoon, I remember.   We were sitting
         in your office when Joe Pickels came in.   He was
         wearing an orange tie, with green in it.   I remember,
         and he offered two-to-one that Dempsey would win.
         You remember, Nod.   I bet him five thousand dollars.
         Five thousand dollars.   Five thousand dollars was a
         lot of money at that time, too.   Bet him five thous-
         and dollars.
TOM: He cetainly has a good memory.   That must have
         been forty years ago.
NOD: He remembers things a long time ago better than
         things that happened yesterday.   But he does have
         a good memory.
ZIGGY: You didn't bet on Tunney, Nod; I did.   You bet on
         Dempsey.   And you bet on Primo when he fought
         Maxie Baer, and you bet on Maxie Baer when he

fought Joe Louis. You always bet wrong, Nod.
Everytime you bet wrong. Admit it, now. Admit it.

NOD: I admit it, Ziggy. I admit it.
(NOD now has pushed the wheelchair to downstage
center, and he stops.)

BURLINGTON: We're certainly glad you both made it tonight.

NOD: We're glad too.

BURLINGTON: We're ready to start if you are.

ZIGGY: What did he say, Nod?

NOD: They're ready to begin.

ZIGGY: I don't care if they are. Wish I were home. It's
lonely here, Nod, lonely, cold, and the lights are
bad.

NOD: Do you want to go back home, Ziggy?

ZIGGY: It doesn't make any difference. Every place is
lonely now--since my Faith left.

NOD: I know, Ziggy. I... I miss her, too.

ZIGGY: It's not the same. It's not the same at all. She
was my wife. Not yours. Mine.

NOD: I know, Ziggy. It's not the same.

ZIGGY: Are we in the right place? Ask that fool if we
are in the right place.

NOD: You'll excuse him, Mr. Burlington.

BURLINGTON: Think nothing of it, Nod.

NOD: Are we in the right place?

BURLINGTON: Well, about. If you could just move the
chair around here. (Goes and starts to help.) The
scene is on that platform there, and sometimes some
of the players like to go out front to see how it looks
at a distance.

ZIGGY: Get your damned hand off my chair.

NOD: I'll push the chair in the right place, Mr. Burlington.
He doesn't like anyone else to touch the chair. (He
has moved chair into position.) Is this all right?

BURLINGTON: That will be fine, Nod. Just fine. Tom,
get Mr. Nod a chair will you?
(Tom goes up on Platform No. 2, takes one of the
bridge chairs and moves it down into a position near
the wheelchair for Nod.)

ZIGGY: What do you want a chair for? Don't see what
you need a chair for.

NOD: You've got a chair.

ZIGGY: I'm not a young man. Last week, I was ninety-
five. That's pretty old. Ninety-five.

NOD: I'm ninety-four.

ZIGGY: It's not the same. Not the same at all. Admit it,

Nod.   Admit it.

NOD: All right, Ziggy.   It's not the same.   I'll stand.

ZIGGY: Oh, sit down.   Sit down and stop your whining.

NOD: No, it's all right.   I'll stand.

ZIGGY: Sit down.   Sit down right now.   I'm older than
you, Nod, and you ought to listen to what I say.
Everytime we get in trouble, I get blamed because
I'm the older.   And then you won't listen to a
damned thing I say.

NOD: You told me to stand up.

ZIGGY: Did not.   I just asked why you needed a chair
It's not the same.   Not the same at all.   Now sit
down.

NOD: (Sitting.)   I could stand.

ZIGGY: And then you'd sulk all day tomorrow, and then
you'll try to cheat me at cards.

NOD: I don't cheat.

ZIGGY: You do, too.   Faith said you did.   She told me
that she saw you cheating.   Are you going to say
Faith lied?

NOD: I don't cheat much.

ZIGGY: Don't cheat at all.   It's not nice.

NOD: What are we supposed to do, Mr. Burlington?

BURLINGTON: Oh.   Well, it's really very simple.   We
are going to act out certain events in your life,
events that you told us about.   We'll do three
scenes tonight, and after each scene, you'll tell us
what we did wrong.   What isn't true.

NOD: I don't know if I remember every detail.

BURLINGTON: We don't try to get all the details or even
to do exactly the same things or say exactly the
same words.   We just try to get the right idea, so
that when you see our little scene, you'll say,
"That's the way it was."   Do you understand?

ZIGGY: What did he say, Nod?

NOD: He wants to know if we understand.

ZIGGY: What actor is going to play me?

BUD: I am, Mr. Ziggy.

ZIGGY: You're not as good looking as I was at your age.
Not by a long shot.   And you, young lady?   I suppose you are playing my wife, Faith?

CYNTHIA: I'm going to try, Mr. Ziggy.

ZIGGY: You're very pretty, young lady.   (To Nod.)   Tell
her she's pretty, Nod.   But she's not as pretty as
Faith was, is she?

NOD: No one ever was or will be.

ZIGGY: It's not your business to say that, Nod.   It's not

your business at all.   You're entirely too free with
your opinions.

NOD: Yes, Ziggy. It's not my business.

ZIGGY: Well, tell the young lady she's pretty.   But don't
spread it on too thick.   Don't over-do it.

NOD: You're a very pretty young lady, Cynthia.

CYNTHIA: Thank you, Mr. Nod.

ZIGGY: Why did you have to say very?   Couldn't you just
say she was pretty.   You always over-do it.   Always did, always will.   (Looks at Clarence.)   You,
Boy, who are you?

CLARENCE: You know me, Mr. Ziggy.   I'm Clarence.

ZIGGY: I never knew anyone in my whole life named
Clarence.   (To Nod.)   They ought to change that
boy's name.   It makes it all sound like a comedy.
I don't remember any Clarence.   Do you remember
a Clarence, Nod? Was Faith's father named Clarence? No, it was Nathaniel. Maybe it was that
shyster from Chicago. He looked like a kind of
Clarence. But I don't want him in my play. I don't
even want him mentioned. Young man, you can't
play any Clarence. I won't permit it.

CLARENCE: My real name is Clarence, Mr. Ziggy. I
play the part of Mr. Nod in the scene.

ZIGGY: Just nonsense. That's all it is. I never promised
her anything. Just paid that lawyer because you
told me to, Nod.

NOD: He won't be in the play, Ziggy. The boy's going to
play my part.

ZIGGY: He is, eh? (To Clarence.) Boy, are you going
to play his part?

CLARENCE: Yes, sir, that's what I was telling you.

ZIGGY: I just wanted to see if he was lying.

NOD: I don't lie, Ziggy.

ZIGGY: You cheat. Everytime we play cards, you cheat.
(To Clarence.) Boy, move down a little. And you,
Boy (Waves at Bud.), you stand next to him. (Bud
and Clarence stand side-by-side, looking at Ziggy.)
Young lady, which one do you think is the best look-
ing?

CYNTHIA: Well, I don't know. They're both all right, I
guess.

ZIGGY: Can't make up your mind, eh? Faith didn't have
that trouble. I was the only one. The only one.
Nod, which one is the best looking?

NOD: The one playing you, Ziggy. But they're both good
looking boys.

ZIGGY: All right. But the best looking one's got to play
    me. (To Bud.) What's your name, Boy?

BUD: Bud, sir.

ZIGGY: Bud! That's not a name. It's a state of being.
    Might as well call a man Puberty as Bud. Might
    better. Puberty has a little dignity to it.

BUD: My real name is Edwin.

ZIGGY: Edwin! You better use Bud. All right, you can
    play me, but you behave yourself.

BUD: Yes, sir. Thank you, sir.

ZIGGY: (To Nod.) He's got nice manners, did you notice
    that? I always had nice manners.

BURLINGTON: We're going to do the proposal scene first,
    Ziggy.

ZIGGY: That's good. That's good. The day I proposed
    was a good day.

BURLINGTON: But one question has come up. Nod was
    there the day you proposed to Faith, wasn't he?

ZIGGY: He sure was. (Laughs.) Course he didn't know
    I was going to propose. I wasn't sure I would my-
    self until the words were out.

BUD: Now, that's interesting.

CYNTHIA: Did Faith know, Mr. Ziggy?

NOD: She knew.

ZIGGY: How do you know that? How do you know that?
    How do you know that she knew?

NOD: Well, she didn't act surprised, did she?

ZIGGY: Well, you don't know. You don't know anything
    about her. You think you do but you don't. I could
    tell you a lot of things. You don't know everything
    about Faith.

NOD: I didn't say I did, Ziggy. I'm sorry I said that.

ZIGGY: You don't know anything about the way she felt.
    Admit it. Admit it.

NOD: All right, Ziggy. I'll admit it. I don't know any-
    thing about the way Faith felt.

BURLINGTON: Is it all right if we start the scene now?

NOD: Yes, it's all right.

ZIGGY: What's all right?

NOD: It's all right if they start, isn't it?

ZIGGY: I don't care. I don't care what they do. I'm
    lonely and I'm cold. I'm freezing.

NOD: I'll go to the car and get a blanket.

ZIGGY: I don't want your dirty blanket. I'm cold on the
    inside, not the outside. Why don't we get started?
    It's all this waiting that's making me cold.

BURLINGTON: All right, take positions. (Cynthia, Bud, and

Clarence take positions on Platform No. 1.) George, will you get the spot over the platform and turn off the stage lights?

GEORGE: (Going off-stage left down.) I'll get them, but I didn't have to come out of the house to turn lights on and off. I could have stayed home and done that. In fact, I just love to turn lights off at home. My wife and her mother look better in the dark. (Exit left.)

TOM: The next time, ask me, Jack. George can't breathe without belching.

BURLINGTON: He's got to have some place to talk. (Yells offstage.) George, turn on the spot before you turn off the lights.

GEORGE: (Off.) My name's not Clarence.

CLARENCE: Now why did he say that? At least, I was here on time.

BURLINGTON: (To Nod.) George is going to turn off the overhead lights, but there will be a spot over the scene. Is that going to be all right?

NOD: That will be fine. Fine.

BURLINGTON: Should you tell Ziggy?

ZIGGY: (Rousing up.) Why don't they turn that light on up there. (Points to spot over scene No. 1.) Look a lot more like a play.

NOD: That's what they are going to do, Ziggy.

ZIGGY: And they ought to turn off the other lights, too. I may want to sleep.

NOD: They are going to, Ziggy. You heard him say it.

ZIGGY: I did not. It was my own idea. I just thought of it.

BUD: Mr. Ziggy, what would you think about doing this scene as a kind of ballet?

ZIGGY: A ballet!

BUD: A ballet. You know, a dance. (He does a twirl.)

ZIGGY: I think I'm going to be sick, Nod. I'm going to be sick and throw up. And that boy ought to have to clean it up. He's going to make fun of me. (The spot light on No. 1 goes on; the stage lights go off.)

NOD: The scene is about to start, Ziggy.

ZIGGY: I'll watch if it's no dance. If they start dancing, like a lot of queers, I'm going to throw up.

GEORGE: (Coming back on stage.) It should be blue. The spot should be blue. I see this as a blue scene.

BURLINGTON: (Going down to director's table.) Flop somewhere, George, we're starting.

BURLINGTON: All, right, Bud let's get going. And no ballet.
 (The play-within-a-play starts. All the actors off
 the platform sit so that platform No. 1 is now the
 center of attention, in clear view of the audience.
 Off-stage, music can be heard -- something quietly
 gay and late Victorian.)
CLARENCE: Now, Mr. Burlington?
BURLINGTON: Now. Let's get started. "The Proposal."
 (There is a pause, the music goes up slightly, the
 three actors on the platform go into character, the
 music is muted, and the play-within-a-play starts.)
CLARENCE: It's a pretty afternoon.
BUD: It is a pretty afternoon, isn't it, Miss Faith.
ZIGGY: I never called her Miss in my whole life. Knew
 her from the time I was three. It was always Faith.
 Just Faith.
BURLINGTON: All right, Bud, cut the Miss.
BUD: It is a pretty afternoon, isn't it, Faith?
CYNTHIA: I'm glad you think so, Ziggy. Or was it Nod
 who thought so?
BUD: I don't have to ask Nod what I think. I think it's a
 pretty afternoon.
CYNTHIA: Well, then I'm glad you think it's a pretty
 afteroon. That means you're happy. Whenever you
 think the weather is pretty, you're happy. Are you
 happy this afternoon, Ziggy?
BUD: I think so. Yes, I'm happy, Faith.
CYNTHIA: And you, Nod, are you happy, too? It's not
 as easy to tell about you, Nod. Sometimes you
 think the weather is pretty and you're not happy at
 all. But you do think it's a pretty day, don't you?
CLARENCE: Pretty enough, I guess.
CYNTHIA: Pretty enough for what, Nod?
CLARENCE: Pretty enough to say it's pretty, I guess.
 (Then in the character of Clarence, to Nod.) Mr.
 Nod, am I doing your character right?
NOD: (Reflectively.) It seems right. It seems right.
 I don't fully remember anymore.
BURLINGTON: Just keep going, Clarence. If it isn't
 right, we can correct it after the scene is over.
CLARENCE: Okay, I just wanted to do it right. (Then in
 character of Nod.) I guess I'd say it's a pretty
 day, Faith.
CYNTHIA: (Laughing.) Then, you boys must be up to some-
 thing. Here we are sitting and talking about the
 weather just as though it were the most important
 thing in the world.

CLARENCE: Well, weather is important.

BUD: It's important to Nod. If it rains, his head might warp.

ZIGGY: I like that. I like that. He says you got a block-head, Nod. That was a good one.

CYNTHIA: Stop picking on Nod, Ziggy, or I'll just leave here this minute. Nod's a lot smarter than you are. You'd never have made it through the university if he hadn't helped you. You told me that yourself.

BUD: Did I really say that, Faith?

CYNTHIA: You know you did. You said it a hundred times.

BUD: That must have been a lie. Nobody bothers to tell the truth a hundred times. It must have been a lie, don't you think so, Nod?

CLARENCE: If you said it, Ziggy, I wouldn't be surprised.

CYNTHIA: I hope that holds you, Ziggy.

(There is a pause.   The off-stage music stops.)

BUD: I guess this will be a hot summer.

CLARENCE: It feels that way already.

BUD: Might even be hotter than last summer.

CLARENCE: That's what they are saying.

BUD: Of course, last summer was hot.

CLARENCE: Hotter than most, that's true.

BUD: Summers seem to be getting hotter all the time.

CYNTHIA: Did you two come over and take me away from my book just to talk about the weather?

(Off-stage music starts again.)

BUD: Why, Lord no.

CLARENCE: Of course not.

CYNTHIA: You used to talk about all sorts of things when we were children together, but now that you are be-coming important men in town--a merchant and a lawyer--all you can talk about is the weather. I was going to go in and fix some cold lemonade for us, but if all I'm going to get is weather reports, you can just stay thirsty.

BUD: Faith, did you hear that Sarah Delaney and Joe Harper are going to get married?

CYNTHIA: Everybody's heard that. It's even been in the papers.

CLARENCE: And Alice Hutchins and Al Wallace, I hear they're going to get married.

CYNTHIA: That was in the papers months ago.

BUD: Seems like just about everybody's getting married these days.

CLARENCE: It does seem that way.

BUD: Faith, what do you think about marriage?

CYNTHIA: I think it's a very proper institution and likely
    to stay popular for at least the next ten years.
CLARENCE: I think so, too.
    (There is a long pause. The music stops.)
CYNTHIA: Well, I guess we've exhausted the subject of
    marriage. Shall we move on to relatives? Poppa
    is well, Mama is feeling poorly. Aunt Claudia has
    a touch of the grip. Uncle Walter....
BUD: Faith, I'm wondering. What do you think about your
    getting married.
CYNTHIA: I think I may. Someday.
BUD: Have you given it any serious thoughts? I mean,
    what kind of a man would you marry? (The music
    starts again.)
CYNTHIA: (Rising and moving down center.) I've thought
    about marriage, yes. Some.
NOD: And....?
CYNTHIA: And I've thought about the kind of man. Oh,
    I haven't thought much about how he would look.
BUD: But you would want him to be good looking, wouldn't
    you?
CYNTHIA: I guess....I guess every girl wants her husband
    to be handsome. Not too handsome, though. But
    mostly, I'd want him to be ...kind. Not sweet, like
    Sam Larkin, but... but kind. Gentle. That's the
    word, gentle. And he should be a man that likes
    to talk to me. Really talk to me. And listen to me,
    too. And I guess I'd want him to have ambition, to
    care about his work. But to care about other things
    too, like books and music and whether it's a pretty
    day or.... (Music stops.) But mostly, I'd want him
    to be gentle.
BUD: That's very interesting. Most interesting. What
    kind of wife do you think I should have?
CYNTHIA: I couldn't begin to guess.
BUD: Well, try. You know me pretty well. Just guess.
CYNTHIA: Well, someone pretty serious, I would think,
    you being a merchant.
BUD: You're pretty serious, aren't you, Faith?
CYNTHIA: Sometimes. Sometimes I am, and sometimes
    I'm not.
BUD: I don't think anyone should be serious all the time.
    Faith, do you think I'm... well that I'm handsome?
CYNTHIA: You're not ugly.
BUD: Do you think that I'm kind?
CYNTHIA: You're not always nice to Nod.
BUD: (Going from bench and kneeling on one knee by Cyn-

thia.) Faith, don't play with me any more. You
know I'm asking you to marry me, to be my wife.

CYNTHIA: Are you, Ziggy?

BUD: You know I am.

CYNTHIA: You haven't asked me yet. He hasn't asked me
yet, has he, Nod?

BUD: Well, I'm asking you right now. Will you marry me?
There, now I've asked you. Will you, Faith?

CYNTHIA: What do you think, Nod?

CLARENCE: I don't know.

CYNTHIA: Do you think I would make Ziggy a good wife?

CLARENCE: You'd make him a good wife, yes.

CYNTHIA: Do you think he'd make me a good husband?

CLARENCE: If you want him. Ziggy generally does pretty
well anything he really tries to do.

CYNTHIA: Do you want us to marry?

CLARENCE: It's not up to me. It's up to you.

CYNTHIA: What about you, Nod? What are you going to
do?

CLARENCE: Me? Well, I don't know. Nothing I guess.

CYNTHIA: You are going to marry someone, aren't you?

CLARENCE: I don't know. I haven't thought much about
it one way or the other. (Pause.) No, I don't
think I will. I don't think I'll ever marry. Probably
no one would ever have me anyway.

CYNTHIA: You're not bad looking.

BUD: Faith, can't we take care of my proposal first before
we start match-making for Nod? This ground is a
little damp, and it's not very comfortable just kneeling here. I feel like a fool.

CYNTHIA: Do you really want to marry me, Ziggy?

BUD: More than anything else in the world, Faith. And I
will make you happy. That I promise you.

CYNTHIA: I do want to be happy. It's very important to
me.

BUD: I'll make you happy, Faith. I promise you.

CYNTHIA: Will he, Nod?

CLARENCE: If Ziggy says he will, he will. Ziggy almost
always keeps his word.

CYNTHIA: You think I ought to marry Ziggy then?

BUD: Say yes, Nod, please. My leg is just killing me.

CLARENCE: Yes, Faith, I think you ought to marry him.

BUD: Thanks, Nod, you're my friend for life. And after
we get married, Faith and I, you'll still be welcome
... all the time. Might even name one of the children after you. All right, Faith, now tell me you'll
marry me.

CYNTHIA: All right, Ziggy, I'll marry you if you like. (Bud rises, brushing off his knee, and then kisses Cynthia on the cheek.)
BUD: You'll never be sorry, Faith. You'll never be sorry. (All three actors stand now, looking out at the audience, with their heads slightly bowed. They have finished the scene. Jack, George and Tom applaud.)
TOM: Good performance, kids. Good performance.
BURLINGTON: (Rising and moving upstage.) That was good. But now let's tear it apart. George, get the stage lights, will you?
GEORGE: (Rising and going off-stage.) Sure. Sure, I'll get the lights. Good old faithful George, he does everything. Leave it to George. (Exit downstage left.)
BURLINGTON: Well, Ziggy... Nod, what do you think? Did the kids bring back the day?
ZIGGY: I didn't kneel. I stood up. I stood up all the time.
NOD: There were blossoms on the tree, white and pink. And Faith wore a blue dress. And she had a blue ribbon in her hair.
BURLINGTON: Then the scene seemed right to you, eh?
FRANCINE: (Coming down from upstage right.) No, it wasn't right. Anyone could see that. It was all wrong. Everything was wrong.
BURLINGTON: Where the hell did you come from, Francine?
FRANCINE: I saw the whole scene from upstage. I would have told you I was there, but you had already started. I didn't want to interrupt.
TOM: Maybe you should have. Since it was all wrong. Personally I thought it was pretty good, considering the talent.
FRANCINE: Oh, I'm not talking about the performance as such. It was a very touching little scene, and aside from the all too obvious fact that young people mumble, I thought they did well enough. But it just wasn't right. The heart wasn't right. (The Stage lights come on and the spot goes out.)
GEORGE: (Off.) Are the lights all right?
BURLINGTON: O.K., George. Come on back.
FRANCINE: (Walking downstage left.) Maybe the scene was all right from a man's point of view, but it was all wrong for the woman. All wrong for Faith. No woman would ever have acted that way.
CLARENCE: This happened a long time ago, Mrs. Eggers.
FRANCINE: Before Eve?

CLARENCE: I don't know if it was that long ago.

FRANCINE: Then it was all wrong. Neither Eve nor any
of her daughters would have acted that way at a
proposal.

NOD: That's the way Faith acted. I remember it all
clearly. That's exactly what she did. But she had
a blue dress and a blue ribbon in her hair.

ZIGGY: But I didn't kneel. And I didn't say anything about
naming any child for Nod.

FRANCINE: (Goes up on Platform No. 1. The young actors
sit on the edges of the platform, giving her the stage.
She sits on one of the chairs and goes into the
character of the young maiden in the garden.) She
couldn't have done it that way. She just couldn't.
Think about it. Think about it. (Starting to create
the scene.) It was summer.

BUD: I think it was spring.

FRANCINE: It was warm, like summer. (Pause and slow
movement.) And yet not too warm. It was that
time of year when trees and bees and women all
begin to feel... to feel funny. To put out leaves
and buzz and tingle. Faith is in her garden. She
has put down her book; perhaps it was that lovely
book by Emily Bronte. I'd like to think so. She
hadn't finished it, but she knew how it would end
for it was the sixth time she had read it. All of
the romance of that book was around her, mixed
with the scent of the flowers, the buzz of the bees,
the beating of her heart.

GEORGE: (Who has returned at the beginning of her speech.)
Sounds rather like a boiler factory, or a love-in.

FRANCINE: Hello, George, I see you've shaved your beard.
It was a horrible beard, but it was a mistake for
you to shave it. Now do sit down and be quiet.

GEORGE: (Sitting down.) I'm pierced.

FRANCINE: So there she was, ready for the day of her
life. And now she is to receive... not one... but
two--two gentlemen callers. Think about that.
Faith did, you can be sure of that.

ZIGGY: She wasn't thinking about two. Just one. Just
me. She didn't even know Nod was coming, and
she didn't pay a bit of attention to him. She didn't
even know he was there.

FRANCINE: (Rising, but still in the character of the young
maid in the garden.) It would seem that way, wouldn't
it? It would seem that way. (Now in character of

Francine.) And that's what's wrong with the whole
scene. Why would she ask Nod if she should marry
Ziggy? A woman doesn't talk to a man of marriage
unless... unless.... Well, take "The Courtship of
Miles Standish." I don't think that Priscilla ever
meant to marry John Alden until that stupid Miles
sent him to her. Women are not simple, but they
are primary. The babe in their arms is theirs.
And only a fool with a grey beard would think otherwise.

GEORGE: It must be so if you say so, Francine.

FRANCINE: Dear George, shut up.

CYNTHIA: Mrs. Eggers, are you saying that....?

FRANCINE: I'm saying, dear girl, that Faith never would
have asked Nod if she should marry Ziggy unless....

CYNTHIA: It seemed perfectly natural to me when I was
doing it.

TOM: Unless what, Francine?

FRANCINE: (Stepping off platform.) I'm probably just
being silly. Clarence is right. It was a long time
ago, and women do change.

NOD: It's the way I remember it. Except for the dress
and the blue ribbon in her hair.

ZIGGY: It's exactly the way it was. And it was a pink
ribbon.

TOM: Cynthia, what did you think about when you were
playing the scene?

CYNTHIA: Gee, I don't know, Mr. Dogget. You know how
it is when you're with it. You don't think about
anything. I guess I just hoped that Mr. Ziggy would
like the way I was playing his wife.

FRANCINE: What did you think about Bud?

CYNTHIA: I didn't think anything about Bud. Except I did
think that his leg probably was really cramped. Bud
doesn't do much exercise, you know.

FRANCINE: Did you feel any emotion... well, love... for
him?

CYNTHIA: For Bud! No, of course not.

BUD: It's not completely impossible, Cynthia. I may not
be all muscle, but it is possible that some women
might find me mildly attractive.

CYNTHIA: I didn't mean it that way, Bud. I just meant
that I didn't feel anything about you at all. Except
as I say, I did wonder if your leg was really cramped.

FRANCINE: For Clarence? Did you feel anything for
Clarence?

CYNTHIA: Well.... (Laughs nervously).   This sounds kind
          of stupid, considering Clarence and all.   But yes, I
          did.   I felt kind of sorry for him.   You know there
          wasn't anything in the synopsis about Faith asking
          Nod if she should marry Ziggy.   I just made that
          up because I felt sorry for him.
CLARENCE: Well, thanks a lot.   No wonder I'm hungry
          all the time.
CYNTHIA: Clarence, I didn't mean you personally.   I
          just meant that... well, there you were.   You didn't
          have anything to do.   You were just stuck there with
          nothing really to say or do.   Your best friend was
          asking a girl to marry him, and you were just stuck
          there.
ZIGGY: I'm cold.   I'm freezing.   And I'm going to be
          sick.   I don't like all this talk.   I didn't come here
          to listen to all this talk.   It's making me cold.   It's
          making me cold.
NOD: (Rising.)   I'll get that blanket, Ziggy.
ZIGGY: I don't want your dirty blanket.   I keep telling you
          and telling you, and you won't listen to me.   I'm
          not cold on the outside.   I'm cold on the inside.
          INSIDE.
BURLINGTON: Look, Nod, we have some coffee back here.
          It's about time we took a break anyway.   Let's all
          go back to the Green Room for coffee.
ZIGGY: It wasn't green, and it wasn't blue.   The ribbon
          was pink, and I didn't kneel, and no one even men-
          tioned a child.   Say, Nod, remember the day we
          played hookey from school to watch the train come
          in?   It was a Wednesday, wasn't it?
NOD: Ziggy, Mr. Burlington has fixed some coffee for you.
BURLINGTON: It's back to the Green Room.   It's warmer
          there, too.
ZIGGY: It wasn't green.   It was pink.   A pink ribbon.
NOD: You want some coffee, don't you Ziggy.
ZIGGY: I shouldn't drink coffee.   I'm an old man.   I'm
          ninety-five years old.   You know that, Nod.   Last
          week I was ninety-five.
NOD: I know, Ziggy.
ZIGGY: You do not.   You didn't even get me anything for
          my birthday.   Faith and I always got you something
          for your birthday, but now that Faith is gone, no-
          body even remembers my birthday.
BURLINGTON: Do you think maybe you ought to take him
          home, Nod?
NOD: No, he'll be all right.   Ziggy's all right.   He just

acts this way sometimes. But he's all right.

ZIGGY: I want some coffee. You promised me some
coffee. Let's all go back to that Green Room and
have coffee.

NOD: (Going into position to push chair.) All right,
Ziggy, we'll go get the coffee now.

ZIGGY: Well, don't just talk about it. Push me there.
I can't walk, you know. Why do you make me wait
all the time, Nod? Why are you mean to me?

NOD: (Starting to push chair.) We'll go right now, Ziggy.

TOM: Just follow me back, Nod. I'll go ahead and get
the lights on. (He starts off down left.)

NOD: All right, Mr. Dogget, we'll follow. We'll follow.
(Nod pushes the chair downstage left, following Tom.)

ZIGGY: (Waving the cane gently in the air.) With rue my
heart is laden... with laden my heart is rue. Laden,
laden, rue, rue. It was a pink ribbon, Nod, and I
didn't kneel. I wouldn't have knelt with you watching me. I'm cold, Nod. Cold inside.

NOD: The coffee will warm you up, Ziggy. You'll feel
all warm inside. Just like you used to. (Exit Nod
and Ziggy.)

GEORGE: I think we ought to change our name from the
Life Players to the Mummy Stealers. Honestly,
Jack, you can really pick the weirdo's. What'll
you do next week, a double bill of Dracula and Fu
Manchu?

CYNTHIA: Don't make fun of them, Mr. Bellows. I like
them, especially Mr. Nod. And they're kind of sad.

FRANCINE: (Rising.) They were almost old men when I
was only a child. But they had dignity. I remember
seeing Mr. Ziggy and Faith... and Nod, too, of
course... riding through town in their buggy. It was
fifty years ago or more. I was only a little girl.
But I can still remember that they seemed such handsome men. Tall, slim, important.

CYNTHIA: And Faith, Mrs. Eggers? Was Faith beautiful?

FRANCINE: Any woman escorted by two handsome men is
always beautiful. (Starts across down left.) Well,
I want coffee, too. Anyone else?

GEORGE: (Rising.) I'll join you, Francine. If two men
made Faith beautiful, I should, at least, make you
half-beautiful.

FRANCINE: Just one-fourth, George. Just one-fourth.
(They start off left.)

GEORGE: Coming, Jack? I need reinforcements with
Francine.

JACK: You two, go ahead. I'll be there in a minute.
(Exit Francine and George.)

CYNTHIA: (Coming downstage to Burlington who is checking a tablet.) Now, how did we really do, Mr.
Burlington?

BURLINGTON: Fine, Cynthia, just fine.

CYNTHIA: I'm sorry about all that talking I was doing
earlier. You know about our doing regular plays.
There is something special about the Life Theatre.
(Pause.) I think I may have seen tears in his eyes.

BURLINGTON: You can't be sure at his age what he's
thinking. But I guess he does miss his wife. She
was his life.

CLARENCE: They were married for about seventy years.
That's a long time.

CYNTHIA: It was Nod. I saw the tears in Nod's eyes.

BUD: Now, I really do feel sorry for him. Ziggy bosses
him around all the time, and Mr. Nod's ninety-four
years old.

CLARENCE: Mr. Burlington, is there anything to eat back
there? Or any Cokes?

CYNTHIA: Oh, Clarence, that's all you do is eat.

CLARENCE: That's because you pick on me. It's a proven
fact that people who eat all the time are suffering
from a denial of love.

CYNTHIA: Try handball, Clarence, it's cheaper.

BURLINGTON: Come on, Clarence, I'll help you find some
food. (Exit Clarence and Burlington left.)

BUD: Boy, that Clarence. He's my friend and all that.
But boy, what a jerk.

CYNTHIA: I don't know. He's deeper than you think.

BUD: Yeah? Is there something going with you two?

CYNTHIA: Oh, shut up, Bud. I'd like some coffee too.
(She starts off left, Bud following her. She stops
downstage left.) Are we just going to leave the
stage as it is?

BUD: I guess so. We'll be back in ten minutes. What
did you want to do?

CYNTHIA: I don't know. It just looks kind of deserted.

BUD: Yeah, it does. I guess we could turn the lights out
on our way back.

CYNTHIA: I guess we could do that.

BUD: Do you think I'm silly, Cynthia?

CYNTHIA: No, I don't think so. I feel the same way.
What are stage lights for except to see actors, and
if there are no actors on stage, well, it looks like
a lighted bathroom window with no shade. Let's turn

the stage lights out.

BUD: Yeah, we can turn them back on before the others get through.

CYNTHIA: Maybe we'd better not. If Bellows sees us turning off lights, well, you'll know what he'll say....

BUD: Yeah, why is it old men have dirty minds?

CYNTHIA: They're just afraid to talk about things they're doing and thinking. They don't even think when they say things like that. Maybe they're trying to remember.

BUD: You think we should leave the light on then?

CYNTHIA: Course we could turn off the stage lights and turn on the house lights.

BUD: That would be all right. I'll go do it. (He exits off left. Cynthia wanders about the stage, obviously half-acting, until she comes to Platform No. 1. The stage lights go out.) The lights are out, Bud.

BUD: (Off.) Okay.
(The house lights come on. She stands looking at the garden scene, and Bud joins her.)

CYNTHIA: It still looks a little sad, doesn't it? These two scenes (Indicates two platforms)--they're rather like Ziggy and Nod, aren't they? Kind of sad. Empty. Dark.

BUD: Yeah. Well, let's get some coffee.

CYNTHIA: (Moving away from scene, but still looking at it.) Bud, let's turn the music on as we leave. It won't be so lonely.

BUD: Okay, but let's go.
(They start off left, and Cynthia, just before she exits, turns back for a moment, looks upstage left and then out over the house.)

CYNTHIA: It's just an intermission. Just a ten-minute intermission. (She exits left.)

THE MUSIC STARTS.

End of Act I

Note: During the intermission, if coffee is served to the audience, FRANCINE, BURLINGTON, and CLARENCE--all in character--should be in evidence.

ACT TWO

AT THE END OF THE TEN-MINUTE INTERMISSION, BURLINGTON, carrying a cup of coffee, comes on stage,

goes to his table, sits down, and looks at some notes.   The
off-stage music grows fainter, and the stage lights come
on.   CLARENCE comes on stage, chewing a stalk of celery.
He looks over Burlington's shoulder.   The off-stage music
flares up and plays at the wrong tempo.

BURLINGTON: God, Clarence, what a noise.
CLARENCE: The music!   Somebody left the music on.
    I'll get it.   (Starts off left.)   Here, hold this.
    (He hands Burlington the stalk of celery.)
BURLINGTON: Damn it, Clarence, I'm not talking about
    the music.
CLARENCE: I got it.   (The music stops.)   (Clarence is
    off-stage.)
BURLINGTON: (Calling off to him.)   Get the house lights,
    too, Clarence.   No sense in running up our electri-
    city bill for nothing.   (He drops the stalk of celery
    on the table and returns to the tablet.   Francine
    comes on left.   Burlington speaks without looking up.)
    I told you to get the damned house lights.   (At that
    moment, the house lights go out, then come on
    again, then go off, on once more, and then off.)
    Clarence, what the hell are you.... (Sees Francine.)
    Sorry, Francine, I thought you were Clarence.   That
    kid will drive me crazy.   (Picks up celery.)   Here,
    you want some celery?
FRANCINE: (Taking Celery.)   Oh, Clarence is a nice-
    enough boy.   Stupid, but gentle.
    (The house lights come on again and then again go
    off.)
BURLINGTON: (Yelling off.)   Leave the damned lights
    alone, Clarence.
FRANCINE: (Walks downstage right, carrying the stalk of
    celery.)   I have always loved calla lilies.   (Drops
    the stalk.)   It's odd, Jack, but when those house
    lights went off and then on, then off--I felt a kind
    of excitement.   Rather like a warning to the audience
    that the intermission is over and the action is about
    to begin again.   Of course, we don't have an audience
    with the Life Players, but....   Well, you know what
    I mean, Jack.
BURLINGTON: I guess.   You know how I feel about plays
    before out-in-the-dark audiences, Francine.   It's a
    kind of exhibitionism, like undressing before a light-
    ed window.
FRANCINE: I don't care for the analogy, but I know your
    objections.

BURLINGTON: Then you don't want the sermon on the
    vitality of the Life Theatre?
FRANCINE: No, spare me. I think there's something in
    what you say, of course, or I wouldn't be here to-
    night. But there's something to be said for (Waves
    her arm toward the audience) the audience out there,
    too. If we had an audience out there now, real
    people who had paid real money to be entertained,
    we wouldn't be just drifting about up here now. We'd
    have a purpose, a tension. Oh, I agree that the
    play might be old, tired, pretentious, impossible.
    The characters we would be playing might be mere
    shadows of men and women; the words merely echoes.
    Out there, they wouldn't believe a thing we were say-
    ing or pretending. But by God, we'd believe it all.
    And it's all in the believing, Jack, all in the believ-
    ing. (By this time, the lights should be settled and
    the audience in place.) Belief, Jack, belief. That's
    what people live by. Not facts, not even truths,
    just beliefs. Take those two old men, two decades
    past their burial. They believe. They believe.
    They believe.
BURLINGTON: Yes, my Lord Hamlet, what do they believe?
FRANCINE: (Relaxing and going toward him.) Oh, I know
    I'm hamming it, Jack. A bit. It goes with the
    territory. But there's something about tonight. I
    hate to admit it, Jack, but tonight I think the Life
    Players might really touch a little life. Those two
    old men, crusted over with age, habit, maybe even
    senility, are like ripe melons, just waiting to split
    open and tell all the secrets of a lifetime.
BURLINGTON: Good God, Francine, they don't have any
    secrets, I wouldn't take a chance if I thought they
    had. Their lives are about as public as Grant's
    tomb... and just about as exciting. In their whole
    lives, they have never had a single... well, only
    one.
FRANCINE: And that...?
BURLINGTON: And that was a long time ago.
FRANCINE: Maybe for us, yes. But probably not for them.
    (George, Bud, and Cynthia come on stage from down
    right.)
GEORGE: I don't object to the theater of the absurd on
    moral grounds. I'm no Puritan. I object as an
    artist. The theater of the absurd is nothing, just
    nothing. Pieces of characters sit around tearing
    metaphors to tatters to please the ears of the purse-

carrying boys.   Take Beckett's <u>Endgame</u>, for example.

CYNTHIA: Have you seen it, George?

GEORGE: I wouldn't waste my time.   And that Albee.
    <u>A Delicate Balance</u>?   Just junk.   An indelicate pile
of junk.

CYNTHIA: And you haven't seen that either, have you,
    George?   (To Bud.)   You like Albee, don't you
    Buddy?   Wouldn't you just love for the two of us
    to do Martha and George in "Virginia Woolf"?
    Like Liz Taylor and Richard Burton, that's what
    we'd be like.

BUD: I don't think my mother would care for that.
    (Burlington and Francine have gone up to Platform
    No. 2. She sits on the davenport, and Burlington
    folds the bridge table and sets it off the platform;
    then he arranges the chairs.)

GEORGE: (To Burlington.)   Can I help you there, Jack?

BURLINGTON: No, it's finished.   I think that's all we
    need.   If they'll just get here, we can get back to
    work.

GEORGE: Ziggy had to go to the bathroom, and Tom is
    staying with them to make sure they make it back
    all right.

BUD: It's really rather remarkable how two men that old
    get around.

CYNTHIA: Tennessee Williams' grandfather used to travel
    all over the country, to New Orleans, Florida,
    everyplace.   Even by bus.   And he was ninety-five.
    And blind.

GEORGE: And I can't stand Williams either.   Doesn't
    have a single role that a really virile man would
    want to play.

CLARENCE: (Entering from left.)   They're coming.
    They're coming.

BURLINGTON: All right, everybody, let's get back to work.
    We'll use the downstage set for this one.   (Francine
    rises and walks down right from platform.)

CLARENCE: Do you want the spot on that scene, Mr.
    Burlington?

BURLINGTON: Yes, but wait until they get on stage,
    Clarence.   And try to get it right the first time,
    will you?

CLARENCE: I always get it right.   (He exits left as Ziggy
    in his wheelchair, being pushed by Nod and Tom,
    comes on from left.)

ZIGGY: That coffee made me sick.   I don't like coffee.

I don't know why I drink.   Do you know what I like?
A glass of milk with an egg beaten in it and some
vanilla flavoring.   I haven't had that since I was a
boy.   Why didn't Faith make that for me?   She
should have known I liked it.

NOD: Where do you want us, Mr. Burlington?

BURLINGTON: (Indicating position upstage left of Platform
No. 2.)   Up there will be fine, Mr. Nod.   We're
going to use the other platform for this scene.
(Nod pushes Ziggy's chair into position, Tom gets
Nod a chair and puts it near the wheelchair, and
Nod sits.   George goes down left to the director's
table and sits on it.   Tom and Francine stand downstage right.   Burlington views the scene on Platform
No. 2, then stands on the platform and continues his
speech.   All this action takes place during Burlington's speech, and after Burlington is on the platform
and a sentence into his speech, the stage lights go
out as the spot on Platform No. 2 comes on.   Bud
and Cynthia are sitting on the floor upstage left,
near Platform No. 1.   After the lights are fixed,
Clarence will come onstage down left and sit down
near Bud and Cynthia.   Both the lights and the direction of the actors should focus attention on Burlington
and Platform No. 2.)

TOM: What scene do we do next, Jack?

CYNTHIA: What about the marriage ceremony?

GEORGE: Or the honeymoon!   My mother-in-law went on
our honeymoon.   Of course, I didn't mind because
I had to stay home and take care of the kids.

BURLINGTON: Our second scene is "Betrayal and Forgiveness."   You can think of it as Act II if you like.

CYNTHIA: Do I play Faith in this one?

BURLINGTON: No, this is Mrs. Egger's scene.   Francine,
do you want to take your position now?

FRANCINE: On the platform?

BURLINGTON: Yes, up here.   I think you'll be sitting on
the sofa.   On the upstage end.   (Burlington watches
her as she takes a position.)   Now, move down just
a little.

FRANCINE: (Moving.)   Is this right?

BURLINGTON: Yes, that's fine.   (He now uses his narrator's voice and speaks almost directly to the theater
audience.)   It is ten years after our first scene.
Ziggy and Faith were married, and in the best
tradition of our grandparents, they live happily ever

after. Well, almost ever-after. Faith was a... a
faithful wife, as befits a wife named Faith. And
Ziggy was a loving husband. A most loving husband.
In fact (Moving up platform, down left, almost beyond the spot), too loving. That was their problem
and our second scene, "Betrayal and Forgiveness."
It should be understood, of course, that Ziggy loved
Faith, but somehow he always managed to have a
little love left over.

ZIGGY: That's a good way to put it. I wish I had thought
of it. That was my whole trouble. I was too loving a man. I had a lot of love in me.

NOD: You had a lot left over. There was that woman in
Chicago. And there was at least one in New Orleans
and one in Kansas City. And your secretary. And
my secretary. And others. Others.

ZIGGY: Nobody asked you, Nod. Nobody wants your comments. Just don't talk. Just don't say anything.
This is my life, not yours.

BURLINGTON: There were--shall we say--other women.
But it was all quiet, and if Faith knew, she never
said a word. Until that day....

ZIGGY: Until that day that damned woman from Chicago
came down and told Faith I wanted a divorce. A
divorce!

NOD: You must have suggested it to her. No woman's
going to come all the way from Chicago for nothing.
You must have given her the idea.

ZIGGY: I never did. I never did at all. I never even
heard the word divorce until she came around. I
never mentioned a divorce. We were moral in those
days. We married for life. For life. It was that
lawyer. He wanted money. He was a lawyer, Nod,
just like you. Just like you.

NOD: I never told her anything. I wanted to, but I didn't.

ZIGGY: That lawyer was a crook. All lawyers are crooks.

BURLINGTON: That's not important now. Let's get on
with the scene. Faith knew about the other woman,
and when Ziggy learned that, he ran away.

NOD: For three days, he didn't go home.

BURLINGTON: And there was Faith, alone, not knowing if
she would ever see him again.

ZIGGY: I wasn't ashamed of what I had done. It was
perfectly normal for any man. I just didn't want
to see Faith's face. I had hurt her, you see. I
had hurt her because she loved me. She loved me
very much.

BURLINGTON: Maybe she cried when she was alone.
NOD: No, Mr. Burlington. Ziggy's right. Faith never
   cried. Never.
BURLINGTON: All right, all right. Faith didn't cry. I
   don't know what you are going to do in this waiting
   scene, Francine. I had thought there would be some
   tears.
GEORGE: I don't care what she does as long as she doesn't
   start tearing her scarf again. I hated you in that
   role of Amanda, Francine.
FRANCINE: Really, George, did you? I thought you liked
   the character. Amanda was the kind of woman who
   flattered men like you. Weren't you the Gentlemen
   Caller in that, George?
GEORGE: Hell, no. I wouldn't be in a Williams play.
FRANCINE: I guess I just thought you were because he's
   your type.
GEORGE: Don't be bitchy, Francine.
BURLINGTON: Can we get back to the business of the play?
GEORGE: I'm willing. Lord knows, I'm trying to help.
FRANCINE: Well, it's all right with me. What am I sup-
   posed to do?
BURLINGTON: I'm not sure. I mean I was so certain
   there were tears. I guess you'll just have to walk
   up and down and suffer, Francine.
FRANCINE: (Moving on platform.) That's what I do best.
BURLINGTON: George, move over with Tom.
GEORGE: What am I supposed to do?
BURLINGTON: I'll want you for Ziggy and Tom for Nod.
GEORGE: (Moving across downstage and joining Tom.) All
   right, I don't know what the hell I'm supposed to be
   doing, but I'll do it.
ZIGGY: I was better looking than that fellow. Let the
   young fellow play me again. He's better looking.
BURLINGTON: For this scene, Mr. Ziggy, you're almost
   forty.
ZIGGY: Don't make any difference. I was always young
   for my age, young and high spirited.
GEORGE: I'll do the part with spirit, old boy.
ZIGGY: (Stage whisper to Nod.) And he talks funny.
NOD: He'll do it right, Ziggy. Don't worry.
ZIGGY: He looks too old.
   (Tom has taken a newspaper from his pocket and
   starts reading.)
NOD: Ziggy, he'll hear you.
FRANCINE: Jack, can't you give me a piece of business
   in this scene. I feel like I'm training for a track

        meet, just running up and down.
BURLINGTON: How would you behave in these circumstances
        normally? I mean if you were Faith.
FRANCINE: I'd cry a little and curse a lot, I suspect.
        No, I'd wash my hair. I aways wash my hair when
        I'm upset.
BURLINGTON: That just isn't practical for this scene.
        (To Tom.) Tom, would you mind putting up that
        paper and joining us?
TOM: (Folding paper and returning it to his pocket.)
        Sorry. I'm probably going to miss the news tonight,
        so I just thought I'd try to catch up. It's last week's
        paper anyway. I found it in the bathroom.
BURLINGTON: All right, this is the scene now. Faith is
        waiting. Tom, you're Nod. After three days of
        searching, you've found Ziggy and now you drag him
        home to Faith. (Tom grabs George by the collar of
        his coat and the two step up on the Platform.) All
        right, start the scene here. (Burlington moves into
        the shadows, and all the action on stage is centered
        around the platform performers, George as Ziggy,
        Tom as Nod, and Francine as Faith.)
TOM: I think he's been drinking, Faith, and he may be
        sick. What will I do with him?
FRANCINE: I don't know. I don't know, Nod. What does
        a best friend do with a runaway husband after he has
        dragged him home? You're an attorney, Nod, our
        attorney. And you're a... friend, our friend. Tell
        me what you think I should do with him.
TOM: Whatever you want me to do.
FRANCINE: What can I do?
TOM: Whatever you want, Faith.
GEORGE: I'm sick. I'm dying. I've got to sit down. (He
        staggers across the platform and drops into a chair.)
        I'm here now, Nod; so why don't you go? Why don't
        you leave me alone? You're not my keeper, you
        know. I'm older than you. No, don't go, Nod.
        Don't leave me alone.
FRANCINE: Would you like to leave, Ziggy? Would you
        like to leave me and go to Chicago? I didn't ask
        Nod to bring you here. If you want a divorce, I
        won't stop you.
GEORGE: Faith, I don't want a divorce. I never wanted
        to be with that woman in Chicago. It was just...
        well, all the buyers were there and... It was just
        a lark?
FRANCINE: A lark, Ziggy? An Indian Summer lark?

TOM: Maybe, I'd better go.

FRANCINE: No, please don't. I... Ziggy wants you to stay. I want you to stay. I need you as a... a lawyer. You are my lawyer, you know.

GEORGE: You don't need a lawyer, Faith.

FRANCINE: There's been talk of divorce, and a woman needs a lawyer when there's talk of divorce. Please stay, Nod.

TOM: All right, I'll stay. But I don't belong here.

GEORGE: We don't need a lawyer. I don't know where all this talk of divorce started. I don't want a divorce. I don't even like the word. I'm telling you, Faith, I don't want a divorce.

FRANCINE: Don't you, Ziggy? Are you sure?

GEORGE: (Rising.) Of course, I'm sure. I'm not drunk. I haven't been drinking. I'm just sick. Faith, I don't want a divorce. I love you, Faith. (Goes to her and pleads.) I've never loved anyone in my life so much.

TOM: (Angrily.) You ought to kneel when you say it. You knelt when you asked her to marry you and promised her you'd make her happy. You ought to kneel again.

ZIGGY: I didn't kneel when I proposed. I don't know why everyone keeps saying I did. It isn't so.

GEORGE: (In his own character.) That's my line. He stole my best line. That's what I was going to say. Jack, I don't like to be prompted. Tell him that.

BURLINGTON: Please, George, stay in character.

GEORGE: (Flatly.) I didn't kneel when I proposed. I don't see why everyone keeps saying that.

TOM: Then you should have knelt. And you ought to kneel now and ask Faith's forgiveness.

GEORGE: I'm willing. I'm willing, Faith. There's no woman in the world that I'd rather kneel down to. It's just that I'm not feeling well. I don't think I could. But if you'll forgive me, Faith, really forgive me, I'll never look at another woman again as long as I live. I don't want a divorce, Faith.

FRANCINE: Well, maybe I do, Ziggy. Maybe I do. Maybe you should be free to chase after all the women you want.

ZIGGY: She never said that. She couldn't. She didn't know about any other women. Nobody knew. Except Nod. (To Nod.) You didn't tell her, did you, Nod? You didn't tell?

NOD: No, Ziggy, I never told her anything. She just knew

about the one.   The woman from Chicago.

FRANCINE: <u>(In her own character.)</u> No one would have
to tell <u>a woman a thing like that.</u>   That's the sort
of thing a woman would know anyway.   I don't know
what makes men think that women are so stupid.
It takes just feeling to know what the man one loves
is up to.   She doesn't have to hear gossip or see
lipstick on his handkerchief.   There's something
that tells a woman that the man she loves is unfaithful.   It's part of loving him.

ZIGGY: She didn't know.   We lived together for fifty years
after that and she never mentioned another woman--
just the one from Chicago.   If Faith had known, she'd
have said something.   She couldn't have helped saying something sometime.   She didn't know.

FRANCINE: All right, all right.   She didn't know.   But a
lot of husbands would be surprised if they knew what
wives know.

BURLINGTON: Stay in character, Francine.

FRANCINE: How can I stay in character?   I can't even
find it.

CLARENCE: I knew someone would get mad.   It happens
every time.

BURLINGTON: Let's get back to the action.   Francine,
pick up the part where you stopped.

FRANCINE: Am I supposed to believe that now Faith forgives the zigging Ziggy and they live happily ever
after?   That would be a zag I couldn't swallow.

BURLINGTON: Stop abstracting, Francine.   Life doesn't
make sense in the abstract.   Just play it scene by
scene, that the way we live our lives, scene by
scene, day by day, hope by hope, fear by fear.
Think.   What would <u>you</u> do now?   In Faith's place?

FRANCINE: I don't know.   <u>I</u> don't know what I'd do.   <u>(In
character of Faith.)</u>   Nod, what should I do?

TOM: It's hard to say, Faith.   You don't owe anyone anything now.   Listen to your own heart.   What is it
<u>you</u> want?

FRANCINE: My heart stopped beating a long time ago.   It
doesn't say anything.   It doesn't even murmur.
Shall I take him back, Nod, and pretend that nothing
has happened?

TOM: You don't have to do that, Faith.   It happened, and
you'll always know it happened.   But you'll know
something else; too.   It will never happen again.

GEORGE: I promise that, Faith.

FRANCINE: On the day he proposed, he told me he'd make

me happy.

TOM: Hasn't he, Faith? Until now?

FRANCINE: There have been happy days, quite a few
really. It hasn't been what I expected, but I have
been happy, yes.

TOM: If you take him back, Faith, I promise you that
this will never happen again.

FRANCINE: And if it does, if it does, what then?

TOM: It won't. I'll kill him if he tries.

GEORGE: You don't have to go that far.

ZIGGY: He would have, too. He would have killed me if
I ever looked at another woman. I don't understand
it. He knew about those other women, and he never
said a word. But when she knew just about one...
he said he'd kill me, and I knew he'd do it.

FAITH: All right, Nod. I believe you. But I don't want
that promise. I don't want Ziggy to stay faithful to
me because he is afraid of you. I don't care whether
he's faithful or not. I don't really care anymore.
But if you think I should, Nod, I'll try again. If
you want to, Ziggy.

ZIGGY: (Almost crying.) There was nothing in the world
I wanted more. Nothing. I didn't want other women.
I just wanted my Faith. And I almost lost her.
Lost her. Nod, if it hadn't been for you, I'd have
lost her. She wouldn't have taken me back again.
I have you to thank for all the good years I've had.
I never even thanked you. You have been my loyal
friend all these years, and I've never thanked you.
I've been mean. I've picked on you. And all these
years, you--just you--have been the only faithful
friend I've had. I'm sorry, Nod. I'm sorry.

NOD: Don't, Ziggy. Don't.

ZIGGY: You were the only faithful one. Just you.

NOD: You're making it harder for me. You're just making
it harder for me to do what I must do. To show you
what I have to show you. Don't, Ziggy.

BURLINGTON: Well, go ahead. Pick up the scene.

FRANCINE: There's nothing to pick up, George. The scene
is over.

TOM: It sure is, Jack. Not only the scene but the play.
We know everything now. So, I guess there will be
no objections if I get on home. I'd like to hear the
news.

BUD: (Rising.) Mr. Burlington, there is one more scene
to do.

BURLINGTON: Well, what is it, Bud?

BUD: Mr. Nod gave Cynthia and me a scene to do.   Can
        we do it now?
BURLINGTON: Well, I don't know.   I'm supposed to be the
        director here, you know.   It's the Life Theatre and
        all that, but the director is still the director, you
        know.
BUD: I know, Mr. Burlington, I know that.   I told Mr. Nod
        that.   But this scene really fits here.   It's the real
        betrayal part, Mr. Nod said.
BURLINGTON: Oh? Well, I don't know.   I guess we might
        as well.   What do you think?
FRANCINE: It's all right with me.   I'm tired anyway.
GEORGE: I'm kind of interested, in a half-interested sort
        of way.
TOM: If we could hurry it up.
BURLINGTON: Okay, Bud, take over.   What scene do you
        want?
BUD: The same scene.   It's the living room of Faith's
        house.
        (George, Tom, and Francine move off the platform,
        and Bud and Cynthia step on it.)
CLARENCE: Am I in this scene, Bud?
BUD: No, just Cynthia and me.
BURLINGTON: Is this the scene with the woman from
        Chicago?
ZIGGY: You're not going to show that woman, Nod.   You
        promised that we wouldn't have to show her at all.
NOD: It's not about that, Ziggy.   It's not about that.   It's
        something else.   Something you didn't even know
        about.
CYNTHIA: Shall we start now?
NOD: Yes, please start now?
CYNTHIA: (In the role of narrator.) Nod knew that Ziggy
        had run away, almost before Faith did.   He knew
        he would.   But he waited two days before he went
        to her.   He found her, sitting alone, not crying,
        not doing anything.   (She sits and then in character
        of Cynthia.)   All right, Bud, it's time for your
        entrance.
BUD: Shall I find him, Faith?   Do you want me to find
        him and bring him back?
CYNTHIA: Why? What good would it do?   What good is
        a husband who must be dragged home to his wife?
        How he must loathe me, how he must hate me to
        send that woman to me.   Have I been so bad a wife,
        Nod?   I didn't know.   I didn't know.
BUD: He didn't send her, Faith.   And he doesn't hate you.

He loves you. He just hates himself. Just himself.

CYNTHIA: And the way that woman looked at me. I felt
a hundred years old with my slip hanging.

BUD: She doesn't mean a thing to Ziggy, Faith. She
doesn't and she never did. He's sorry. I know he
is.

CYNTHIA: Maybe if I hadn't lost the baby. It's important
to a man like Ziggy to have children. They're
visible assets to show that his marriage was a sound
investment. With no child of his own, nothing to
show for our life together, our love together, the
marriage couldn't seem real to him. Without a
child, he has to act like a child. I understand
that, Nod, I understand. Buy why didn't he come
to me himself? Why didn't he tell me? Why did
he send that woman? She's an awful person.

BUD: He didn't send her. He didn't even know she was
in town. She's just a woman, the kind that business
men meet when they are out of town. Maybe she
was a model. I don't know. But I do know that if
Ziggy had met her when he was single, she would
have meant nothing to him. Nothing at all.

CYNTHIA: If the baby hadn't died. He needed the baby.

BUD: The baby's got nothing to do with it. A man doesn't
need children to grow up. What children did Washington have?

CYNTHIA: He needed the child.

BUD: A man's not like a woman. Men like children, sure
--even love them, perhaps. But to a man a child
is like a visitor, someone who comes to live for
awhile. It's not something that grows inside him,
feeding off him. A man's not a woman, Faith. You
can't blame yourself for this. You can't blame yourself for the child, and you don't owe Ziggy any
special allowance.

CYNTHIA: If I had gone to Chicago with him....

BUD: And to Omaha? And to New York? And to the office
every day? You're his wife, not his mother.

CYNTHIA: I failed him.

BUD: He failed you. That's the only failure, .and Ziggy
knows it. That's why he's sorry, and that's why
he should be ashamed. He betrayed you.

ZIGGY: You did tell her, Nod. You told her about the
others.

NOD: I didn't tell her anything, Ziggy. Wait. Wait and
let them finish the scene.

ZIGGY: You betrayed me.

NOD: Not in what I told her about you. Wait.

CYNTHIA: Shall we go ahead, Mr. Nod?

NOD: Go ahead, please.

CYNTHIA: (In character of Faith.) No, Nod, he didn't
betray me. Not on purpose. He's like a boy who's
been stealing apples. But I have done all the real
betraying. For a long time now, I have... I don't
know how to say this easily... I have not been a
wife to Ziggy. Oh, there's been no open break! I
smiled when he came home, reminded him to wear
an extra coat. But inside... deep inside... I've
not been faithful. I could have understood if he had
come to me, telling me that he was leaving me because I had been unfaithful. It's just my pride--that
woman! I didn't know I had any pride left.

NOD: Stop it, Faith. Your pride is hurt, and it should
be hurt. Ziggy has done wrong, and when he comes
back. . . .

CYNTHIA: If he comes back?

NOD: He'll come back if I have to drag him by the scuff
of his neck.

CYNTHIA: I don't want him back that way. I don't know
if I want him back at all.

NOD: I thought... I thought you had already forgiven him.

CYNTHIA: If there is anything to forgive, I forgive. But
living with him again, I don't know. Even before
this... even before my pride was hurt... I had
thought... I had wondered if I shouldn't go away.
For good.

BUD: Forgive me for asking this, Faith. Is there someone else?

CYNTHIA: For me?

BUD: I'm sorry, Faith. I had no business asking such a
question. Of course, there could never be anyone
else.

CYNTHIA: Oh, are you so sure?

BUD: There never was and there never could be. I know
that.

CYNTHIA: There has never been anyone else, Nod. Not
in the sense that you mean. But maybe there could
be. Why not?

BUD: Do you mean that, Faith?

CYNTHIA: At this moment, I feel nothing for Ziggy. Not
even fondness, and I always felt that before. A
woman needs to have someone for whom she has
feeling. Some feeling of some kind.

BUD: I shouldn't speak. I shouldn't say this. But... Faith, could you ever have any... feeling for me?

CYNTHIA: For you, Nod?

BUD: I'm sorry I asked that. I just had to.

CYNTHIA: Do you feel sorry for me, Nod? That sorry?
Or is it Ziggy? Do you think that you have to make
up for all Ziggy's mistakes. You may have passed
him through college, but you can't pass him through
marriage. That he has to do for himself.

BUD: This has got nothing to do with Ziggy. I love you,
Faith. I've always loved you.

CYNTHIA: And did you love me the day you told me to
marry Ziggy?

BUD: That day most of all.

CYNTHIA: You have a strange way of showing love.

BUD: He was my friend. What could I do?

CYNTHIA: And now he is no longer your friend?

BUD: I'm sorry, Faith. I'm sorry. I should have known
that you still love... that you could only love.... I
should never have said this. I should never have...
Please, forgive me.

CYNTHIA: Nod, I don't know what to say. Everything is
coming out differently from what I intend.

BUD: You don't need to say anything. And I've said too
much. But... if you... I'll never speak this way
again. (Starts off.)

CYNTHIA: Nod, please, I do want to say something.

BUD: You don't need to say anything. I'll find Ziggy.
I'll bring him back. I'll bring him back because
he wants to come back.

CYNTHIA: Wait, Nod, wait....
(Bud steps off the platform and moves a few steps
downstage, almost as if to address the audience.
Cynthia stands with her hands reaching out.)

BUD: (In the style of Tom Wingfield of "The Glass
Menagerie". I didn't wait. I didn't go back. I
didn't listen. For the next twenty-four hours, I
didn't sleep or even think. And I found Ziggy. I
didn't tell him what I had done, and I guess Faith
never did either. For over fifty years, I haven't
told anyone. Night after night, we sat together...
talking, playing cards, just the three of us together.
Went for rides together. Grew old together. She
never mentioned that night again. But I knew. I
had betrayed my best friend, my only friend. And
... you'll understand this Ziggy, now... I betrayed
the woman I loved. I betrayed her at the moment
when she most needed someone she could trust.

Faith may have forgiven Ziggy.   I think she did.
But I know that she died without forgiving me.   And
now, Ziggy knows.   Now, he knows what I did.
(Bud walks back over and sits down on the platform:
Cynthia sits down next to him.   There is silence
for a moment.)

FRANCINE: Well! Now this is something.

BURLINGTON: Turn on the stage lights, will you, Clarence?

CLARENCE: (Rising and going off-stage, down left.)   Sure,
Mr. Burlington, I sure will.   (Exit Clarence.)

TOM: Well, what do we do now? I knew I should have
stayed home tonight.   I'm getting too old for this
business.   It's all a lot of crap.

BURLINGTON: Well. Well, now.   This does come as a
little bit of a surprise.   This wasn't in the original
synopsis.   We should stick to the synopsis.   I've
always said that.

FRANCINE: (Moving downstage and stepping up on platform
No. 2.)   I'm not surprised.   I suspected it right
from the start.   I told you that first scene wasn't
right.   I just knew it couldn't have happened that
way.

GEORGE: Come on, Francine, you didn't even suspect
Nod.   It was Faith's part that bothered you.

FRANCINE: I knew something was wrong.   I just sensed it.
(The stage lights come on.)

ZIGGY: You betrayed me, Nod.   You betrayed me.   All
these years, I've been feeling guilty, blaming myself.
And you--you're the real Judas.   (He rises and
starts out of the wheelchair.)

NOD: Please, Ziggy, sit down.   You'll fall.   (He starts
toward him.)

ZIGGY: Stay away from me, and keep your hands off me.
I don't need this chair, and I don't need you.   For
ninety years, you've been my friend.   But no more.
No more.   You betrayed me.   You tried to run away
with my wife.   My Faith.   I spit you out.

NOD: Please, Ziggy, sit down.   You'll tire yourself.

ZIGGY: I'll never be tired again.   A man can't be tired
in this god-damned world.   He can't.   His friend
will wait until he sleeps and then rob him.   I spit
you out, Nod.

NOD: Please, Ziggy, let me take you home.   We can talk
there.   It will be warm and we can talk.   Now that
you know, we can talk, talk the way we did before....

ZIGGY: You're not coming home with me.   I'm never going to see you again, Nod.   You betrayed me.   I

trusted you and you betrayed me. (Starts upstage
right off.)   I'm going to leave here now.   Alone.
You try to follow me and I'll kill you.

NOD: Wait, Ziggy.   Wait.

ZIGGY: You come near me, and I'll kill.   I'll do what I
should have done sixty years ago.

TOM: Wait a minute, Mr. Ziggy.   If you want to go home,
I'll take you home.

ZIGGY: I don't want any of you to come near me.   You're
all friends of his.   I don't trust any of you.   You
just brought me here tonight to laugh at me, to make
fun of me, to spit on me.

TOM: No, we didn't know anything about this, Mr. Ziggy.

ZIGGY: Stay away from me.   I spit you out.   All of you.
You hate me, Nod, you hate me because you couldn't
take Faith away from me.   She loved me.   Only me.
You remember that, you son-of-a-bitch.   (Starts out,
upstage left.)

CYNTHIA: Would you like me to take you home, Mr. Ziggy?

ZIGGY: I don't want anything to do with any of you.   And
you don't even look like Faith.   You never did, and
you never will.   Even if you live to be ninety-five.
Only the good live long.   You may live to be ninety-
four like Nod, but you won't live to be ninety-five
like me.   You haven't got the stuff in you.
(Ziggy exits through upstage entrance, and the others
now move upstage right to follow him, except Nod
who moves downstage and sits down.)

FRANCINE: Someone go after him.   The old fool will hurt
himself.

NOD: Let him go.   Let him go!   He needs to be alone for
a bit.   He'll be all right, and he'll come back.
He'll come back after a bit.   I've got the key.   The
key to the apartment.   He won't go without the key.

TOM: He may hurt himself out there all alone.

GEORGE: He may kill himself.   And if he takes that car,
he will surely kill someone else.

NOD: (Muttering.)   Let him go.   Let him go.   He needs
to be alone.

TOM: If he's killed out there, he'll be alone.

NOD: No.   No, then he won't be alone.   She'll be waiting
for him, just as she's always waited for him.

BURLINGTON: Nod, we're going to have to go after him.
Something serious might happen to him.

NOD: Something serious has happened to him.   Last week
he was ninety-five.   Do you know what that means?
There's no juice left at ninety-five.   We're old

banana peels, both of us, empty, brown, spotted,
and still a little slimy.   What can happen to a banana peel?   (Laughs.)   Sometimes, at night, I think
about all the times I worried about something going
to happen to me.   There was a war in Cuba, and I
worried and worried and finally decided I couldn't
worry any more.   So I made up my mind to go, and
then it was over before I could even go down to en-
list.   You worry a lot in a long lifetime.   The war
in Europe and poison gas.   And the flu epidemic.
And the bonus marchers.   And the reds.   And the
black shirts.   And Hitler.   Ziggy and I worried a
lot about Hitler.   And the big bomb.   Faith worried
about that, because of the children, you know. Everyone was going to be the one that got me.   I don't
need to worry about what's going to get me.   I'm
already got.   I'm alive, and nothing is worse than
that.   (Rises suddenly.)   I've got to go to the bathroom.   (He hurries off, downstage left.)

CYNTHIA: Well, somebody had better go with Nod.
GEORGE: Stop giving orders.   If you want to go with him,
    go.   The old boy may have more juice than we think.
CYNTHIA: You're a dirty old man.
TOM: I'll go and take car of Nod.   But somebody had better
    find Ziggy.   (Tom exits down left after Nod.)
FRANCINE: Well, if none of you men care, I do.   I'll go.
GEORGE: I'll go with you, Francine.   He can't have gotten
    far by this time.
FRANCINE: Let's try the back street first.   Then we can
    double back and look in the theater.   He's probably
    still on the steps.   (Exit Francine and George up
    right.)
BURLINGTON: There's not much chance, but I'll go check
    up front.   Clarence, turn on the house lights, will
    you.   He might just wander into the front and fall
    asleep.
CLARENCE: Okay, Mr. Burlington.   I'll get the lights.
    I don't like the idea that maybe that old character
    is out there staring at us.   It makes me uncomfort-
    able.   (He speaks as he exits downstage left.)
BURLINGTON: God, I hate this.   I hate mess.   I hate not
    knowing what's going on.   It's just a mess.   A fine
    director of life I am.
CYNTHIA: It's not your fault, Mr. Burlington.   I guess
    Bud and I should have told you about that scene, but
    Mr. Nod asked us to keep it a secret.
BUD: I'm sorry, too.

BURLINGTON: Forget it. I'd probably have gone along
    with it. It's not just tonight. It's the whole busi-
    ness. I'm beginning to have some doubt about this
    Life Theatre idea. Real life may be just too rotten
    to put on stage. Nobody ought to parade in front
    of a mirror in the altogether. Some things are
    better left in the dark. (All the stage lights go out
    and the theater is in darkness.) Damn it, Clarence.
    Turn on the lights.
CLARENCE: Sorry. I made a mistake. (The house lights
    now come on, but the stage lights are still off.)
BURLINGTON: Clarence, turn on the....(To Bud and
    Cynthia.) What's the use. We don't need the stage
    lights anyway. (Starts down off-stage into the audi-
    ence.) I'll go around front, in case he went that
    way. You kids might look around in the scenery
    shop. (Burlington goes down the aisle and disappears
    into the front of the theater. Bud and Cynthia watch
    him for a moment.)
BUD: I don't think we can do much good. He would never
    make it back to the scenery shop.
CYNTHIA: We'd better look anyway.
BUD: It's dark back there.
CYNTHIA: We can turn on the lights.
BUD: I guess so.
    (The two go off-stage, down right. The stage is
    empty for a moment, then Ziggy comes on dragging
    a blanket after him. He pauses under the "Miss
    America" sign, looks about carefully, then pushes
    the wheel chair upstage left, sits in it, and covers
    himself completely with the blanket. This should
    be almost a clown routine. Then Clarence comes
    on stage, talking loudly as he comes.)
CLARENCE: What do you say to a little music? It will
    cheer us all up. (Looks around.) Everybody's
    gone. And I'm hungry. Maybe it's intermission.
    I think I'll find something to eat. (He exits down-
    stage left. The music starts, and

END OF ACT II

During the intermission between Acts II and III, the curtains
remain open and Ziggy remains onstage in the wheelchair.
Tom walks from downstage left to downstage right and returns once during intermission, and occasionally, Ziggy
comes up for air from under his blanket. Music plays
throughout the intermission, and at the end of the inter-

mission, the music will go out of control--sounding like a warning signal. At that point, Act III will begin.

ACT THREE

WHEN THE MUSIC BECOMES A WARNING, Ziggy jumps up, looks around the stage, then goes to the director's table and takes paper and pencil. He shakes his head several times at the sound, starts off left to stop the record, hears Clarence off-stage, and then races back to his wheelchair, and covers himself with the blanket.

CLARENCE: (Off-stage.) Who's playing our song? Never mind. Never mind. I'll get it. (The music stops and a minute later, Clarence comes on stage, talking.) You know, I'm not the only person here. Someone else can take care of things once in a-while, too. (Looks about.) I am the only person here. God, it's lonely.
(He exits off down left. The house lights flick on and off several times and then come on again. Clarence comes back on stage and looks out at the audience, and then goes off-stage down left. Ziggy comes up for air and starts writing on the pad. Cynthia and Bud come on-stage, down right; and Ziggy again covers himself with a blanket.)

BUD: You, know, I really couldn't care less where that crazy Ziggy has gone.

CYNTHIA: Oh, he's all right. He's just old.

BUD: All decent people are in their graves at his age. Why would a normal, decent, fun-loving man want to live after ninety? It's obscene.

CYNTHIA: (Sits down, on the downstage end of Platform No. 2.) It's kind of spooky here. Sit down with me, Bud.
(The lights go out, leaving the theater in darkness.)

BUD: Cut that out, Cynthia. I'm not that kind of boy.

CYNTHIA: Turn on the lights, Clarence.

CLARENCE: (Off.) Sorry!
(The spot over Platform No. 2 comes on, spotlighting Cynthia and leaving Ziggy completely in the shadows. He peeks out for a moment and then covers himself with his blanket again.)

BUD: How did you know it was Clarence?

CYNTHIA: It figured.... And what do you mean you're not that kind of boy? You've been around these dirty old men here tonight for so long, you're even beginning to think like them.

BUD: I wasn't even thinking about that.   It was just a joke, for God's sake.

CLARENCE: (Coming on from down left.) Did someone call me?

CYNTHIA: I trust you heard joke and not God, Clarence.

CLARENCE: Where is everybody?

CYNTHIA: That's a stupid question to ask anybody.

BUD: I guess they are all looking for Ziggy.

CLARENCE: Nod's in back. In the men's room. I think he's sick.

BUD: I think this whole night has been sick.

CYNTHIA: It's this Life Theatre that is really sick. You know, for a moment tonight I was beginning to think this might be a good idea. But now I wish we were back doing regular plays again.

CLARENCE: I guess I'd better go back and see how old Nod's feeling. (Starts off.) I'm hungry. There should be something back there to eat. Maybe an old stale sandwich if the cockroaches leave anything. (Clarence exits down left.)

CYNTHIA: I really mean it. I wish that we could go back to doing regular plays.

BUD: Yeah, anything would be better than this.

CYNTHIA: Even high school plays. Bud, do you remember that play we did in high school?

BUD: I remember it.

CYNTHIA: That was the first time I ever noticed you, really noticed you, I mean.

BUD: Yeah, me, too.

CYNTHIA: Did you notice me then, Bud?

BUD: I had to. You gave me the measles, remember?

CYNTHIA: Oh, Bud, I'm serious.

BUD: I'm worried. I'm joking. I'm joking. My father told me to say that anytime a girl said she was serious. But I do remember the play. "The Moon's Up There."

CYNTHIA: That's the one. Who wrote it, do you remember?

BUD: It was one of those things nobody writes. It was non-royalty.

CYNTHIA: Yeah, I remember. I had hoped that Thornton Wilder had written it. Or Tennessee Williams. I know Albee didn't. He doesn't believe in moons. It was non-royalty. Albee doesn't write non-royalty plays.

CYNTHIA: I guess it wasn't very good.

BUD: I guess not.

CYNTHIA: I liked it.

BUD: It was all right, I guess.

CYNTHIA: Do you remember that part where I'm sitting on a bench, trying to climb aboard the rocket to get away.

BUD: And I go up to you and start talking.

CYNTHIA: And I thought you were trying to keep me from going.

BUD: And all the time I was trying to sneak aboard myself.

CYNTHIA: (Now in character of Joan in the play, rises, and walks down and looks out at audience.) That's it, isn't it?

BUD: (Sitting down on platform, watching her.) Yes, that's the moon rocket.

CYNTHIA: It looks very clean.

BUD: Oh, yes, I'm sure it is.

CYNTHIA: And it is going to the moon tomorrow?

BUD: No one has said, but I think so.

CYNTHIA: Well... well, I don't want to keep you.

BUD: I wasn't going any place. But don't stay on my account.

CYNTHIA: (Turning back toward him.) You're just going to stay here?

BUD: Why, yes. I'm just going to stay here.

CYNTHIA: But why?

BUD: I just want to, that's all.

CYNTHIA: Are you going to stay here long?

BUD: Oh, I don't know. Quite a while, I think. Does it bother you that I'm staying here?

CYNTHIA: No, no, of course not. It's none of my business if you want to act like a fool and just sit there.

BUD: I don't see why you have to insult me. If it's so foolish, what are you doing here?

CYNTHIA: I just have something to do that's all. (She sits down on the end of the platform.) I can stay here just as long as you can. (Pause.) I don't see why you don't go home. Somebody is probably waiting for you.

BUD: (Sitting down a little distance from her.) Waiting for me? That's a laugh. Nobody even knows I have a home. I work all day at the shoe store. Then I go to my room. Nobody's there. I just sit and write poetry.

CYNTHIA: (Turning toward him and moving a little closer.) Are you a poet?

BUD: As a matter of fact, I am. Although I guess I

should say, as a matter of fancy.
CYNTHIA: Oh? I've never known a poet before. (She
    now moves so close they are almost touching.) I
    read poetry.
BUD: Longfellow, I guess.
CYNTHIA: I like... well, somebody like Yeats.
BUD: (Looking into her face.) Oh?
CYNTHIA: Yes, you know.... "Suddenly I saw the cold and
    look-delighting heaven..."
BUD: "That seems as though ice burned and was but the
    more ice ... " My name's John.
CYNTHIA: I'm Joan.
    (Burlington has started down the darkened aisle of
    the theater, and now he shouts at them from the
    dark.)
BURLINGTON: Hey, you two, cut out that necking!
BUD: (Jumping up.) Who's necking?
CYNTHIA: (Rising.) Who's that?
BUD: (Peering out.) Oh, it's Mr. Burlington.
CYNTHIA: Have you found Mr. Ziggy?
BURLINGTON: (Climbing up on the stage.) He's nowhere
    around front. I looked everywhere, even in the
    trees. God, old men are worse than children.
CYNTHIA: He's kind of sweet, in a way.
BURLINGTON: He's rich anyway. Go back to your neck-
    ing. My congratulations were premature. (Goes
    back over to table.)
CYNTHIA: We weren't necking. We were doing a scene
    from an old high school play.
BURLINGTON: Who took my damned pencil?
BUD: We really weren't necking, Mr. Burlington. We
    were just trying to remember a scene we did in a
    high school play.
BURLINGTON: I said my congratulations were premature.
    Why the hell aren't you out looking for Ziggy?
CYNTHIA: We did look. We looked all over.
BUD: He must have gone home.
BURLINGTON: Where is everybody?
CYNTHIA: I still think that's a stupid question.
BUD: Clarence and Mr. Dogget are with Nod.
    (George and Francine enter from upstage right.)
GEORGE: Is he back yet?
BURLINGTON: Hell, no. He's disappeared.
BUD: I can't figure out any place he could have gone.
FRANCINE: (Going up to platform and sitting on davenport.)
    Well, I know where he can go. I work all day at a
    damned dull job, and then for leisure-time activity I

spend my nights streetwalking for an old man.   God, what I haven't done for Real Life Theatre here in Centerville.

GEORGE: I should say so.

FRANCINE: George, just once before you die, would you try to resist saying the obvious?   Just once, George, for me?

GEORGE: (Seriously.)   I may, Francine, just once.   Just for you.

FRANCINE: I'm only joking, George.

GEORGE: I know.   I should be laughing.

FRANCINE: Now, George, don't be that way.

BURLINGTON: We just can't stand around here doing nothing.   We've got to find Ziggy.

FRANCINE: Why?   The play was over anyway.

BURLINGTON: That old man is ninety-five years old, Francine.   We can't just let him roam the streets alone.

FRANCINE: I feel ninety-five, and you let me roam the streets alone.   And it's a lot safer for a ninety-five-year-old man on the street at night than it is for me.   At least, it used to be.

GEORGE: It depends on how dark the streets are, Francine.

BUD: George was with you, wasn't he?

FRANCINE: That's what I said.

CYNTHIA: We ought to call the police, that's what we ought to do.

BUD: Yeah, I guess that's what we ought to do.

BURLINGTON: I guess so.   But maybe we'd better tell Nod first.
    (Enter Nod, Tom, and Clarence from up-center.)

NOD: Don't tell Nod anything.   I'll use it against you.   I'll betray you.   If not this year, next, or seventy years from now.

CLARENCE: Seventy years from now, I'll be dead.

NOD: Don't count on it, Son.   You may not be that lucky.

GEORGE: (Rises, takes a chair across stage, and gives it to Nod.)   Anyway, Nod, one betrayal a century seems modest enough.   Stop worrying about it.

NOD: (Sitting.)   Thank you.   Thank you, I am tired.

GEORGE: It's been a tiring night.   But stop worrying.

NOD: I do worry.   I worry all the time.   It's not an easy thing to betray a friend with his wife.

TOM: You can't really say it that way, Nod.   She didn't do anything.   I mean there was no....

NOD: I did.   I did.   I did the worst thing a man can do to a friend.

TOM: Ziggy wasn't exactly Mr. Clean himself. Chasing around with your secretary, among others, wasn't he?

NOD: It's not the same.

GEORGE: Why not? Why not? Why isn't it the same?

NOD: She wasn't my wife. She wasn't even a good secretary. Faith was a good wife. She was a wonderful wife, a perfect wife. One wouldn't even want to think such things about Faith. It was different.

TOM: You really do feel bad, don't you, Nod?

NOD: I thought of killing myself. I thought about it a lot--then... a long time ago. And then I thought about it again tonight. It's not that I'd mind dying.

GEORGE: Well, don't kill yourself yet. Wait a week, at least. It won't kill you to wait a week, will it?

FRANCINE: George, do you have to rob the best lines from every play you've ever seen? Honestly, I don't know what a man with your thieving principles is doing with the Life Players.

GEORGE: That's what life is about, Dear Francine. Thieving. Didn't you know?

BURLINGTON: Nod, we want to call the police. To find Ziggy.

NOD: Don't. Not yet at least.

BURLINGTON: We're going to have to do something soon.

NOD: It would shame him, and he's already been shamed enough tonight.

BURLINGTON: We've got to do something.

NOD: We can wait, that's something. He'll be back.

BURLINGTON: All right. We'll wait another half hour, but that's all. If he hasn't returned then, we call the police.

FRANCINE: Is there any coffee left?

CLARENCE: No coffee, no food, nothing.

GEORGE: What are we going to do for a half hour? Just sit and contemplate our navels?

CYNTHIA: Bud and I were doing a scene from a play--a regular play. Would you like us to do it for you?

TOM: No.

GEORGE: Hell no.

FRANCINE: No, thank you.

BURLINGTON: I guess not, kids.

TOM: If we had some cards, we could play a little bridge.

GEORGE: If we had a bridge, we could cross over Jordan.

TOM: It was just a suggestion, George.

CLARENCE: Why don't we do some more of Ziggy's story? That's what we oame here for.

BURLINGTON: There isn't any more.

CYNTHIA: There must be something.   They're still alive.

BURLINGTON: I was going to do one more scene, "The
   Golden Sunset."   Seems stupid to do that now.

NOD: It wasn't stupid.   There were some good years there
   later.   For Ziggy, for Faith, and--for me.   In a
   long life, you pay for mistakes, but not every minute,
   not every day.   There were some good times,
   especially in the last years.   Lots of them.   Every
   evening after I had my supper, I would walk down
   Pine Street, stop at the store and get some candy
   or flowers and sometimes cigars.   Ziggy loved
   cigars then.   He doesn't smoke now that Faith is
   dead.   Then I would go to their apartment.   The
   card table would be set up, and we would play
   rummy--just the three of us.   Then at ten o'clock,
   we'd have some cheese and crackers and coffee.
   And then a glass of brandy.   It was almost like a
   service in church, always the same and yet always
   a little different.   I would lift the glass of brandy
   (As though drinking a toast.) and drink to them,
   "To Our Best Friend."   Then Faith would drink to
   Ziggy, "To the Only Man I've Ever Loved."   (Pause.)
   She was very gentle about it, almost as if she were
   talking to herself.   She didn't look at Ziggy and she
   didn't look at me.   It was a funny feeling, and I
   guess Ziggy wondered about it.   He might even have
   thought she was chiding him for his unfaithfulness,
   but she wasn't.   She was reminding me that I must
   never think of her... think of her as I did that
   night.

TOM: You're probably reading too much into it, Nod.
   People don't mean much.

NOD: No, it was there.   You could tell.   But do you know
   something?   I pretended to myself that she was
   drinking to me, that I was Ziggy.

BURLINGTON: Did anything happen in those years, anything
   like the proposal or the betrayal.   Maybe we could
   do one more scene, just while we're waiting.

NOD: Nothing ever happened.   Nothing you could put in a
   play.   It was all quiet--like the background for those
   old paintings--like the pauses between pieces at a
   concert.   Quiet, satisfying, enough.   (Pause.) Ziggy
   misses her very much.   It was after her death--even
   before the funeral--that he took to his bed.   Then
   months later, I got him to try the wheelchair.   But
   he doesn't need it.   You saw tonight.   There's noth-

ing wrong with his body. He can walk when he
wants to. As well as I can. But when Faith died,
he didn't want anything anymore. He doesn't even
care when I cheat at cards. I just do it to try and
make him care. It's better when he's complaining.

TOM: You've moved in with him, haven't you, Nod?

NOD: I had to take care of him. He doesn't have anyone
else. It might have been different if there had been
children. If the baby had lived, he would be a man.
Then, maybe, he wouldn't. He'd be seventy years
old, if he had lived. That's pretty old for your
generation. I never see anyone in your generation
that lives to be our age.

BURLINGTON: Yes, that might have made a difference.
A child, I mean. That's all there is then? The
story has been told?

NOD: It's all told. It's all through.

ZIGGY: (Throwing off the blanket and wheeling the chair
into the action.) You lie, Nod. And you're a fool.
There's one scene left, and I'm the only one who
knows about it. (Waving a paper in his hand.)
I've gotten it all written down. . . .

BURLINGTON: Where the devil have you been? (To Clarence.) Clarence, go turn some more light on.

FRANCINE: We've been looking all over for you.

CYNTHIA: He must have been back there all the time,
hiding?

ZIGGY: I wasn't hiding. I was just sitting there, minding
my own business, when you too were necking.

BUD: We weren't necking.
(Spot over No. 2 comes on.)

ZIGGY: Damned fool. Why not? What are you going to
do, wait until you're my age before you nibble a
little of that? It won't do. Your dentures will slip
when you try, and sex ain't worth a damn when your
dentures are slipping.

CYNTHIA: You're disgusting. You're a nasty vile old man.

ZIGGY: All old men are nasty. Most of us are just too
damned tired to do anything about it. You've got
to be nasty to live as long as I have. Last week,
I was ninety-five.

TOM: Nod, shall we help you get him home?

ZIGGY: Might not go home. Might just take off and go
to Chicago and see Kitty. That was her name--Kitty.
You didn't know that, did you?

NOD: She'll be dead by this time, Ziggy.

ZIGGY: Did you kill her?

NOD: No, I didn't kill her. She's just dead.

ZIGGY: Wouldn't surprise me if you killed her.

CLARENCE: (Comes on eating a banana.) There was one left.

ZIGGY: He even looks like a monkey.

NOD: Ziggy, let's go home. Kitty's dead. Chicago's blown away.

ZIGGY: I don't believe you. And I'm not going home. There are other towns than Chicago and other girls than Kitty. I'll find them, and I don't need you.

GEORGE: This is the hero of "The Golden Years?" Chee, if this is real life, Ethel is a natural blonde.

NOD: (Rising.) We're going home, Ziggy. I want you to come with me. When we get there, we'll talk. If you want me to leave then, I'll leave. But first let's go home.

ZIGGY: I like it here.

NOD: We don't belong here.

ZIGGY: They asked me to come here and tell my story.

NOD: We have nothing more to tell them.

ZIGGY: A lot you know. A lot you all know. I've got another scene. (Waves paper.) I've got it all written down here, and it makes fools of you all. Not me. You. All of you. But I'm not going to let you see it. I'm going to keep it just for me, and when I die, I'm going to burn it.

CYNTHIA: If you take it with you when you die, it'll burn. You're a terrible old man.

ZIGGY: (Looking at Cynthia.) You know, Nod, she reminds me of that secretary you had. I'm sorry she wasn't a good secretary. She wasn't good for anything else. This girl reminds me of her.

CYNTHIA: (Rising.) I don't know about anyone else. But I'm leaving. I'm tired of nasty old men. (To Burlington.) It's been an interesting evening, Mr. Burlington. If you want me to come back again for some other performance, just call.

BURLINGTON: All right, Cynthia. Perhaps you had better run along. We'll all be leaving soon.

CYNTHIA: You will call me again? For something different?

BURLINGTON: If we keep the Life Players going, I'll call you.

CYNTHIA: Thank you. I don't want to be a poor sport, but.... (Starts off right.)

ZIGGY: (To Cynthia.) Better stay, young lady. I might decide to tell all, and if you leave, you'll never know. Everyone else will know, and you won't.

CYNTHIA: I'd rather not know anymore about you. (To
Bud.) Would you like to take me home, Bud?

BUD: (Rising and going to her.) Sure, Cynthia, I'd be
glad to. (Starts off right.) Mr. Burlington, if
you do find out any more, tell me later, will you?

ZIGGY: You'd better stay too. If you go, you'll never
find out what I have on this paper. You'd better
stay, Boy. You'd better stay.

CYNTHIA: Are you coming, Bud?

BUD: Yeah, I guess I'd better. (He follows her almost
off, right, but looking back.)

TOM: So long, Bud.

BUD: Good night, Mr. Dogget. Good night, Mr. Burlington. Good night, Mrs. Eggers. Good night, Mr.
Bellows. Good night, Mr. Nod. (Pauses.) If I
had anything to do with hurting your feelings, I'm
sorry, Mr. Ziggy.

ZIGGY: Don't worry about my feelings, Boy. And don't
worry about her feelings either. Old men and
young wenches don't have feelings.

BUD: (Shaking his head.) You really are something.
Clarence, are you coming with us?

CLARENCE: Yeah, I guess so. If that's what you want.
(Crosses down right.) Good night, everyone.

FRANCINE: Good night, Clarence.

GEORGE: Good grief. The god-damned movie is starting
over.

TOM: Good grief is right.
(Cynthia, Bud, and Clarence exit.)

ZIGGY: (Yelling after them.) You're going to be sorry
you missed this. You'll never know what happened.

TOM: For which they should thank God. Look, let's get
finished here so I can get. I'd like to watch the
late news.

ZIGGY: The news is never late. It's always too soon and
it's always a lie anyway.

TOM: Maybe so, but I like lies.

ZIGGY: It will be bad news.

TOM: It would be good news for me, Ziggy, if you'd stop
all this bull so we can go home.

BURLINGTON: Take it easy, Tom. We asked him to come
here.

ZIGGY: That's right, you did. And if you want to know my
real story, you've got to see what's on this paper.
You'd better be nice to me.

BURLINGTON: All right, Ziggy. We'll be glad to listen

to you. But hurry up.

ZIGGY: No. I'm not going to tell anyone.

GEORGE: (Rising.) Well, that's it. I've had it. I'm
    going.

ZIGGY: I don't want to tell you about it. I want you to
    act it out--like you did the other stuff.

TOM: Hell no.

ZIGGY: Why not? You acted out the lies, why not the
    truth?

BURLINGTON: Ziggy, we're all tired now.

ZIGGY: You won't be when you see this.

FRANCINE: We might as well do what he says. What
    have we got to lose?

TOM: The last of my sanity, that's what.

ZIGGY: (Wheeling his chair to Francine.) Mrs. Eggers,
    I want to give this to you. (Hands her paper.) I
    want you to be the one to do this scene. You're
    the only one here who hasn't been mean to me.

FRANCINE: All right, Ziggy, I'll try. I'm not sure that
    I can even read this without my glasses.

ZIGGY: I write very neatly. And I can spell, too. Nod
    can't spell worth a damn. Never could.

FRANCINE: (Walks upstage to Platform No. 2 reading
    paper.) All right, I'll try. But my feet are tired.

GEORGE: (Sitting again.) I wish we had some coffee.

TOM: I wish I were home.

ZIGGY: It's a death scene. That's always good in a play,
    isn't it.

BURLINGTON: Ziggy, it's not that we aren't interested.
    It's just that we are tired. We wouldn't do it
    justice.

TOM: You'd want us to do your life justice, wouldn't you
    Ziggy?

ZIGGY: I don't give a damn about justice. I want you to
    know the truth. It's about the night Faith died. It's
    very important.

BURLINGTON: It must have been very sad, Ziggy, we
    know. And if you had told us about it at first....

GEORGE: I hate death scenes, especially with women.
    Women are such hams.

FRANCINE: I think we ought to do the scene.

TOM: God damn it, why?

FRANCINE: Tom, put the spot on here, will you?

TOM: Hell... all right. But then I'm leaving. (He goes
    off up center.)

GEORGE: Now, wait a minute, Francine, I'm not going to
    be in any more damned life scenes. Just count me

out.
FRANCINE: I don't want you to, George. (To Ziggy.)
You were alone with Faith when it happened, Ziggy?
Nod wasn't there? Is that right?
ZIGGY: Just the two of us.
FRANCINE: Jack, will you take Ziggy's role? (The spot
on No. 2 comes on.)
BURLINGTON: It's getting awfully late, and I'm tired.
It's not easy directing a bunch....
FRANCINE: It will only take a few minutes. It's a short
scene.
BURLINGTON: All right. Anything to get this night over.
(Goes up on Platform No. 2 with Francine.) Now,
what am I supposed to do?
FRANCINE: (Handing him the paper.) Just read this.
(She goes to davenport.) I'll use this for the death-
bed. (Spot on No. 1 goes out.)
ZIGGY: She wasn't in bed when she died. She was sitting
up. In a chair. Straight up. She didn't even fall
when she died. She just sat there, looking at me.
GEORGE: (Putting chair on platform.) Here's your death
chair, Francine.
(Tom enters and stands downstage left.)
NOD: (Starts to rise.) I'm going to go. I don't want to
see this scene, and I don't have to look at it. It's
got nothing to do with me.
ZIGGY: You stay. You weren't there when she died. You
should have been there, and you weren't. You were
there every night when she lived. You should have
been there when she died. So now you stay.
(Nod sits down.)
BURLINGTON: (As announcer.) Last Scene! "The Death
of Faith." As we know, it hasn't been quite a year
since Faith died--one night, early in the evening.
Nod was out of town. Ziggy was with her. (Burlington sits in role of Ziggy.) It was a quiet, calm
evening, just like any of the 2,000 other calm, quiet
evenings we had spent together. Except that Nod
wasn't there. I should have known something would
happen when Nod wasn't there. I didn't. Faith's
death came as a surprise. When you're young, you
expect the old to die. It's never a surprise. It's
not that way for the old. Faith's death surprised
me, and I guess it surprised Nod, too. But it
didn't surprise Faith.
FRANCINE: Ziggy, I'm going to die.
BURLINGTON: Suppose you will one day. We all go, thank

God.

FRANCINE: I'm going to die now.

BURLINGTON: Right this minute?

FRANCINE: Maybe not this minute.   But the next or the
next.   Not more than ten.

BURLINGTON: You're up to something, Faith.

FRANCINE: No, Ziggy, I'm not up to anything.   I'm down
to dying, and I want to tell you something.

BURLINGTON: You're just pouting.   You're just talking.
You've got your nose out of joint because Nod didn't
send flowers tonight.

FRANCINE: Nod should have sent flowers tonight, that's
true.   More tonight than any night.

NOD: I left an order for flowers.   They didn't arrive
until after she was dead.   But I sent them.

BURLINGTON: Nod should have sent you flowers.   A man
has no business sending a woman flowers for fifty
years and then forgetting.   It's fickle.   I'll tell
him about it tomorrow.

FRANCINE: No, Ziggy, I don't want you to.   I don't want
you to say anything to him about it at all, and I
don't want you to make fun of him anymore.   You
understand me, Ziggy.   I want you to stop abusing
Nod.

BURLINGTON: I don't abuse him.   He's my friend.

FRANCINE: You do.   He's been your friend, but you
haven't been his.   You've used him.   And I want
you to stop.   You promise me, Ziggy.

BURLINGTON: If you'll stop this talk about dying, I'll
promise.

FRANCINE: I won't talk about it anymore, Ziggy.

BURLINGTON: And you won't die.

FRANCINE: I've got to do that, Ziggy.   I've just go to.

BURLINGTON: Faith, I don't like your playing jokes like
this.

FRANCINE: I've never played jokes on you, Ziggy.   And,
except for one thing, I've never lied to you.

BURLINGTON: I don't want to hear anymore.

FRANCINE: You listen to me, Ziggy.   You listen to me
now.

BURLINGTON: I'm listening.

FRANCINE: And hear me, Ziggy.   Hear me.

BURLINGTON: I hear you, Faith.

FRANCINE: I never loved but one man in my life.

BURLINGTON: I know it, Faith.   I know it.   And I never
loved but one woman.   Faith, we don't have to say
these things to each other.   Why have we lived to-

gether all these years except to tell each other that?
FRANCINE: And that man--the only man I loved--I love--
   is Nod.
BURLINGTON: (<u>Rising.</u>)   Nod?
FRANCINE: You owe me something, Ziggy.   You owe me
   for the years I didn't tell you, for the years I didn't
   tell Nod.   You owe me for my hurt, for Nod's
   sorrow, for your pride.   You owe us, Ziggy.
BURLINGTON: Why are you saying this to me, Faith?
   What have I ever done to you?
FRANCINE: I'm not trying to hurt you, Ziggy.   I just want
   you to give Nod a message for me.
BURLINGTON: I'll be damned if I will.   Faith, you don't
   know what you're saying.   (<u>Faith curls into her soul</u>
   <u>and dies without changing position.</u>)   Faith.   Faith,
   listen to me.   What the hell are you trying to do to
   me?   What have I got now if all our life together
   was a lie?   Faith.   Faith.   (<u>Then turns to audience,</u>
   <u>in character of Burlington.</u>)   <u>Faith was dead.</u>
NOD: (<u>Rising, turning on Ziggy.</u>)   You knew this?   You
   knew this and for a whole year you haven't said a
   word?
ZIGGY: I was going to tell you.   Sometime.
NOD: When?   When were you going to tell me?   For
   seventy years I loved her and never said a word--
   except just that once.   And you stood between us.
   You used me, just like Faith said.   And now, now
   that it doesn't even make any difference, you wouldn't
   tell me.
ZIGGY: Why should I tell you anything?   She was my wife.
   Right to the end, she was my wife.   I didn't lose.
   I never lost.
NOD: But she loved me.   She loved me.   (<u>Gets into the</u>
   <u>wheelchair and pulls the blanket around him.</u>)   <u>All</u>
   these years, she loved me.   She loved me.   She
   loved me.   I'm cold.   I'm freezing.
ZIGGY: I'll get you another blanket, Nod.   I'll get it right
   now.
NOD: I don't want another blanket.   I'm not cold on the
   outside.   I'm cold on the inside.   Oh, Ziggy, I miss
   her.   I miss my Faith so much.
ZIGGY: I know, Nod.   I miss her too.
NOD: It's not the same.   She loved me.   She loved me.
   It's not the same.   I want to go home, Ziggy.   It's
   lonely here.   It's lonely every place... since Faith
   left.
ZIGGY: I know, Nod.   I know.   I really do miss her.

NOD: It's not the same.

ZIGGY: No, it's not the same. I'll take you home, Nod. I'll take you home now.

TOM: I'll help you with him, Ziggy.

ZIGGY: (Pushing wheelchair upstage through the "Miss America" sign.) No, I'll do it alone. I'll have to take care of him now. Alone. (Looks up at sign.) Say hello to Miss America for me when she arrives.

NOD: And, Ziggy, I want you to stop cheating at cards.

ZIGGY: I don't cheat much, Nod.

NOD: I don't want you to cheat at all. I don't want you to cheat at all, ever again. (Exit Nod and Ziggy.)

BURLINGTON: Well, I guess that finishes it. Get the lights, will you, George.

GEORGE: Okay, I'll get them on my way out. Can I give you a lift home, Francine?

FRANCINE: I don't want to take you out of your way, George.

GEORGE: It's not out of my way. I'd kind of like to talk to you. (Pause.) About that last scene.

FRANCINE: All right, George. (Francine and George start off down left.)

BURLINGTON: Get the curtain, too, will you, George.

FRANCINE: I thought you didn't like curtains, Jack.

BURLINGTON: I don't know what I like. But tonight... tonight, closing the curtains seems right. (Francine and George exit off left. Tom walks downstage to Jack, looking after them.)

TOM: Every night, they have to go through the same business of pretending to leave together by accident. I wonder why it's worth the effort. At their age, there can't be much passion left.

BURLINGTON: I don't know. But then there's lots I don't know tonight. Especially about men and women and passion.

TOM: Well, I'll be on my way. Maybe I can still catch the late show. (Laughs.) You know, Jack, it's a funny thing. I have been coming here every night. All the time I'm here, I just can't wait to get home. I don't like the Life Players, but if we do another of these next week, call me.

BURLINGTON: Next week? Hell, Tom, next week we might just do "East Lynne."

THE CURTAIN CLOSES: THE STAGE LIGHTS COME

ON, AND THE PLAY COMES TO

THE END

4.   Encouraging Academic Skills

Justice for Andy Jackson
A One-act Play
for Upper Elementary School Children

CHARACTERS:

JUDGE DOMINICK HALL	MISS LOUISIANA
RENATO BELUCHE	JOHN REID
JEAN LAFFITE	DISTRICT ATTORNEY
PIERRE LAFFITE	GENERAL ANDREW JACKSON
DOMINIQUE YOU	CLERK OF COURT,
MISS LIBERTY	CITIZENS OF NEW ORLEANS,
MISS JUSTICE	BARATARIANS.

TIME: March 31, 1815.
PLACE: The Courthouse on Royal Street, New Orleans.
SCENE: The interior of the courtroom.   Upstage center
is the judge's bench.   In front of it is a small desk for
the clerk of court.   Above it are a flag and a picture of
George Washington.   Downstage right from the bench is
the witness stand.   Two tables, downstage right and left,
with chairs facing toward the judge's bench, are for the
district attorney and the defendant, respectively.   Two
rows of chairs, on each side of the stage, are for the
spectators.

AS THE CURTAIN RISES, several of the Baratarians are
gathered in the courtroom, standing amid the chairs in the
spectators' section.   They are looking offstage right, as
though waiting for someone to enter.

RENATO: If the Judge thinks that Andy Jackson will stand
        for this, he doesn't know the General.
DOMINIQUE: I say we should take the Judge and the
        bloody courthouse and pitch them in the river.
PIERRE: Little Brother, why do you want to dirty up the
        river?   Let us just cut the Judge into small pieces.
DOMINIQUE: That's true, Pierre.   Old Dominique You is
        not thinking clearly.   What have the little fishes in
        the river done to us that we should fling our garbage
        into their living room?   It is better we cut him in-
        to small pieces.
JEAN: Do not worry about the Judge.   He will not come.

Did not the General have Judge Hall arrested and
taken out of town?

DOMINIQUE: Oui.   And he told him not to return.

PIERRE: But he did return.   He waits until the celebration
is over, and he returns.

DOMINIQUE: He did not fight the British, but now he wants
to fight General Jackson.

JEAN: He will wish that he were with the British.

PIERRE: Maybe the Judge will not come, no?

JEAN: He will come.   But maybe the General will not
come.

DOMINIQUE: Is the General such a man that an old man
on a bench can say, "Come," and he will come,
and "Go," and he will go?   I do not think so.
(There is a shout offstage.)

DOMINIQUE: It's the General.   He has come.   Now we
shall see a fight.

PIERRE: (Standing on a chair.)   No.   No, it is not the
General.   It is the citizens of New Orleans.   They
come to stand by the General.
(Enter Misses Liberty, Justice, and Louisiana,
followed by some of the citizens.)

MISS LIBERTY: (To Baratarians.)   Has the General come
yet?

DOMINIQUE: Not yet, little Miss Liberty.   Are you here
to save him?

MISS JUSTICE: Last January in the Place d'Armes, we
stood to pay him honor.

MISS LIBERTY: We put wreaths on his head because he
saved the city from the British.

MISS JUSTICE: Today, we again bring wreaths.

MISS LOUISIANA: So he will know that the love in our
hearts lives longer than the petals of a flower.

PIERRE: Then you'd better stand on chairs so that you
can reach his head.
(Chairs are arranged so that General Jackson will
pass between them as he enters.)

A NEW ORLEANS CITIZEN: Of course, the General may
not come.

MISS JUSTICE: I think he will come.

BARATARIAN: Little Miss Justice, do you think that General Jackson is afraid of this little mean judge?

MISS JUSTICE: This is a courtroom, the home of justice.
The General will come to throw the Judge out.

DOMINIQUE: By gar, I think that little Miss Justice speaks
the truth.

ANOTHER CITIZEN: Here comes the General.

ANOTHER CITIZEN: John Reid is with him.

JEAN: That John Reid is one smart man. He will make
that Judge Hall sorry he did not stay in the country.

MISS LOUISIANA: The General does not have his uniform
on.

DOMINIQUE: What! He is unclothed! This is a great
disgrace.

MISS LOUISIANA: He is wearing his everyday clothes.

A CITIZEN: On the chairs, girls. Be ready with the
wreaths. Everybody make way for the General.

ALL: Hurrah for General Jackson. Hurrah for Old Hick-
ory. Hurrah for Andy Jackson.
(Enter Jackson and John Reid. Jackson passes
through the arch, and the girls put wreaths on
his head.)

JACKSON: Thank you, my friends, thank you. It does
an old soldier's heart good to see that the friends
he made in the war are still friends in peace.

DOMINIQUE: General, say the word and we pitch the judge
and the bloody courthouse in the river.

ALL: (Shouting.) Let us throw the judge in the river!

JACKSON: (Moving with Reid upstage until they reach the
defendant's table. He tries to raise his hand to
stop the shouting; then he stands on a chair.) My
friends, hear me, if you are my friends. Good
people of New Orleans. My good friends, the
Baratarians. We are not here for war. We shall
hear what this court has to say.

DOMINIQUE: We shall hear. Then we throw the judge in
the river.

ALL: (Shouting.) In the river! In the river!

JACKSON: If you are my friends, hear me. (They are
silent.) If you are my friends, make no more disturbance than I shall make.

PIERRE: We shall wait for your lead, General.

JACKSON: Good, then let us sit down. (He sits down,
placing his coat and wreaths on the table. John Reid
sits beside him.)
(Judge Hall, the Clerk of Court and the District
Attorney enter from behind the judge's bench. Jackson rises, and the others, seeing him do so, follow
his example. The judge takes his place on the
bench; the District Attorney and the Clerk of Court
go to their tables. The judge sits, and then all,
except the Clerk of Court, sit.)

CLERK OF COURT: The case of The United States versus
Andrew Jackson is now in session.

JEAN: That's a funny one. Andy Jackson is the United
States.
JUDGE: Order in the courtroom. (There is silence, all
looking to Jackson for an example.) Is the defend-
ant ready?
JOHN REID: He is, Your Honor.
JUDGE: Is the state ready?
DISTRICT ATTORNEY: It is, Your Honor.
JUDGE: Then the trial will proceed.
DISTRICT ATTORNEY: It is the contention of the State,
Your Honor, that one Andrew Jackson, Major General
of the Army of the United States, did wilfully and
without due process of law usurp authority and show
contempt for the court and its legal representatives.
JUDGE: So be it.
REID: May I be heard, Your Honor?
JUDGE: Proceed.
REID: It is the argument of the defense, Your Honor,
that no such charges are binding, for if a contempt
were committed, it is beyond the jurisdiction of
this court. No act of contempt was performed within these walls and these proceedings are illegal and
unconstitutional. Moreover, Your Honor, if General
Jackson is to be tried, we demand his right to trial
by jury, not by a single judge.
JUDGE: Your appeal is denied. Proceed with the trial.
DISTRICT ATTORNEY: I would like to call General Jackson
to the witness box.
JACKSON: I decline.
DISTRICT ATTORNEY: Then I would ask the General these
questions: Did you not arrest Louallier? Did you
not arrest the judge of this court? Did you not
seize the writ of habeas corpus? Did you not say
all manner of disrespectful things to the Judge?
REID: I protest, Your Honor. General Jackson is not on
the witness stand.
JUDGE: Then let him take the stand.
JACKSON: I refuse to speak before this court. You would
not hear my defense.
DOMINIQUE: General, now we throw him in the river, no?
JACKSON: Please my friends. I would speak. (The room
is quiet.) Under these circumstances, I appear before you, to receive the sentence of the court, and
have nothing further to add.
PIERRE: He is going to let the Judge tell him what to do?
JEAN: This cannot be.
JACKSON: My friends, you promised to make no more

disturbance than I shall make. I am ready for
sentencing, Your Honor.

JUDGE: General Jackson, the court is not ignorant of
what this city--nay, the whole nation--owes to you.
You have been our savior in an hour of need. Your
service is not on trial here. The only question is
whether the Law should bend to the General or the
General to the Law. If we are ever to be a great
people, respect for the Law must lead the way.
You are fined one thousand dollars.
(The judge rises, all follow; and the judge leaves
the courtroom. Jackson turns around and starts
out upstage exit. There is silence for a moment.)

BELUCHE: Hurrah for General Jackson.

DOMINIQUE: Hurrah for the next President of the United
States.

JEAN: Come, General, let's go to the Exchange Coffee
House.

JACKSON: Yes, all of you come. You shall be my
guests.

JEAN: You'd better be our guest, General. It's already
cost you a thousand dollars today, and you did not
even get breakfast.
(All, except the Clerk of Court and the District
Attorney, start to leave.)

JACKSON: I shall be your guest, but let me say this
first. During the invasion I exerted every one of
my faculties for the defense and preservation of
the Constitution and the laws. On this day I have
been called on to submit to their operation under
circumstances which many persons thought sufficient
to justify resistance.

DOMINIQUE: Now, shall we throw the Judge in the river?

JACKSON: No, my friends, obedience to the laws, even
when we think them unjustly applied, is the first
duty of a citizen. I do not hesitate to comply with
the sentence. I ask you to remember the example
I have given you of respectful submission to the
administration of justice. Now let us have our
coffee.

ALL: (Exiting.) Hurrah for Andy Jackson. Jackson
for President.
(As the last one leaves, Judge Hall re-enters the
court.)

CLERK OF COURT: He's still their hero, isn't he? Still
the great man.

JUDGE: He still is.

DISTRICT ATTORNEY: They even want to run him for
    President of the United States.
JUDGE: And when they do (pause)... I think I'll vote for
    him.

(Curtain)

THE END

PRODUCTION NOTES:

Characters: 7 boys, 3 girls, and as many others as are
available.
Costumes: Early nineteenth-century New Orleans.
Settings: One.
Stage Properties: Chairs and tables, 1815 flag of United
States for the wall behind judge's bench, picture of George
Washington.
Hand Properties: Wreaths for girls, cloak for Andrew
Jackson, gavel for judge.
Playing Time: 15 to 18 minutes.

VI

The Teacher as Self-Critic

It is the thesis of this collection that there are
natural ways in which the classroom instructor can continue
to function as a "teacher who writes," thus stimulating his
imagination for a better classroom performance and, also,
performing some educational service beyond his classroom.
Even those who protest most loudly against the teacher-
writer would probably agree that such activity, if not of
any great value, is, at least, of no harm. The complaint
against the teacher as writer comes for two reasons.
First, many think that he is too richly rewarded for an
educational service of dubious value. Secondly, many
think--not altogether without some basis--that he takes
himself too seriously. Any teacher, not merely the teacher
who writes, needs to distinguish between the seriousness
of his intent and the importance of his accomplishment.

The teacher who is asked by a student if he missed
anything important by cutting the last class should answer,
"I don't know. I don't know what you know--or need to
know--about the material covered in that class." Teachers,
like actors and writers, however, are prone to think that
every performance they give is well worth the time of the
audience, a dangerous way of thinking for teacher, actor,
or writer.

In this last selection in this collection, a spoof of
academic writing which was published in The Serif, IV
(December 1967), on pages 3 to 18, Dr. Nolan pokes fun
at the pretensions of the teacher who writes. His target
is, of course, not the PMLA article by Professors Cargill,
Charvat, and Walsh. In fact, in the first finished version
of this essay, titled "A Handbook for Academic Hacks,"
that article was never mentioned. "In the main," he says,
"I have used my own publications as the subject of my
satire. It is not that I don't write as well as I can; it is
not that I do not take my writing seriously. It is rather
that I am aware the seriousness of my intent does not

insure any literary worth in what I have written.   The
teacher who writes--like the teacher in the classroom--
simply does the best he can with what he knows with all
the skill he has.   Sometimes the results are not merely
disappointing; they are downright bad.   I find it useful to
look at my work with some objectivity, not because I have
any desire to be humble, but because I know I can never
teach any better than I do unless I also realize that I
frequently teach worse than I should. "

A New Short View:
Some Animadversions on Professors Cargill,
Charvat, and Walsh's "The Publication of
Academic Writing"

In a recent issue of PMLA--sometimes carelessly
called Publications of the Modern Language Association of
America--Professors Oscar Cargill, William Charvat, and
Donald D. Walsh, all distinguished scholars and members
of an ad hoc Committee appointed by the MLA Executive
Council--gave their view of "The Publication of Academic
Writing. "[1]

I certainly have no intention of quarrelling with the
generally good intention of this view.   Their report has,
among other things, the support of other equally distin-
guished scholars in the field of academic letters: Richard D.
Altick, Herbert S. Bailey, Jr., Chandler Beall, Fredson
Bowers, Germaine Bree, Ashbel G. Brice, George Brock-
way, W. W. Norton, Vincenzo Cioffari, D. C. Heath, Leon
Edel, William B. Edgerton, August Frugé David Horn,
Howard Mumford Jones, Lawrence B. Kiddle, George
Metcalf, John E. Neill, W. W. Norton, William R. Parker,
Henri Peyre, Dana J. Pratt, Gordon N. Ray, Macha L.
Rosenthal, Mark Shorer, Oskar Seidlin, Archibald K.
Shields, Roger W. Shugg, Jack M. Stein, George Winchester
Stone, Jr., Henry Thoma, Claude Simpson, Jr., B. J.
Whiting, Thomas J. Wilson, and Carl Woodring.   These
men read and criticized the drafts of "The Publication of
Academic Writing" in three forms, and those whose names
are underlined "were unusually painstaking and helpful. "[2]

Obviously one does not even beg to differ in such
august company.   When one makes an animadversion with
men like Leon Edel, Howard Mumford Jones, Henry Thoma,
and W. W. Norton (who for some reason is listed twice, but
neither time with italics), one must be quite certain that
he is unusually painstaking and that he makes clear that
he is trying to be helpful.

Their report starts with a sentence that none would
challenge for either its truth or clarity, to wit: "Publication
continues to be one of the more important activities of the

scholar-teacher. " What follows, however, is obviously
written for a rather narrow audience. For example, these
three gentlemen make this comment about style: "By the
nature of his profession, the scholar is supposed to be
able to write clear expository prose"; and then they conclude, "If he has difficulty in doing so, he should not seek
publication. "[3] Further, they argue: "He [the scholar]
should write to express what he feels, to convey his enthusiasm for knowledge or ideas lucidly and in concise
and vigorous prose. ... The most effective scholars make
use of all the skills and stratagems of creative writing. "[4]

All of which, I will admit, is all very well for the
one in a hundred in the academic profession, but what of
the rest of us? It is all very well for them to argue that
we should not seek publication, but the brute facts of life
demand that we do.

There are about 800, 000 faculty members on the
2, 700 college and university campuses in the United
States. [5] Unfortunately, there is only money to pay living
wages to about 200, 000. Two solutions come to the minds
of the prosaic. First, those charged with financing higher
education should increase their support four-fold. This
proposal is called "getting juice out of an orange without
a squeezer. " The second solution is to spread the available funds among all faculty members evenly, this insuring
one meal a day, per faculty member. Since, however,
man does not live by breakfast alone, this solution seldom
pleases anyone.

What has resulted, therefore, is not a solution, but
a problem: how does one become distinguished enough to
earn three meals a day? The answer is rather simple:
publication.

To be fair, some schools do have other means of
deciding value. Some reward long service, but they find
it difficult to recruit new faculty members, since it is the
rare new faculty member who brings long service to the
job with him. Some, to solve the recruiting problem, pay
high salaries to beginning teachers and low salaries to
those already established. Unfortunately, however, this
gives a campus a gypsy-camp atmosphere. Some attempt
to reward good teaching, but this system favors the prestige
fields in which the presidents' children enroll. Some reward
service to the community or loyalty to the administration, .

but one can trust so few people these days. [6]

In truth, there is no standard that works so well
as publications, and it is essentially a sane system.   Obviously, a man who spends his time writing wisely about his
field is interested in education.   He can be trusted not to
be a drone, idling away his time at golf, stirring up faculty
trouble through the AAUP, [7] or politicking for the dean's
job.

Moreover, he lends prestige to the institution.   Go
to any meeting of the Rotary Club and listen when Professor
Higglebotham enters, assuming, of course, that Professor
Higglebotham is a publishing professor.

"By George, " one of the Rotary members will say
to another, "there's old Higglebotham.   A damned fine man
and a good scholar.   He had a ripping analysis of Finnegan's
Wake in the last issue of the James Joyce Quarterly.   A
sound man, too.   You don't need to worry about his poli-
tics. "[8]

The professor, of course, should not be interested
in publications merely for the financial returns.   There
are all sorts of other rewards, some almost spiritual.

For one thing, the academic profession respects
its members who produce.   Some professors, to be sure,
view with alarm the over-eager graduate student who would
leap into print before he is dry behind the ears, to coin
a phrase.   They may even sneer at publications by others
in the same discipline, but the writer must simply assume
that these sneers rise from a stomach sick on envy and
jealousy.   The publishing professor must expect to be hated
by those who know him and his work best, but the open
adulation of the rest of the faculty and administration is
worth a few summers of discontent.

It gives a man a sense of his own moral worth to
publish.   No man can resist swelling a little when he can
end his lecture with the comment, "And for those of you
who are serious students, I'd suggest that you look at my
book (article, review, note, or query) for a more detailed
comment on the problem. "[9]

Publication also leads to invitations to speak for
money.   It is a social advantage.   A publishing professor

is much in demand at cocktail parties, and many a hostess
has succumbed to the man who has clearly demonstrated
his manliness by his vigorous prose.   Bookmen are eager
for his comments on their latest wares, and review copies
can be sold for almost half the retail price.

In fact, there is damned little in the academic world
or the adjacent community that is not open to that man a-
mong men, the scholar who publishes.   He teaches fewer
classes, grades fewer papers, and gets more money, easier
promotions, and other special rewards.

The self-evident truth of the value of publications
is, of course, not really at issue.   And this essay would
be of little value if it were merely to urge those who can
to publish.   Of the 800,000 faculty members in the United
States, fewer than 99,000 publish anything between gradu-
ation and retirement; and fewer than 49,995 publish enough
to earn the right to be called "publishing" professors. [10]

This statement is not meant to hurt anyone's feelings, but, in truth, one note in the Times, one query to
Life, and one review of Barry Goldwater's Why Not Victory?
in the state education journal does not qualify one for
membership in the distinguished ranks. [11]   One has, in the
precise terms of the academic world, got to grind it out--
two or three books (preferably with hard covers and
indexes), twenty or thirty articles (at least two or three
in reputable journals in one's own field), and thirty or
forty reviews, queries, letters-to-the-editor.

There are few of us in the academic world that have
much to say that has not already been said better.   In fact,
there are few of us that have anything to say that we haven't
read.   But that condition is the readers' problem, not the
professors'.   The professors' problem is simply to get in
print, and the professor who confuses this problem with the
problem of creativity is headed for a long, sour career unless,
of course, he is one of the small groups for whom Professors
Cargill, Charvat, and Walsh write their advice.

We professors have not been trained to be creative,
nor to think or say anything new.   If here and there one
wants to try it, that's his business--and a damned poor
business it is likely to be, too.   No one likes a man who
makes waves, and we have more new ideas than we can
understand or exploit as it is.

We professors are trained to read, repeat, and qualify. It is cunning, not talent, that is developed in our educational system; and it is through cunning that we learn how to use friends and influence administrators.

The young academic on his way to being a distinguished scholar must, first of all, develop the proper attitude. He must understand the moral superiority of scholarship over original thinking; he must seek community service that is performed by repeating the familiar rather than experimenting, wildly, with the new. He must understand, too, that in the final analysis, his obligation is to the length of his bibliography, not to some nebulous entity called quality.

Those who prize the publishing scholar most--administrators, the general public, students--do not have time to read anything longer than the bibliography. Nor is there any great need for them to do so. After all, if a man's works are published, wiser men than you and I-- editors and boards of readers--have guaranteed the worth of that work.

There are, of course, certain bibliographical qualifications to be made. A long book is more impressive than a short book, but two short books are more impressive than one long book. An important book has an index. A major book has illustrations. The best books are published by the major publishing companies and the university presses. Books published by foreign presses suggest the author is a man with international stature, but perhaps a little un-American and superficial. But books--anything published as a separate edition--are more important than articles.

The most important articles are the lengthy ones, placed at the front of the journal; they appear in the house organs of the largest academic societies--the Modern Language Association, the American Studies Association, the American Association of University Professors, and the like. The next most important are the same articles when they appear in the journals like The Yale Review, New Mexico Quarterly, and The William and Mary Quarterly. Some might argue that an article in one of the academic journals, say The Yale Review, has an advantage over the article in such a house organ as the American Journal of Physics. [12] I wouldn't wish to take sides in such a debate, but the advantage of publication in the house organs, rather than in the academic quarterlies, lies in the sub-titles, "the official publication of ...!" This sub-title not only makes the bibliographical entry longer, sometimes by as much as two lines; but it also suggests that the article published in the journal has the full support of the whole membership of the organization.

Ideally, one should have a few of each, but they should be viewed as the olives at the brunch. The real meat and potatoes of one's bibliography have to be the general journals--the several thousand general-article magazines that are published fitfully across the country, journals like The Ball State Teacherlies Forum, Western Speech, The English Record, the fifty state educational magazines, the fifty proceedings of the state biology societies, the fifty state historical journals, the journals of the state mathematics teachers, the state drama teachers, and the state chemists.

There probably are differences within these groups. The Chronicles of Oklahoma is perhaps a better journal than The Alabama Review. (I use this only as an example, not meaning to offend anyone.) Louisiana Schools is perhaps a better state educational journal than The Arizona Teacher. (Again I say perhaps, not meaning to offend anyone.) The Forum is perhaps a better journal than the McNeese Review.

But not many people read any of these journals, and no one reads more than a few of them. Thus, the publishing professor--unless he has some special reason for wanting to draw a considerable amount of attention from the few readers of one journal--does better to scatter his fire over as wide a range of journals as possible. 13

Judge for yourself which sounds better. "I've had five articles in The Southern Speech Journal," or "I have published in a variety of journals, including The Southern Speech Journal, The South Dakota Review, Western Speech, The English Record, and The Alabama Review." The second statement gives a sense of being desired, wanted, sought after. It is plain that a man who has published in five journals is more in demand than a man who has published in one.

The first article in a journal is seldom meant to indicate a value judgment by the editor. Some editors like to start each issue with their longest article; some, with their shortest. Some build each issue by first getting rid of the stuff left over from the last issue. Whatever the editor's reasoning, however, with a few modest disclaimers, any professor lucky enough to have his article appear first can make that accident appear to be a wise choice.

If it happens to you, simply chuckle and say, "I don't know why the editor selected that article of mine for the lead. I personally didn't consider it that important when I wrote it."

Of course, no matter where your article appears, make sure that it finds its way to the standard yearly bibliographies. The easiest way to insure that all of your things are listed is to volunteer to be a member of the bibliography committees on all the journals in which you are interested. You can assign the actual work of collecting all the bibliography entries except your own to one of your students.

Finally, after the books, after the articles, finally comes the yeast--those things that can make two books and six articles into a five-page bibliography: the notes, the queries, the reviews, the exercise exchanges, the comments, the letters to the editor.

It helps if you can entitle them in some way so that when you list these items in your bibliography, they have a pleasant sound. Let us say for example that you have missed the last two issues in your subscription of School and Society. You write the editor expressing your displeasure, but instead of merely addressing the letter with a formal salutation, you give the letter a title, like, "A Problem in Communication for the Non-Reader: A Critical Examination of Editorial Confusion." Now you have an entry that would be a credit to any bibliography.

All of this is not meant to suggest that one may become a distinguished publishing professor without any real effort. A mere understanding of the situation is only the starting place. The books, articles, and reviews must be written; once they are written, they must be accepted and published; after they have been accepted and published, they, in turn, must be reviewed, must become a part of the literature of the field with an exciting future in footnotes and bibliographies; finally, they must be brought to the attention of those we wish to influence.

It is these matters that this essay now treats, and
I believe, sincerely but modestly, that this is the first
such full-length analysis ever made of the problem.

I

One of the disguised blessings for the academic
writer is the generally low reputation of academic prose.
Frederic W. Ness, in his A Guide to Graduate Study, for
example, comments upon the poor writing found in scholarly
works. "Even many works by mature scholars suffer from
awkwardness of expression,"[14] he says, putting the matter
in the best possible light.

Poor writing may make learning wearisome for the
students, but thank God, our student days are behind us;
and while it may not be easier to write poorly--academically
poorly--than well, there are certainly more of us who can
do it. Triteness and dullness are the qualities that identify
the true scholar. Mr. Ness, for example, in an enlighten-
ing footnote, writes, "The writer [Mr. Ness, I guess] knows
of one instance of a brilliant master's essay [title not
cited] that contained many quotations [specific quotations
not cited] but without a single identification or reference.
Fortunately, a team of fellow graduate students [names not
given] lent a hand [metaphor not explained] and, after ap-
proximately two weeks, managed to supply the necessary
footnotes,"[15] getting rid of the vulgar brilliance, one would
hope.

But if the academic author is not concerned with
writing, he must be concerned with his reputation--his
image as a writer. Academic writing is the only literature
in the world that is accepted on the demonstrated competence
of non-writers. No one but a raw novice ever builds his
reputation by the submission of naked manuscripts. In
fact, the successful academic writer should learn to submit the manuscript itself almost as an afterthought, a kind
of note to document the virtues of the author.

Before one may even hope for success, he must
first become an academic personality, a serious scholar,
a profound thinker, a "solid man." Some of this image-
making can be done, of course, at the national meetings
of the various academic organizations in formal papers;
but most of it must be done on the level of personal contacts.

The ultimate customer for the academic author is the editor, but he must be reached through indirection. The first step is to establish a reputation for profundity in one's own community, and one cannot start at too low a level.

A professor of my acquaintance, for example, started his career as a bumbling sort of fellow, easily embarrassed, pathetically anxious to get on. He was accepted by his co-workers as a good, average fellow, and everyone from the president to the janitor felt on easy terms with him. The president and the janitor both called him by his first name, "Sam." His students called him "Prof" and "Teach." But he had the right idea. His children never called him anything but "Dr. Professor Samuel Samuelson," which, as a matter of fact, is not his real name. [16]

The obvious respect of his children was contagious and soon everyone, even his wife, was calling him Dr. Professor Samuel Samuelson--a name, quite obviously, to reckon with.

It wasn't only his name, moreover; it was his appearance, too. Even in the heat of a Georgia summer, he wore tweeds. He smoked a pipe. He carried a pocketful of notes. And the words he selected carried with them the sound of authority, the perfume of scholarship: in the final analysis, seemingly, reputable authorities in the field.

He became a man whose opinion was valued. He was chairman of the committee to name the new library. He was the president's personal representative at the installation of the president at a sister institution. He developed two responses to all students: he chuckled when he was pleased, and he frowned when he was annoyed.

In his relationships with his colleagues, he developed the greatest tact. All younger people in the department were "bright young fellows"; all the older ones were "the good, old guard." He, himself, stood safely between, sympathetic to both--a man to mediate.

His natural qualities of leadership on his own campus were further developed at the regional meetings in his field. At first, of course, he was simply the host for the parties held by his group and their friends. Then he was elected to various offices in the smaller sections. He read papers;

he served as critic.   He was a popular choice for a major
office.

No one really could remember what papers he had
read.   But it didn't make any difference.   At the various
academic annual conventions, one goes to be identified.
True, one has an obligation to listen to those papers
delivered by friends and people of worth; but one does
not need to listen closely.   His papers were masterpieces
of acknowledgments and brevity.

The book men started talking to him about doing a
book; the editors of the regional quarterlies asked him for
articles and reviews.

Dr. Samuelson's next step should have been to the
national meetings, but unfortunately, he got ambitious and
he began to believe in his own image.   He accepted a contract to write a book in his own field, got a sabbatical from
his university to do the research.   All that was several
years ago, and as far as I know, he is still collecting his
materials.   In fact, he has grown quite embarrassed by
his failure to meet the deadline on the contract, and he
no longer attends even the regional meetings.   Even at his
own institution, he is no longer named to the important
committees; his colleagues moved him into the ranks of the
old guard; and his children now call him "Pop. "

But he had the right idea.   He had the recipe, but
he rushed the baking.   He needed to follow the slow progress of the careful scholar, not the mad race of the fated
genius.   It would have been all right, of course, if he had
started a book as a major project--but to sign a real contract with a deadline was rash.

Although one book--even a small one without an
index--is worth four articles and six reviews, letters, and
exercises, one must move up the ranks one step at a time.
George Custer, who wasn't really a professor but who might
have learned from association with the more thoughtful in
our ranks, made his big mistake when he jumped from
lieutenant into the ranks of general.   Can anyone imagine
a cautious major, who had moved up step by step from
Pfc. , rushing off to the Little Big Horn?   Of course not.

Every professor worth his salt must understand that
he has two reputations to create.   One is undocumented.

It is his personal reputation, created by image, by student
approval, by the prose of the public relations office.   It is
the reputation that makes any thoughtful man who has read
"Hamlet" twice a Shakespearian authority, any man who
can spell "Einstein" an atomic scientist.   It is a reputation
that must be protected with all the pomp that one can
create, all the evasions that one can learn.

If one is certain that he intends to remain with a
single institution--especially one that limits its faculty
records to impressions--he can be concerned only with
this first reputation.   He must be prepared, of course,
to wage war against all assaults on professional privacy
and academic freedom.   The publication of a faculty bibliography, for example, must be viewed as the worst sort of
academic dishonesty. With the intrusion of accrediting
associations into the private affairs of the various institutions,
however, he has picked a major battle.

He can, of course, refuse to cooperate and make
himself the champion of the unbibliographed.   "I have no
intention of submitting my annual bibliography.   Anyone who
is genuinely concerned can check the standard bibliographies
in the field.   Scholarship should not be used for personal
self-aggrandizement.   What are we doing, selling Coca-
Cola?" He may, further, point to many excellent men who
have not published, thus suggesting that he has and at the
same time insuring the support of others who haven't.   He
can speak of the hours and hours that "many good men"
spend in counseling students and preparing lectures, "rather
than rushing into print with every half-baked idea they can
think of. "   He may even be able to get Life Magazine to
run the story of his life, but, of course, if he is going to
go to this trouble--and if he has this talent for managing
editors--he would probably find it more convenient--(and
certainly much easier) just to publish.

The publishing reputation is not merely broader than
the non-publishing one, giving the professor greater visi-
bility in the field.   It is safer.   Few administrators have
the courage to suggest that a publishing scholar has classroom responsibilities.   Only colleges of education, dance
studios, and business schools could be so gauche.

But enough of these battles with straw men.   By
this time, we are all agreed that publication is the only
means of salvation--both personally and professionally;

so let's get down to business and start to work.

II

There is, it is commonly agreed, no need for any more new books in one's own field, unless one writes them himself. In the first place, in the academic world new books are merely old books with different qualifications, current applications, or historical restatements. Yet academic books continue to appear, and they must be reviewed.

When one is asked to review a book, he should realize that in the lowly review lies a golden opportunity to add a little luster to one's image, a little muscle to one's professional power, and a few cents to one's income. I would not appear greedy, but one must eat.

Always accept a book-reviewing assignment. It is well, of course, to ask for several months to do your work. You won't need the time, but it will inform the editor that you are a busy man, and yet one who takes the art of reviewing with high seriousness.

Elmer Rice's Dream Girl gives the formula for reviewing: thumb through until you find several typographical errors, carp at the style, and then give at least half of the review to the kind of book the author should have written rather than the one he wrote. In the main, this is good advice.

In the first place, there is never any sense in reading a book one is to review. Academic books are so constructed that a close analysis of the table of contents, a survey of the sources, and a judicial testing of the style should give one all he needs for his review.

If the book itself deserves little attention, however, the review one is to write should be of great concern. One should plan it with the same detail with which Hannibal planned the invasion of Rome, the daring with which Napoleon planned the Battle of Waterloo, the confidence with which Hitler planned the Battle of Britain. The reviewer is, after all, a lonely soldier attacking an entire regiment.

It might be fitting, in fact, to list the objectives of the review. First, of course, a review is one more item

in one's bibliography.   For this reason, the review article--
three or four reviews jammed together under one heading--
is better than a single review.   One should, it hardly needs
to be said, fight for all the space he can get.   So many
editors habitually set limits on reviews--1,000 words, 500
words, even 250 words--that it is no longer an easy matter
to pad a review into a minor article; but it can be done.
Use the longest words you can find; count compound words
as a single word; cite authorities with long names; and
always add a few words--never more than ten percent how-
ever--to the limit that the editor has given you.

Secondly, a review should build your image as a
major scholar.   The author of the book, obviously is some
sort of scholar or he wouldn't have written a book.   Chances
are--and I mean to offend no one--the author is better
known than the reviewer.   But the reviewer is in a position
to place himself in a superior position to the writer.   The
reviewer, after all, has been asked to judge the author's
work; and the act of judgment implies some sort of superiority.

There are many poses that the critic may adopt in
dealing with the author.   He may speak as an amateur of
his love for the work of the professional.   He will thus
endear himself to the author, but for all the rest of the
world he will appear to be a graduate student reviewing
the work of his major professor.   If you are reviewing
the book largely to endear yourself to the author, this is
obviously the pose you need, and do not haggle over the
terms.   As the late Adlai Stevenson said, in much better
form, "In the art of flattery, one cannot be too fulsome. "
Let your review drip with honeyed words: superb, reveal-
ing, touching, engrossing, select, unerring honesty and
perception, reality, human association, outstanding major
development, fabulous (reserved for the arts), lively
(reserved for sociological studies), frank (reserved for
theological studies), virtually definitive, gracefully written,
complete, influential, poignant (reserved for theatre arts),
profound, original, creative, scholarly, and a worthwhile
addition.   There is one advantage to such reviews.   They
will be picked up by the publishers, and thus your name
will be spread about.

Fortunately, most of the books are not written by
friends; so the pose of the amateur is one we need use
only sparingly.   Most of the academic books are written

by fat, sleek, youngish men at fat, sleek, oldish universities. One may speak of their work without the slighest
fear of retaliation, for it is a pose among the fat, sleek
youngish men at fat, sleek oldish universities to pretend
they never read reviews.

One should be careful, however, not to show a
bias. One is tempted, of course, to open a review of
such books with a rather frank statement: "Why this book
was written only God, the author, and the publisher (and
it is assumed that the author and the publisher are one
and the same) know. " Such a statement is probably fair
enough, and if one were in a position to deal justly, it
would be the only decent statement to make.

Unfortunately, however, a review of this nature
coming from one relatively unknown will not be taken in
the spirit of honest scholarship in which it was intended.
The editor--who is probably a friend of the author--might
even reject the review; he would certainly not invite you
to do a second. And the casual reader might mistakenly
judge your response to have its origin in envy, not high
standards.

This is not to deny that one purpose of the review
is to damn the book. It is rather to say that damnation
through fain praise is more effective. More important
than your reader's opinion of the book is his opinion of
the reviewer.

Patronize, don't condemn. For example, you might
start with something like this: "This is a nice little book
by one of our younger scholars. "[17] Or if he is not so
young: "This is another nice little book by one of our
established scholars, more a work of love than of scholarship. "[18]

One, of course, should demonstrate that he has read
the book carefully. Your secretary or one of your better
students can read the book for you and mark any typographical errors, lapses in grammar, or misspellings. Note
these, of course, in your review, but do not scold the
author. Rather suggest, kindly, that his editor failed in
his responsibility to the author by general sloppiness. Such
a defense shows that you are really on the author's side,
a gentle, humane man roused to anger only by professional
incompetence.

After you have established the self-evident fact that
you should have been the man to write the book, explain
to your readers how you would have done the job--and don't
be modest.   Keep in mind that the real scholar is willing
to spend fifteen hours a day for twenty years to do the job
right, and that's the kind of a job that you would do.
Incidentally, there is one sure way of demonstrating that
you already have all of the scholarship at your command.
There is usually a lapse of about a year at the least between the completion of a manuscript and the publication
of a book.   During this time, something somewhat related
to the subject of the book must have appeared.   Find it
and lament, gently of course, that the author had not included it as representative of a "significant amount of
current scholarship" in his study.   It is a real windfall,
of course, if the author has missed an article that you
have written, but--it should be noted--one cannot count a
work in progress or an unpublished manuscript as a missed
article.

If you have an unpublished manuscript, you may, of
course, call attention to its existence.   Such a manuscript
not only demonstrates that you are a working scholar, but
it might make it a little easier for you to place the manu -
script the next time you send it out.   It is entirely ethical,
in fact, to append a note to your manuscript: "Although
recent mention has been made of this article in the spring
issue of The Sociological Review, this is the first time
that the article itself has been offered for publication. "
An editor may, of course, check your reference and find
that you made the only mention; but it is not likely.   Editors have all they can do with their own work, and they
have no desire to stick their noses into other people's
business.

The review is also a good place to demonstrate that
you are keeping up in your field.   Sprinkle your review with
allusions to other books that have recently appeared.   It is
recommended that you read the reviews of such books carefully before citing them.   Titles are so deceptive these
days--especially those written by historians--that one cannot
judge a book by either its title or cover.

In selecting your allusions, keep in mind that this
is an opportunity to dispense favors and repay neglect.   Use
every opportunity to compare books by friends with that of
the author for things you do not like about the book you are

reviewing. And if you should find something you do like, select the book of one you do not like as a contrast.

Establish quickly and in as many ways as possible the fact that you are the judge. Once you have demonstrated that your words carry authority and that no one is beyond your judgment, you will discover that you have won the respect and affection of every other author in your field.

Finally, the review itself is only half of your reason for accepting a reviewing assignment. There is, also, the book. Needless to say, a clean book sells better than a dirty one. Don't write notes in the book. Don't underline, not even errors. In fact, it might be a good idea to make your examination of a library copy so that your review copy remains virginal clean for resale.

III

Finally, of course, after the reviews, after the image-making, after the contacts, and "so much more, " it is necessary to come to the writing itself; and it seems safe to say that perhaps more than any other aspect of being the writer-scholar, it is writing that seems to stall otherwise perfectly competent academic authors. To fill page after page with words can be a bother. Academic people are primarily trained in criticism, not in creativity. We are experts in what should not be written, not in what should. Once started, of course, we can flow on like the best of the academic drop-outs--William Faulkner, Eugene O'Neill, and Edward Farthingale. [19] The problem, then, seems to be in getting started.

Professors Cargill, Charvat, and Walsh suggest that the academic writer start with his dissertation. "If it has been well written, " they comment, "and written to interest as well as to inform the reader-critic, the dissertation may be publishable with few or no changes. " Unfortunately, as they observe, "... not many dissertations are in this happy category. "[20]

If the dissertation is publishable as is, the academic writer needs no words of counsel from me. He should rather read Professors Cargill, Charvat, and Walsh for instructions on contracts, proofreading, and publishing schedules, being prepared to drop into the editor's office, from time to time, for chats.

For the academic writer with a dissertation that is not publishable, however, (and this condition may be the result of a scrupulous concern for the niceties of academic style), there are still ways and means of achieving immortality and becoming internationally famous, at least on one's own campus.

Perhaps, the work merely needs a breezy style. Try dropping every other footnote, all the <u>howevers,</u> and two out of three <u>moreovers.</u> If the manuscript is still a little bulky, take <u>out all the</u> adjectives and adverbs and then boil.

It may be, of course, that the dissertation is too complex, too profound, for a broad audience. If so, try borrowing a semester of lectures from it, putting your pure prose into the popular jargon of the classroom. Then take each lecture, return a little of the pure prose, and read it as a paper before a learned society. Then take each paper read, add a few footnotes, and submit it as a separate essay to one of the journals. When the dissertation has been exhausted, collect the published essays into one manuscript again; and now you have a publishable book.

There are, of course, a few problems. Some academic presses, like Indiana University, have a policy against publishing dissertations. Other presses, like the University of Oklahoma, have a policy against publishing anything in book form that has already appeared in journal form.

It is necessary, obviously, to discover such biases before submitting your manuscript. If you submit the manuscript to Indiana, comment that some of this material <u>in a different form</u> has appeared in journals of the highest repute. If you submit the manuscript to Oklahoma, comment that a large part of the manuscript, <u>now completely revised,</u> appeared in your dissertation. You have now confessed the full sordid history of your manuscript, and your conscience is clear.

Any revisions of the dissertation are, of course, more painful than this brief account suggests. When one considers that there are about a half-million words in the English language, counting recent coinages, one must realize that the problem of putting the right word in the right place is tremendous. Thus, you may prefer a collaborator--some-

one who will make these changes for you for the privilege
of becoming one of the co-authors, the last one listed, of
course.   You may feel that you are giving away your rights
of parenthood after you alone have borne the child, but unless you have been able to publish the dissertation alone,
you must realize that your role is essentially that of an
unwed mother, looking for someone to share the blame.

The entire business of collaboration, in fact, deserves
more attention than it has thus far received. [21]   Professors
Cargill, Charvat, and Walsh and their thirty-three able
consultants, for example, say nothing on the subject, probably convinced that people wno should be published do not
need collaborators.

I had a friend who worked many years trying to do
a book on Old English poetry without much success.   It
was not that he could not find a market for his manuscript.
He could not finish the manuscript.   In fact, he could not
even get started.   Then, when computers became popular,
he had a really brilliant idea.   He would combine his study
of Old English metrics with the new computer science.

He went to the young lady in charge of programing
for the campus computer and broached the idea.   She was
most willing.   Although he has not yet finished the book,
or I should say, although they have not yet finished the
book, he has a renewed vigor that is bound to spill over
into his prose.   Obviously, judging from this example,
whatever the pitfalls of collaboration, it does serve to
stimulate a fresh interest in scholarship, a feeling of
comradeship that one does not find in the lonely work of
being an individual writer.

As Professors Cargill, Charvat, and Walsh, so
wisely, point out, "The creation of textbooks is a legitimate, meaningful, and often profitable activity for a
teacher." [22]   So make the most of it. [23]

Notes:

1.   PMLA, 81 (September, 1966), 39-45.
2.   Ibid., Note *, 39.   In an "Introduction" to this
article, the authors comment that they were aided by thirty-
three consultants.   In Note *, however, a total of thirty-
six consultants is listed, if one counts Professor W. W.
Norton twice, which seems reasonable for Professor Norton

is listed twice.

    3. Ibid., 39.
    4. Ibid., 40.
    5. These figures are based on an actual nose-count of colleges and their faculties, made under a grant from the Essex Motor Car Company.
    6. Personal interview with college and university recruiters at the annual MLA Convention in New York, New York, December 27-29, 1966.
    7. AAUP are the initials for the American Association of University Professors, not to be confused with the American Association of University Women.
    8. This spelling of Joyce's novel is based on Higglebotham's essay, the first instance, to my knowledge, of a correct spelling. The title appears Finnegans Wake in the Dublin, Texas, edition and as Finnegan Woke in the Little Rock, Arkansas, edition.
    9. See, for example, John C. Hodges and Mary E. Whitten, Harbrace College Handbook, 5th ed., New York: Harcourt, Brace, and World, 1962.
    10. It should be noted that the recent issues of Vacancies in College and University Departments of English, published by the Association of Departments of English and the Modern Language Association of America, are most specific on this point. In nine of ten colleges, "pub." are "desired" and in three of ten colleges, "pub." are "required." (It should be noted that pub. has a period.) Obviously if one "pub." would do, a plural verb would not be used, not in a publication of the Association of Departments of English and the Modern Language Association of America.
    11. Ranks here means one's general reputation as a writer-scholar, not merely his rank in the university, i.e., instructor, assistant professor, associate professor, or professor.
    12. Professors Cargill, Charvat, and Walsh, "The Publication of Academic Writing," p. 40, suggest that it is not entirely disreputable to publish in such journals as the Hudson, Kenyon, Partisan, and Sewanee reviews, for while these journals "publish mostly critical essays," they "... are hospitable to scholarly writing of certain kinds."
    13. See the List of Useful Addresses in the annual directory issue of PMLA. Cited in Cargill, Charvat, and Walsh, "The Publication of Academic Writing," p. 40.
    14. Frederic W. Ness, ed., A Guide to Graduate Study: Programs Leading to the Ph.D. Degree (Washington, D.C.: American Council on Education, 1960), also, comments: "... unfortunately even many English majors arrive

in graduate school with but an uneasy control of the language, " p. 25.

15.   Ibid.

16.   As a matter of fact, the man's name was David Davidson.

17.   See Arthur Hobson Quinn, A History of the American Drama, II (New York: Harper & Brothers, Publishers, 1927).

18.   See Edward Albee. "Who's Afraid of Virginia Woolf?" New York: Mimeographed, not published, 1966.

19.   Faulkner and O'Neill both, eventually, won Nobel Prizes in Literature; and although it is not generally known, Edward Farthingale was also a college drop-out, having failed English 100 three times.

20.   "The Publication of Academic Writing, " p. 39.

21.   I presently have a work in progress on this subject, tentatively titled, How To Collaborate With Nothing To Produce Something. When completed, it will probably be published by the Oxford University Press.

22.   "The Publication of Academic Writing, " p. 39.

23.   This essay does not have the support of the ad hoc Committee. It does, however, have the "personal endorsement" of John Hurt Fisher, executive secretary of the Modern Language Association of America. In fact, in a letter dated 8 March 1967, Professor Fisher told me that he had recommended that this study be published in PMLA, "but I can't get my editorial committee to support me. " This comment raises an interesting point. While the advice offered in this study is not intended to help the writer-scholar publish in PMLA, I see no reason that one could not succeed--if one had the sense to submit his manuscript during a season when Professor Fisher's editorial committee was on vacation. I would recommend July or August.